# INHERITANCE
# AND FAMILY LIFE
# IN COLONIAL
# NEW YORK CITY

# INHERITANCE AND FAMILY LIFE IN COLONIAL NEW YORK CITY

David E. Narrett

CORNELL UNIVERSITY PRESS

ITHACA AND LONDON

NEW YORK STATE HISTORICAL ASSOCIATION

COOPERSTOWN, NEW YORK

First published 1992 by Cornell University Press.

International Standard Book Number 0-8014-2517-4
Library of Congress Catalog Card Number 92-7680

Printed in the United States of America

*Librarians: Library of Congress cataloging information*
*appears on the last page of the book.*


⊗ The paper in this book meets the minimum requirements
of the American National Standard for Information Sciences—
Permanence of Paper for Printed Library Materials, ANSI Z39.48-1984.

*To my parents*

# Contents

# Preface

The conception of this book began some years ago when I was a graduate student at Cornell University and taking a research seminar taught by Michael Kammen. Professor Kammen, ever alert to the possibilities for future research, suggested that I might base a paper on an analysis of the *Abstracts of Wills* published in the Collections of the New-York Historical Society. After all, the field of social history was just then beginning to expand our knowledge and broaden our perspective on the early American past. Though the then recent books by John Demos and Philip Greven were illuminating about New England family life, no similar work had been attempted for New York—a colony that had generally been neglected in historiography.

Since my seminar paper was a success, I decided to continue my research in New York probate records. My work led me initially to examine some 2,400 original wills written in three culturally diverse regions of New York—Manhattan, Suffolk County on eastern Long Island, and Ulster County in the mid–Hudson River Valley. I later went on to investigate family papers and court records pertaining to such important subjects as the relationship between law and social custom, primogeniture, and the settlement of estates.

As my research progressed, I realized that the study of early New York history depended on a thorough understanding of the New Netherland era. One of my foremost goals in this book is therefore to trace the influence of Dutch social customs and legal traditions on family life, especially the position of colonial women. The book assesses Dutch social practices in relation to those of other ethnic groups by analyzing the evolution of inheritance from the founding of New Netherland to the outbreak of the American Revolution. But while my focus is on New Amsterdam and subsequently New York City, this book is also informed by my extensive reading of wills and related documents in other regions of the province. I have attempted as well to relate my findings to the most recent historiography concerning inheritance and family life in colonial America. This book contributes to that scholarship by being the first published work that systematically investigates inheritance in New York and indeed in any major urban center in the English colonies.

I am indebted to many scholars who have worked in the fields of early American social, family, and legal history, but my foremost debt is to Michael Kammen, my mentor who has set such a wonderful example of teaching and scholarship for his students. I am deeply grateful for his many kindnesses and for all that I have learned from him over the years.

I thank Marylynn Salmon for her invaluable help in critiquing the entire book manuscript. I am also in the debt of Mary Beth Norton and Douglas Greenberg for offering me assistance and encouragement at several stages of my work on this book. Other scholars who deserve special mention are Daniel Scott Smith and Jessica Kross for their useful criticisms of my work, and Charles Gehring, who gladly shared his knowledge of the colonial Dutch. I also thank Wendell Tripp, editor of *New York History,* for his long encouragement of my work and his unfailing support of the book's publication. I am honored that Cornell University Press is publishing this book, and I am grateful to Peter Agree, my editor, for all his assistance, and also to Elizabeth Holmes for her skillful copyediting.

For permission to use material from essays that I've published, I thank the New-York Historical Society and the University Press of Virginia. The essays concerned are "Dutch Customs of Inheritance, Women, and the Law in Colonial New York City," in William Pencak and Conrad Edick Wright, eds., *Authority and Resistance in Early New York* (New York: New-York Historical Society, 1988); and "Men's Wills and Women's Property Rights in Colonial New York," in Ronald Hoffman and Peter J. Albert, eds., *Women in the Age of the American Revolution* (Charlottesville: University Press of Virginia, 1989).

I have incurred debts to many archivists over the years. Two stand out as being extremely helpful. Leo Hershkowitz, Professor at Queens College, City University of New York, long ago guided my entry into the original New York probate records and other sources on file in his university's library. I could not have progressed in my work without his active support. Thomas Dunnings of the New-York Historical Society offered me highly personal and skillful assistance during the entire course of my research.

The University of Texas at Arlington has supported my research in several important ways since I joined the faculty in 1984. Robert Perkins, Dean of the Graduate School, helped to provide summer research grants on two occasions, and two successive chairs of the History Department, Stanley Palmer and Kenneth Philp, have continually encouraged my progress. In fact, I thank all my friends and colleagues at UTA for being there when I needed them. Special thanks go to Stephen Maizlish and Joyce Goldberg as well as to Alex Weiss and Juli Hobdy for all we've shared.

Two friends and former students were of tremendous help in typing and word processing: Kit Goodwin and the late Pat Kinkade. I am grateful for the devotion and good cheer of them both, and I will always remember Pat for her mix of Texas toughness and kindness.

Finally, I express my gratitude to my family for their continual love and support: to my brothers, Eugene, Zach, Seth, and Matthew, and to my dear parents, Sidney and Beatrice Narrett, to whom I dedicate this book. In the simple and true phrase of colonial times, I offer this gift to them out of "natural love and affection."

DAVID E. NARRETT

*Arlington, Texas*

# Note on Sources

The Historical Documents Collection, Paul Klapper Library, Queens College, New York City, includes the following colonial probate records:

Wills, Surrogate's Court, New York City, 1st series, 1662–1761; 2d series, 1736–75. Although the two series have overlapping dates, the first consists almost entirely of wills probated before 1735. These records are numbered according to the listing in Kenneth Scott, "Early Original New York Wills," *National Genealogical Society Quarterly* 51 (1963): 90–99, 174–78, 185; Julius M. Bloch, Leo Hershkowitz, and Kenneth Scott, "Wills of Colonial New York, 1736–1775," *National Genealogical Society Quarterly* 54 (1966): 98–124.

Wills, Surrogate's Court, New York City, Libers, vols. 1–43, 1665–1800. These volumes include official copies of the great majority of original wills and also record many testaments for which no original is extant.

The New-York Historical Society has published abstracts of the wills recorded in the Surrogate's Court Libers. See William S. Pelletreau, ed., *Abstracts of Wills on File in the Surrogate's Office, City of New York, 1665–1801,* 17 vols., in Collections of the New-York Historical Society, 25–41 (New York, 1893–1909). These volumes also include a valuable listing of letters of administration in cases of intestacy. Since the abstracts of wills include numerous errors, they should be used only with the utmost care. My own research is therefore based on Queens College microfilm of the original wills and the Surrogate's Court Libers. The wills in the Libers have been checked against the original whenever possible. All citations of wills list the date that the document was drafted.

The Surrogate's Court records include most colonial wills written in downstate counties (Westchester, Richmond, Kings, Queens, and Suffolk) as well as Manhattan. For upstate wills (formerly on file in the Court of Appeals), see Court of Probates, Wills, 1671–1815 (series J0038), New York State Archives, Albany. These wills are listed in Berthold Fernow, ed., *Calendar of Wills on File and Recorded in the Offices of the Clerk of the Court of Appeals, of the County Clerk at Albany, and of the Secretary of State, 1626–1836* (New York, 1896; rpt. Baltimore: Genealogical Publishing Co., 1967). The Court of Probates records also include Administration Papers, ca. 1700–1823, and Inventories and Accounts, 1666–1823.

In all quotations from colonial wills and other sources, I have followed the original spelling as closely as possible. I have also dated documents according to colonial practice, with one exception—the new year is considered to have begun on January 1 rather than on March 25 as was customary before 1752.

# Introduction

The study of inheritance—the transmission of property at death—has become an important tool for understanding the dynamics of family life in early America. By analyzing probate records, particularly wills, historians have not only unearthed information about family size and structure; they have also assessed the nature of basic human relationships—the bonds between husbands and wives, parents and children, and the less intimate ties between kin or neighbors. Inheritance was a complex and variable process in colonial society because it was governed by individual choice as well as by custom or law. Testators—those men and women who prepared wills—often served their own personal needs and desires while implicitly expressing commonly held social values or attitudes.[1]

The bequest of property in early America was shaped by economic circumstances, demographic realities, and cultural traditions within particular communities or regions. Unfortunately, our knowledge of social development in the middle colonies, particularly New York, has lagged behind scholarship concerning New England and the Chesapeake. Philip Greven's pioneering study of Andover, Massachusetts, was among the

[1]Carole Shammas, Marylynn Salmon, and Michel Dahlin, *Inheritance in America: From Colonial Times to the Present* (New Brunswick: Rutgers University Press, 1987). For a good overview of colonial historiography, see Daniel Blake Smith, "The Study of the Family in Early America: Trends, Problems, and Prospects," *William and Mary Quarterly* (hereafter cited as *WMQ*), 3d ser., 39 (1982): 3–28. One among many significant European contributions to this field is Jack Goody, Joan Thirsk, and E. P. Thompson, eds., *Family and Inheritance: Rural Society in Western Europe, 1200–1800* (Cambridge: Cambridge University Press, 1978).

first systematic and detailed examinations of inheritance in an early
American community. Disproving the idea that New World conditions
liberated the young from family constraints, Greven contended that
inheritance in seventeenth-century Andover was a profoundly conser-
vative social force. The Puritan founders acquired far more extensive
landholdings than their English counterparts and also used their property to maintain their patriarchal authority. Since men commonly lived
until their seventies, their heirs were generally well into adulthood before gaining independent control of land. The postponement of inheritance depended on the transmission of real estate by last will and testament rather than by deeds executed during the father's lifetime.
Patriarchal power eventually weakened because of the colonial preference for partible inheritance—an English yeoman custom of dividing
land, the most valuable family resource, among as many sons as possible.
As the average size of farms diminished, fathers could no longer satisfy
all male heirs with real estate in their native town. Transmission of
property in eighteenth-century Andover became characterized by im-
partible inheritance (the descent of land to a single male heir), the payment of legacies in cash or other forms of personal property, the settlement of sons in outlying towns or counties, and the transfer of legal title
to land before the patriarch's death.[2]

Although Greven's study of Andover capably analyzed father-son relations, it nearly ignored other crucial aspects of family life, notably female
property rights. Toby Ditz is one historian who rejects the notion that
early New England inheritance practices were exclusively patrilineal, or
concerned only with the transmission of property through the male line.
Though sons inherited the bulk of family wealth in land, daughters
often received substantial portions of personal property. The inheritance of real estate was, moreover, often linked to the assumption of
familial obligations, since male heirs might be required to pay their
sisters' legacies or to support their mothers during widowhood. Connecticut yeomen's wills by no means encouraged simple economic indi-

---

[2]Philip J. Greven, Jr., *Four Generations: Population, Land, and Family in Colonial Andover,
Massachusetts* (Ithaca: Cornell University Press, 1970). John J. Waters has also emphasized
the patrilineal nature of New England inheritance practices. See "Patrimony, Succession,
and Social Stability: Guilford, Connecticut in the Eighteenth Century," *Perspectives in American History* 10 (1976): 131–60; "Family, Inheritance, and Migration in Colonial New England: The Evidence from Guilford, Connecticut," *WMQ*, 3d ser., 39 (1982): 64–86; "The
Traditional World of the New England Peasants: A View from Seventeenth-Century Barn-
stable," *New England Historical and Genealogical Register* 130 (1976): 3–21. See also Linda
Auwers, "Fathers, Sons, and Wealth in Colonial Windsor, Connecticut," *Journal of Family
History* 3 (1978): 136–49.

vidualism, but instead established a series of overlapping social rights and duties.[3]

Seventeenth-century settlers of the Chesapeake confronted a physical and social environment far less conducive to stable family life than that of New England. Given the shortage of women among early colonists, many men were unable to marry at all. Diseases, especially typhoid and malaria, contributed to an appallingly high mortality rate, leading to the premature end of marriages and to the presence of many orphans. Since most testators lacked extensive kinship ties, men tended to rely principally on their wives to care for their minor children. It is therefore not surprising that planters' widows often received more substantial property rights from their husbands' wills than mandated by colonial intestacy law. The widow's privileges often amounted to control of the entire estate throughout life, irrespective of whether she married again.[4] Inheritance practices became increasingly complex as the colonial economy developed and social classes became more distinct. By the early eighteenth century, wealthy men devoted their energies to conveying land and slaves to their lineal descendants, especially sons. This goal was commonly linked to the reduction of widows' property rights and to the requirement that daughters' legacies pass eventually to grandchildren. Inheritance in Virginia therefore reflected the emergence of a more stable, coherent social order founded on the plantation regime and slavery.[5]

[3]Toby L. Ditz, *Property and Kinship: Inheritance in Early Connecticut, 1750–1820* (Princeton: Princeton University Press, 1986). See also Ditz, "Ownership and Obligation: Inheritance and Patriarchal Households in Connecticut, 1750–1820," *WMQ*, 3d ser., 47 (1990): 235–65. For other studies concerning widows' property rights in colonial New England, see Kim Lacey Rogers, "Relicts of the New World: Conditions of Widowhood in Seventeenth Century New England," in Mary Kelley, ed., *Woman's Being, Woman's Place: Female Identity and Vocation in American History* (Boston: Hall, 1979), 26–52; Alexander Keyssar, "Widowhood in Eighteenth-Century Massachusetts: A Problem in the History of the Family," *Perspectives in American History* 8 (1974): 83–122. Keyssar emphasizes the marginal nature of many widows' property rights and material welfare.

[4]Lois Green Carr and Lorena S. Walsh, "The Planter's Wife: The Experience of White Women in Seventeenth-Century Maryland," *WMQ*, 3d ser., 34 (1977): 542–71. The impact of high mortality rates on family relations is examined in Lorena S. Walsh, " 'Till Death Us Do Part': Marriage and Family in Seventeenth-Century Maryland," in Thad W. Tate and David L. Ammerman, eds. *The Chesapeake in the Seventeenth Century: Essays on Anglo-American Society and Politics* (Chapel Hill: University of North Carolina Press, 1979), 126–52; and Darrett B. Rutman and Anita H. Rutman, " 'Now-Wives and Sons-in-Law': Parental Death in a Seventeenth-Century Virginia County," in ibid., 153–82.

[5]James Deen, Jr. [Jamil Zinaildin], "Patterns of Testation: Four Tidewater Counties in Colonial Virginia," *American Journal of Legal History* 16 (1972): 154–76. While eighteenth-century Virginia planters generally favored sons in the succession to land, they tended to circumvent primogeniture in their wills. See C. Ray Keim, "Primogeniture and Entail in Colonial Virginia," *WMQ*, 3d ser., 25 (1968): 545–86. The relationship between inheri-

Ethnic and religious loyalties influenced inheritance practices and family life in the socially heterogeneous middle colonies of Pennsylvania and New Jersey. For example, Quaker men in the Delaware Valley expressed an especially strong commitment to their children through their wills. They often provided special care for minors and relied on other Friends as trustees to assist their widows in managing their property after death. Both Pennsylvania Quakers and Scots settlers in New Jersey were more apt than Anglicans to distribute land among all their sons, rather than to one or two male heirs. A. G. Roeber maintains that German immigrants in Pennsylvania followed fundamentally different traditions concerning inheritance from those of English settlers. English law countenanced the idea of a written will by which the individual bequeathed his own property according to his personal preferences. Most German yeomen originated, however, from regions where custom rather than individual choice dictated the descent of the family estate. These settlers gradually learned how to use the English form of will in order to circumvent colonial intestacy law, notably provisions allowing the eldest son a double share of his deceased father's wealth.[6]

New York history is especially complex given the colony's Dutch origins, subsequent English conquest, and ethnic and regional diversity. Unfortunately, our knowledge of family life under both Dutch and English rule has depended too long on a few colorful, highly impressionistic accounts written during the late nineteenth century.[7] These books

---

tance practices and family values is capably analyzed in Daniel Blake Smith, *Inside the Great House: Planter Family Life in Eighteenth-Century Chesapeake Society* (Ithaca: Cornell University Press, 1980). Widows often received the use of a major portion of their deceased husbands' real estate, but not the right to alienate that property. See Linda E. Speth, "More Than Her 'Thirds': Wives and Widows in Colonial Virginia," In *Women and History* no. 4 (1982): 5–41. The emergence of a more stable social order in the eighteenth-century Chesapeake is discussed in Jack P. Greene, *Pursuits of Happiness: The Social Development of Early Modern British Colonies and the Formation of American Culture* (Chapel Hill: University of North Carolina Press, 1988), 94–95.

[6]Barry Levy, *Quakers and the American Family: British Quakers in the Delaware Valley, 1650–1765* (New York: Oxford University Press, 1988); Ned C. Landsman, *Scotland and Its First American Colony, 1683–1765* (Princeton: Princeton University Press, 1985), 155–59; A. G. Roeber, "The Origins and Transfer of German-American Concepts of Property and Inheritance in the Eighteenth Century," *Perspectives in American History*, new ser., 3 (1987): 115–71. Unlike Roeber, Stephanie Grauman Wolf finds little that is distinctively German about wills written in one Pennsylvania town. See *Urban Village: Population, Community, and Family Structure in Germantown, Pennsylvania, 1683–1800* (Princeton: Princeton University Press, 1976), chap. 8. Daniel Snydacker finds that Germans were less likely to leave wills than English or Scots-Irish Pennsylvanians. See "Kinship and Community in Rural Pennsylvania, 1749–1820," *Journal of Interdisciplinary History* 13 (1982): 41–61. The studies mentioned above have begun to meet the scholarly challenge raised by Douglas Greenberg in his important essay "The Middle Colonies in Recent American Historiography," *WMQ*, 3d ser., 36 (1979): 396–427.

[7]See, for example, Mrs. John King Van Rensselaer, *The Goede Vrouw of Mana-ha-ta: At*

offer fine portraits of colonial women's domestic and social roles, but scarcely touch on broader issues of historical change or development. Richard B. Morris was among the first scholars to contend that married women enjoyed a more privileged legal status in New Netherland than in any of the English mainland colonies.[8] Linda Briggs Biemer has more recently argued that the institution of English common law after 1664 led to a sudden decline in women's economic, political, and social role. Her thesis is not proved, however, because it examines the social experience of only four wealthy women in any detail.[9] In contrast to Biemer's approach, William J. McLaughlin's thorough study of colonial Flatbush, Long Island, emphasizes continuities in Dutch rural family life. Firth Fabend's book on one particular family, the Harings of New York and New Jersey, also indicates the lasting impact of Old World traditions.[10] Given the limited nature of this scholarship, we still need to know more about the persistence of Dutch social customs related to inheritance and women's property rights.[11]

My own goal is to examine the relationship between inheritance and family life in New York City from the beginnings of Dutch settlement in the 1620s until the American Revolution. An analysis of Manhattan probate records and related documents is especially important because we have lacked any thorough study of inheritance in a major colonial city. From its origins as an outpost of the Dutch West India Company, New York was its province's most populous town, center of government, and most ethnically diverse community. Unlike Dutch burghers in Albany or yeomen in the mid–Hudson Valley, Dutch residents of Manhattan had to adjust to a growing English presence within a generation after the conquest of New Netherland. New York City wills are therefore

---

*Home and in Society, 1609–1760* (New York: Knickerbocker Press, 1898); Alice Morse Earle, *Colonial Days in Old New York* (1896; reissued, New York: Charles Scribner's Sons, 1915). For a survey of recent scholarship in the general field of Dutch settlement, see Eric Nooter and Patricia U. Bonomi, eds., *Colonial Dutch Studies: An Interdisciplinary Approach* (New York: New York University Press, 1988).

[8]Richard B. Morris, *Studies in the History of American Law*, 2d ed. (1930; rpt. New York: Octagon Books, 1964), 176–78.

[9]Linda Briggs Biemer, *Women and Property in Colonial New York: The Transition from Dutch to English Law, 1643–1727* (Ann Arbor: UMI Research Press, 1983).

[10]William J. McLaughlin, "Dutch Rural New York: Community, Economy, and Family in Colonial Flatbush" (Ph.D. diss., Columbia University, 1981). Firth Haring Fabend, *A Dutch Family in the Middle Colonies, 1660–1800* (New Brunswick: Rutgers University Press, 1991). For an analysis of an English town in the province, see Jessica Kross, *The Evolution of an American Town: Newtown, New York, 1642–1775* (Philadelphia: Temple University Press, 1983).

[11]It should be noted that Marylynn Salmon's overview of colonial women's legal status is based primarily on evidence from New England, Pennsylvania, and the southern colonies. See *Women and the Law of Property in Early America* (Chapel Hill: University of North Carolina Press, 1986).

especially revealing about the extent of ethnic assimilation and the changing nature of communal ties within a pluralistic society.[12]

The legal history of colonial New York is usually divided into two phases—first, the chaotic years of proprietary government and political turmoil between 1664 and 1691; second, a process of Anglicization beginning in 1691 and culminating in the colonial assembly's wholesale adoption of English statutes just before the Revolution. Legal historians have viewed 1691 as a turning point because that year marked the establishment of a new court system based on English procedures and precedents. Before that point, ethnic diversity and local particularism ruled throughout the province. Legal institutions differed significantly among the Puritan settlers of eastern Long Island and the Dutch-speaking inhabitants of the Hudson River Valley. The Mayor's Court of New York City meanwhile administered a curious mixture of English legal procedures and Dutch civil law. A hybrid province initially developed a hybrid body of law.[13]

The issue of inheritance can be understood partly through this interpretive framework. The pre-1691 era was indeed a period characterized by uncertainty in law and legal institutions. The provincial government instituted English laws of inheritance, but it made little attempt to impose them on the Dutch population in either New York City or other areas. Most court officials—though appointed by the governor— were local men who administered law with respect to popular needs. The new laws of succession were neither efficiently nor widely enforced, particularly in Dutch areas of settlement. Kingston and Albany court records during the 1670s and 1680s include many instances of marriage contracts and settlements of estates drafted according to Dutch customary law. Dutch colonists in most regions, including New York City, pre-

---

[12]My own preliminary research into colonial New York probate records is presented in David E. Narrett, "Preparation for Death and Provision for the Living: Notes on New York Wills (1665–1760)," *New York History* 57 (1976): 417–37. This research culminated in my doctoral dissertation, "Patterns of Inheritance in Colonial New York City, 1664–1775: A Study in the History of the Family" (Cornell University, 1981). Two essays of mine focus on the issue of women's property rights in early New York. See "Dutch Customs of Inheritance, Women, and the Law in Colonial New York City," in William Pencak and Conrad Edick Wright, eds., *Authority and Resistance in Early New York* (New York: New-York Historical Society, 1988), 27–55; "Men's Wills and Women's Property Rights in Colonial New York," in Ronald Hoffman and Peter J. Albert, eds., *Women in the Age of the American Revolution* (Charlottesville: University Press of Virginia, 1989), 91–133.

[13]Herbert Alan Johnson, "The Advent of Common Law in Colonial New York," in George Athan Billias, ed., *Selected Essays: Law and Authority in Colonial New York* (Barre, Mass.: Barre Publishers, 1965), 74–91. See also Johnson, "English Statutes in Colonial New York," *New York History* 58 (1977): 277–96; Martin L. Budd, "Law in Colonial New York: The Legal System of 1691," *Harvard Law Review* 80 (1967): 1757–72. An important study dealing with the criminal legal system is Douglas Greenberg, *Crime and Law Enforcement in the Colony of New York* (Ithaca: Cornell University Press, 1974).

pared wills based on their own legal tradition of community property within marriage. Many of these testaments were jointly written by husband and wife—a practice that was valid under Roman-Dutch law, but contrary to English legal practice.

Two seemingly contradictory trends characterized Dutch-English relations in late seventeenth-century New York City. While Dutch resentment at English dominance fueled political unrest and even rebellion, Dutch colonists began to assimilate English culture and to acquire familiarity with the English language.[14] Many Dutch burghers initially feared that English rule would lead to the imposition of foreign customs, especially primogeniture, that were contrary to their own ethnic traditions. This anxiety diminished as the Dutch and other non-English colonists learned how they might serve their own needs through the new political and legal system. The pursuit of self-interest as well as the need for communal harmony eventually led many Dutch townsmen to adopt some English ways, though only after an initial period of distrust and enmity.

Dutch assimilation of English law proceeded gradually from the fall of New Netherland to the 1720s. Because the surrender terms of 1664 guaranteed Dutch customs of inheritance, many colonists initially felt free to follow their own ethnic traditions. It should be emphasized that Dutch adoption of English legal forms preceded the acceptance of English concepts of property. Consider, for example, the case of the mutual will drafted by husband and wife. While this type of testament all but disappeared from use by 1700, the Dutch concept of community property continued to influence the succession to wealth. Men assumed sole authority over will writing within marriage, but they still respected their widows' property rights much as previous generations had done. During the first sixty years of English rule, Dutch burghers as well as yeomen generally bequeathed the use of the entire estate to their spouses. The

[14]Dutch-English ethnic tensions are analyzed in Thomas J. Archdeacon, *New York City, 1664–1710: Conquest and Change* (Ithaca: Cornell University Press, 1976); Robert C. Ritchie, *The Duke's Province: A Study of New York Politics and Society, 1664–1691* (Chapel Hill: University of North Carolina Press, 1977); and John M. Murrin, "English Rights as Ethnic Aggression: The English Conquest, the Charter of Liberties of 1683, and Leisler's Rebellion in New York," in Pencak and Wright, *Authority and Resistance in Early New York*, 56–94. While Archdeacon, Ritchie, and Murrin emphasize Dutch-English political and economic rivalry, Joyce D. Goodfriend stresses the gradual and voluntary assimilation of English culture within the Dutch community. See "'Too Great a Mixture of Nations': The Development of New York City Society in the Seventeenth Century" (Ph.D. diss., UCLA, 1975). Goodfriend's research has recently culminated in her book *Before the Melting Pot: Society and Culture in Colonial New York City, 1664–1730* (Princeton: Princeton University Press, 1992). A distinctive approach to Dutch culture is offered in Donna Merwick, *Possessing Albany, 1630–1710: The Dutch and English Experience* (New York: Cambridge University Press, 1990).

transfer of wealth and authority to widows took precedence over other family concerns.

While Dutch colonial wills of the late 1600s conform to a nearly uniform pattern, a far greater diversity of practices is apparent over time. By the mid-1700s, economic status rather than ethnic background alone had become a major influence in determining how urban men balanced their widows' and children's needs. Testators within the wealthiest occupational groups—irrespective of their ethnic origin—increasingly restricted their widows' authority over property and speeded the transfer of wealth to their children. The adoption of English inheritance practices occurred more rapidly among the Dutch mercantile elite than among either urban artisans or rural farmers.

By 1700 the English rulers of New York had instituted a new legal framework governing many areas of family life, including the guardianship of children and the distribution of wealth among kin. There was, moreover, a fundamental shift in the law of descent. Whereas Dutch practice sanctioned equal division of family property among children, English law instituted primogeniture, the descent of all real estate to the eldest son. Though primogeniture was the official rule in intestacy cases, it was circumvented by the great majority of landowners who left wills. Indeed, hostility to primogeniture was expressed by nearly all ethnic and economic groups throughout the province, excepting a few great manor lords of the Hudson River Valley. Colonial testators did not necessarily distribute property equally among their children, but they had little use for an English aristocratic custom that favored the eldest son to such a pronounced degree.

While early New York wills are an important source for an understanding of Dutch-English relations, they disclose as well the experience of other ethnic or religious groups such as the French Huguenots, Scots-Irish, and Jews. Each of these groups had distinctive ways of expressing their communal loyalties through charitable gifts or bequests to kin. Colonial wills offer much evidence about the influence of English law and culture, but they also indicate how diverse colonists sought to retain their own ethnic customs within a pluralistic society. These documents are, moreover, revealing about social relations among ordinary colonists as well as among the elite.

This study of inheritance is based primarily on a quantitative, computer-assisted analysis of colonial wills. These documents include all extant testaments (37 in number) recorded in New Amsterdam court registers and notarial papers from 1638 through 1664. (There were apparently no wills executed in Manhattan before 1638.) I have also analyzed all 1,619 testaments prepared by Manhattan residents from the English conquest of New Netherland through 1775. These testaments fall into two distinct groups: 1,572 wills left by residents of New York City's urban areas, and 47 testaments written by inhabitants of the city's rural outskirts, mainly the Bowery and Harlem. The urban wills comprise 97 percent of all 1,619 testaments and therefore are the major source for this book. My goal in examining virtually all extant wills is to distinguish between typical and exceptional methods of bequeathing property, not only among the entire population but also within important economic and ethnic subgroups. Because this book spans the entire colonial era, I have been able to trace important changes as well as continuities in family life as New York City developed from a small Dutch trading outpost to the second largest urban center in British North America—a town of 22,000 by the time of the Revolution. Dutch-language as well as English sources have been analyzed for these purposes.

In addition to New York City wills, I have also examined for comparative purposes more than 800 testaments written in two rural regions of the province: Suffolk and Ulster counties. These documents include all 557 wills executed in three Suffolk County towns (East Hampton, Southampton, and Southold) and all 228 testaments declared in five Ulster communities (Hurley, Kingston, Marbletown, New Paltz, and Rochester Township) between 1664 and 1775. These areas were selected for comparison because of their distinctive settlement patterns. Suffolk County, located at the eastern end of Long Island, was first colonized by New Englanders in the 1640s and retained its Puritan loyalties and character throughout the colonial era. The Ulster County towns, located from sixty to ninety miles north of Manhattan and west of the Hudson River, were predominantly Dutch and French Huguenot in population. Though this book's scope does not permit a detailed analysis of Suffolk and Ulster County wills, I offer some comparisons between urban and rural inheritance practices as well as between Dutch and English social customs in farming regions.

I have supplemented my analysis of New York City wills by the extensive use of other sources, particularly vital records, tax lists, administration papers relating to intestacy, inventories of estates, deeds, court records, and family papers. Each of these sources has proved important for specific purposes. Registers of births, marriages, and deaths yield information about such crucial matters as the age of persons who wrote wills, how old they were at marriage, whether they and their spouses wed more than once, and the number of children they had. Tax lists provide data relating to economic status while inventories of estates list the personal possessions that men and women left behind at death—the appraised value of clothing, household goods, merchandise, cash, and sometimes debts and credits. New York inventories are replete with information about personal property but seldom mention real estate. Deeds record transfers of family property that may have preceded or followed the writing of wills. Court records disclose inheritance disputes while family papers reveal the intricacies of inheritance among middle- to upper-class New Yorkers.

While this book is organized topically rather than strictly chronologically, each chapter emphasizes changes that occurred over time in various areas of law, social customs, and family relations. The first chapter examines the ways men and women actually went about preparing their last wills and testaments. In it I trace changes in notarial practice and probate from Dutch to English rule, consider the colonists' physical condition when declaring their testaments, and analyze the religious content of the will. Chapter 2 is devoted exclusively to marriage and inheritance in New Netherland. Because of the limited number of wills and marriage contracts written before 1664, this chapter presents evidence for the Dutch colony as a whole, including Beverwyck (Albany) and nearby settlements, rather than for New Amsterdam alone. In Chapters 3 through 5 respectively I analyze the following aspects of inheritance in colonial New York City: widows' property rights; the transmission of property from parents to their children; and kinship and communal ties (including charitable bequests and the treatment of slaves). Each of these last three chapters spans the entire period from 1664 to 1775.

An Appendix offers largely statistical evidence concerning a key question: Who left wills in colonial New York City? Here I analyze the frequency of will writing among the general population and present data concerning the testators' social and economic background: their age, gender, wealth and occupational status, family size and characteristics, as well as their degree of literacy. Although will writing was naturally most common among the upper classes, it was by no means confined to that group. Indeed, 65 percent of all male testators belonged to the middling or lower orders of society. Craftsmen as well as common sailors were heavily represented. It is also significant that widows left nearly 15 percent of all colonial New York City wills—a much higher percentage than was common in rural areas. Rather than devote a separate chapter to women's wills, I present comparisons between female and male approaches to inheritance within particular chapters. This method offers the best opportunity to view women's social experience within the overall context of family life.

Only about one-fifth of white men and a much smaller percentage of women left behind wills at death. Despite this fact, wills offer our most detailed and reliable guide to inheritance practices and social customs in colonial New York City. Though a considerable majority of colonists died intestate, only a small fraction of their estates passed through official intestacy procedures. Because the courts often failed to appoint administrators in cases of intestacy, many families probably settled questions of inheritance according to their own preferences rather than by complying with a uniform legal code. Those cultural preferences were commonly expressed through the provisions of wills, testaments that allowed men and women to prepare for death by providing for the living.

# Chapter 1

# Preparing a Last Will
# and Testament

On August 29, 1664, the English captured New Amsterdam without meeting any armed resistance from the city's inhabitants. Fearing for their lives and property, a deputation of burghers virtually compelled peg-legged Governor Pieter Stuyvesant to sue for peace despite his desire to fight the enemy. Although the Dutch were forced to surrender the entire province of New Netherland, they managed to obtain several concessions from the colony's new rulers. The English guaranteed the property rights of all settlers and granted special privileges to the Dutch, including religious liberty and an exemption from fighting against any nation in a future war. The surrender terms also recognized the Dutch settlers' desire to maintain their distinctive social customs and legal practices under English rule. The Articles of Capitulation pledged that the "Dutch here shall enjoy their own customs concerning their inheritances" and promised the safekeeping of all public records relating to that subject.[1]

These rights remained unchallenged until the chaotic events of 1673–74 stemming from the brief Dutch reconquest of New York during the third Anglo-Dutch war. Though most Manhattan residents were jubilant at the arrival of a Dutch fleet and the overthrow of English rule, they

[1]Edmund B. O'Callaghan, ed., *Documents Relative to the Colonial History of the State of New York,* 15 vols. (Albany: Weed, Parsons, 1856–87), 2:251. For an account of the conquest, see Robert C. Ritchie, *The Duke's Province: A Study of New York Politics and Society, 1664–1691* (Chapel Hill: University of North Carolina Press, 1977), chap. 1. The Dutch surrender occurred on September 8, 1664, according to the modern calendar. All dates in the text reflect the older Julian calendar until September 1752 when the Gregorian calendar was adopted in England and its colonies.

were soon disappointed when the Dutch States General returned the colony to the English under the Treaty of Westminster in 1674. Considering the topsy-turvy fortunes of New York, it is scarcely surprising that Dutch colonists chafed at the arrival of a new English governor, Sir Edmund Andros, later that year. Their frustration stemmed partly from feelings of wounded national pride. They also wondered about the legal standing of their own social practices, including their customs of inheritance. Dutch residents of New York City were not satisfied by Andros's pledge that the surrender terms of 1664 would be respected. On March 15, 1675, eight prominent burghers refused to take an oath of allegiance to the new government until they received a more specific guarantee of their civil rights. Their petition listed four basic demands, including a plea that "the Article of Inheritances" be confirmed.[2] Governor Andros responded to this demand in a manner consistent with his military training—he jailed the petitioners. Although one protester soon capitulated to the governor, seven remained unrepentant. In October, an all-English jury found these men guilty of promoting rebellion and ordered the seizure of all their goods and chattels. This penalty was subsequently reduced to one-third of their personal wealth after the group submitted to the oath.[3]

Although Andros's policy toward the Dutch was initially severe, he had no intention of imposing English inheritance law by fiat upon an unwilling populace. Given his need to encourage Dutch political cooperation, he was prepared to tolerate the maintenance of local customs that did not directly threaten English rule. The introduction of English law in late seventeenth-century New York coincided with the persistence of Dutch legal traditions from the New Netherland era.

Dutch colonists correctly perceived significant distinctions between their own customs of inheritance and those of English settlers. These differences pertained to both the bequest of property by will and intestate succession. But before we can consider the question of property rights, it is important to understand the procedural issues relating to inheritance, particularly to the drafting and legal validation of wills.

Within twenty years after the fall of New Netherland, the Dutch began to utilize English legal procedures that served their own communal and individual needs. Considering the uncertain nature of provincial law during this period, colonists could not assume that their own inheritance customs would be respected if they died intestate. By the 1680s, the

---

[2]O'Callaghan, *Documents Relative to the Colonial History of New York*, 3:216–19, 227. Kenneth Scott, ed., *Minutes of the Mayor's Court of New York, 1674–1675*, New York Historical Manuscripts: English (Baltimore: Genealogical Publishing Co., 1983), 29–30.
[3]Ritchie, *The Duke's Province*, 140–43.

execution of a testament had become an important means of preserving Dutch notions of family property and avoiding the English rule of primogeniture. While the Dutch retained certain distinctive customs, they relinquished some practices that were at variance with English law, especially the mutual will prepared jointly by husband and wife. It should be emphasized that the adoption of new legal procedures preceded the assimilation of English concepts of property and family relations. By 1700 Dutch colonists throughout the province had accepted the English form of will, but not primogeniture or English concepts of marital property.

## WILL AND TESTAMENT IN DUTCH
## AND ENGLISH LAW

Beginning in the 1650s, the leading jurists of Holland referred to their province's legal system as Roman-Dutch law. They thereby recognized the diverse sources of law in the Netherlands: Roman law, particularly the Justinian code; the Canon law of the medieval church; Germanic customs; statutes of the Dutch Union and the provincial governments; and local ordinances, charters, and privileges. Although Roman law influenced the jurisprudence of all seven provinces within the United Netherlands, its impact varied from region to region. Judges relied on Roman law when neither statute, custom, nor privilege offered any solution to a case. While the term "Roman-Dutch law" applied strictly to the legal system of Holland alone, Roman law served as a form of common law throughout the Netherlands. Hugo Grotius, the foremost jurist in seventeenth-century Holland, wrote the first systematic treatise of Roman-Dutch law about 1620, some forty years before this legal system became generally identified by its distinctive name.[4]

The terms "will" and "testament" were closely and necessarily related in Roman-Dutch law. Grotius defined a will as a "declaration of what a person wishes to happen to his property after his death."[5] A testament referred to any will, whether written or oral, that appointed an heir or at least intended to name one. As in Roman law, the testator instituted an heir or heirs who succeeded to all of his or her assets and liabilities, legal

[4]R. W. Lee, *An Introduction to Roman-Dutch Law*, 5th ed. (1953; rpt. Oxford: Oxford University Press, 1961), 2–3; J. W. Wessels, *History of the Roman-Dutch Law* (Grahamstown, Cape Colony: African Book Co., 1908), 6, 96–127, 201–11. See also Hugo Grotius (Huig de Groot), *The Jurisprudence of Holland*, trans. and ed. Robert Warden Lee, 2d ed., 2 vols. (1953; rpt. Aalen, W. Ger.: Scientia Verlag, 1977). Grotius's treatise, written while the author was in prison, was first published in 1631.

[5]Grotius, *Jurisprudence of Holland*, 1:138.

rights and duties. While testators transferred the estate as a whole to their heirs, they commonly granted specific gifts or legacies to particular individuals. Roman-Dutch law regarded heirs as successors to the deceased but not necessarily as the sole recipients of the wealth. It is significant that the testator's freedom to bequeath property was restricted in the interest of family members, particularly children. These lawful heirs were entitled to receive at least a fractional share of the estate unless they were disowned for just causes. If the deceased failed to leave a will, the heirs by law succeeded to all his or her property.[6]

English jurists of the early seventeenth century conceived of the relationship between will and testament in a somewhat different manner than did their Dutch counterparts. While the terms "will" and "testament" were used jointly and interchangeably in English law, they also might refer to distinct types of legal instruments. Jurists commonly understood a testament to be a will that bequeathed personal property or movable goods alone. The term "will" or "last will and testament" was used whenever real estate as well as personal property was involved. The *bequest* of personal property was a distinct legal procedure from the *devise* or conveyance of land by will. As in Dutch law, a testament of personal property might assume either a written or an oral form. Only a written will, however, could transfer a valid title to land in England.[7]

The appointment of executors was as basic to the English law of testaments as the institution of heirs was to Dutch law. Since the early thirteenth century, English wills generally named one or more executors to be personal representatives of the deceased. Executors presented the will for probate, assumed title to the chattels or movable goods, paid the testator's debts and the legacies specified in the will, and accounted for their administration of property. They had the right to sue and were also liable to be sued on behalf of the estate.[8] While it is needless to explain all the technical distinctions between the English executor and the Dutch heir, several points merit emphasis. Executors carried out their duties without necessarily receiving any substantial legacy or material benefit from the will. While testators often chose executors from among their principal beneficiaries, they selected disinterested persons as well. During the seventeenth and eighteenth centuries, executors were legally

---

[6]Ibid., 144–51.

[7]Ibid., 26. For the eighteenth-century English law concerning wills, see Sir William Blackstone, *Commentaries on the Laws of England*, ed. James DeWitt Andrews, 4th ed., 2 vols. (Chicago: Callaghan and Co., 1899), 1, bk. 2:500–502. For seventeenth-century law, see Henry Swinburne, *A Briefe Treatise of Testaments and Last Willes* (London, 1611), 3–11 (first published in 1590, and reprinted by Garland Press, New York, 1978).

[8]W. S. Holdsworth, *A History of English Law*, 3d ed. rewritten, 13 vols. (Boston: Little, Brown, 1922–[52]), 3:563–90.

bound to administer personal property while having little or nothing to do with the real estate. They might only sell or convey land at the testator's express command.[9] Under Roman-Dutch law, heirs assumed ownership over both real estate and personal property. They necessarily succeeded to some portion of the estate unless they renounced all interest in their inheritance.

Adapting to the new legal system after 1664, Dutch New Yorkers began to appoint executors in order to guarantee that their last wishes would be respected under English rule. By the 1680s, the selection of executors had become a standard feature of New York City wills. Dutch colonists in rural Ulster County adjusted to English law more slowly than did city residents. Between 1665 and 1695, men and women of Dutch origin drafted thirty-two last wills in five Ulster County towns. Only three of these documents appointed an executor. The selection of executors became the general rule during the next twenty years. Twenty among twenty-four Dutch testators chose executors between 1696 and 1705.[10]

By the early 1700s, the legal phrasing of wills had changed throughout the province as the practice of "instituting heirs" fell into disuse. The decline of this custom is evident even in Dutch-language wills prepared by men and women in rural areas. Dutch colonists no longer appointed a single person or a number of persons to be their universal successors (*universele Erfgenamen*). They instead adopted the English procedure of bequeathing personal property, conveying realty, or granting the use of their estates to particular individuals.[11] These changes in legal phrasing occurred without necessarily altering the substance of the will itself. Dutchmen in the city and countryside enjoyed considerable freedom under English law to dispose of property by last will and testament.

[9]Swinburne, *Treatise of Testaments*, 242; Blackstone, *Commentaries* 1, bk. 2:507–13.

[10]The thirty-two wills drafted in Ulster County between 1665 and 1695 include eleven testaments prepared jointly by men and women. The last testament of this type in Ulster County was written in 1683. All wills were drafted by residents of Kingston, Hurley, Marbletown, New Paltz, and Rochester Township. For these documents, see Court of Probates, Wills, New York State Archives, Albany (hereafter N.Y. Archives). See also the following records in the County Clerk's Office, Kingston: Secretary's Papers and Court Records, 1663–84; Deeds, Libers AA-GG, 1685–1780. Abstracts and translations of county records can be found in Gustave Anjou, ed., *Ulster County, N.Y. Probate Records* (1906; rpt. Baltimore: Genealogical Publishing Co., 1975).

[11]See, for example, the will of Wilhelmus D'Myer drafted in Kingston in 1704. He followed the English custom of conveying real estate to his children as individuals, guaranteeing possession to each "heir and his heirs and assigns forever." The Dutch equivalent of this phrase was expressed in a grant of real estate ("Vaste Staat") to son Nicholas "en sijn ordre of Erfgename voor Euwigh." Court of Probates, Wills, N.Y. Archives, AD 11, Jan. 10, 1704. The provincial assembly in 1710 recognized the validity of Dutch-language marriage contracts, deeds, and wills using words equivalent to "real estate." See *Laws of the State of New York*, 2 vols. (New York: Hugh Gaine, 1789), appendix to vol. 1.

Their wives, however, soon lost that power except in special circumstances.

## TESTAMENTARY CAPACITY—THE RIGHT
## TO DECLARE A WILL

Dutch and English jurists regarded the declaration of a will as a serious act to be undertaken only by persons of sound judgment and sufficient maturity. Roman-Dutch law provided that males had to be at least fourteen years old and females had to be twelve before making a valid will. The younger legal age for women was derived from the notion that girls attained maturity at an earlier point than boys.[12] (This allowance was, however, largely of theoretical significance since no minors apparently prepared any wills in New Netherland.) English law followed the same age requirements for testaments of personal property, but not for wills concerning land. Only persons who had reached age twenty-one could lawfully declare a will that devised land. The New York Assembly adopted this rule by statute in 1684, thereby affirming the fundamental distinction between real estate and personal property in English law.[13]

Seventeenth-century Dutch law authorized married women to prepare a will either by themselves or with their husbands. Married couples in the Netherlands frequently utilized the mutual will in order to dispose of their common property—the family estate.[14] By contrast, English common law permitted wives to bequeath personal property only if they obtained their husbands' express consent. They were, moreover, prohibited at common law from conveying real estate by will under any circumstances. The common law grouped married women with felons, drunkards, and lunatics, as persons who could not prepare a will because of legal dependency, lack of freedom, or mental incapacity. Though the English Court of Chancery recognized married women's right to declare a will under certain circumstances, this tribunal benefited only a small minority of women, primarily among the upper classes.[15]

Although Dutch colonists in New York continued to prepare mutual

[12]Grotius, *Jurisprudence of Holland*, 1:133.

[13]Charles Z. Lincoln, comp., *The Colonial Laws of the State of New York*, 5 vols. (Albany: J. B. Lyon, 1894), 1:145. See also Herbert Alan Johnson, "The Prerogative Court of New York, 1686–1776." *American Journal of Legal History* 17 (1973): 108–9.

[14]Grotius, *Jurisprudence of Holland*, 1:133, 139; Sherrin Marshall Wyntjes, "Survivors and Status: Widowhood and Family in the Early Modern Netherlands," *Journal of Family History* 7 (1982): 399–401.

[15]Blackstone, *Commentaries* 1, bk. 2:497–99. Lawrence Stone, *The Family, Sex, and Marriage in England 1500–1800* (New York: Harper and Row, 1977), 331.

wills for some years after the English conquest, they seldom did so after 1695. As discussed below, only a handful of married women throughout the colony left wills of any type during the eighteenth century.[16] The Dutch custom of the mutual will declined as English legal procedures shaped the drafting of testaments.

## THE DRAFTING OF WILLS

The first statute regulating inheritance in New Netherland was passed just prior to the settlement of Manhattan Island. In 1625, the directors of the West India Company ordered that all marriage contracts, wills, and settlements of estates in the colony be based on the ordinances and common written law of Holland and Zeeland. The earliest extant wills, drafted in the 1630s, were recorded by the provincial secretary, a court officer who served the company's director-general and council in Manhattan. An official record of Albany wills and related documents—those written at Fort Orange or in nearby areas—begins in 1656. At least five notaries emigrated from the Netherlands to the colony between 1650 and 1664 as the need for professional legal services increased, especially in the growing town of New Amsterdam. Dutch notaries themselves were generally better educated, were more professional, and exercised greater legal authority than men who assumed that title in English law. It should be emphasized that colonists in New Netherland were obligated to utilize these professionals or other court officers if they desired to execute a valid testament.[17]

From 1664 to the mid-1690s, the English provincial government licensed notaries and court secretaries who served the Dutch community in much the same manner as they had in New Netherland. Dutch colonists therefore prepared wills with the assistance of Dutch-speaking public officials who understood their special needs. William (Willem) Bogardus, the most active notary in seventeenth-century New York City, began his career in 1656 as a clerk to the provincial secretary in New Amster-

[16]See below, Chap. 3.
[17]Arnold J. F. Van Laer, trans. and ed., *Documents Relating to New Netherland 1624–1626 in the Henry E. Huntington Library* (San Marino, Calif.: Henry E. Huntington Library and Art Gallery, 1924), 113–14. For the provincial records, see Arnold J. F. Van Laer, trans., and Kenneth Scott and Kenn Stryker-Rodda, eds., *Register of the Provincial Secretary, 1638–1660*, 3 vols., New York Historical Manuscripts: Dutch (Baltimore: Genealogical Publishing Co., 1974). Early Albany wills are found in Jonathan Pearson and Arnold J. F. Van Laer, trans. and eds., *Early Records of the City and County of Albany and Colony of Rensselaerswyck*, 4 vols. (Albany: University of the State of New York, 1869–1919). Vol. 1 includes wills written prior to the English conquest of New Netherland.

dam. He drafted twenty-four city wills in his official capacity as notary public between 1669 and 1691—40 percent of all testaments left by Dutch colonists and other non-English settlers during these years.[18] Dutch New Yorkers trusted Bogardus to draft or witness their wills because he spoke their language, understood their legal traditions, and acted with government approval. The notary himself assumed an important role in the maintenance of Dutch social customs under English rule. The preamble to a Dutch-language mutual will implies a personal bond between Bogardus and his clients:

> Know all men whoe Shall See this present publick instrument, That after ye nativity of our Lord and Saviour Jesus Christ 1686 ye 24th July, did appeare in their owne persons before me Wm. Bogardus publick notary residing in New Yorke . . . Mr. Dirk Vanderclyf and Mrs. Gessie Hendrix married people, Living within this Citty, very well known to me . . . both in good health, makeing full use of their understanding and reasons, whoe Considering the fragility and mortality of men, the Certainty of death, and ye uncertain time and houre thereof, and desiring to prevent the Same with due disposition of their temporall goods, therefore . . . did declare, to have made, ordained, and Concluded, this their present . . . mutuall Testamt. . . . First recommending their immortall Soules in ye gracious and Mercifull hands of God Almighty their Creator and Redeemer, and their Corps to ye Earth and Christianlike Buriall for a blessed resurection at ye Last day.[19]

Unlike Roman-Dutch law, English law did not require that notaries or other public officials be responsible for drafting wills and other legal instruments. A written testament might be drawn by any person who possessed sufficient legal knowledge, including the testator himself. If one person wrote a will for another, the scribe prepared the document in the testator's name without identifying himself. Since the scribe was not obligated to sign the testament, his role can usually be inferred only when he acted as one of the subscribing witnesses. Unlike the Dutch notarial will, an English testament was not considered valid simply because it was declared before a legal official and witnesses. The will had to be subsequently proved or affirmed by witnesses in court before it was probated.

[18]Bogardus's role was complemented by other men during this period. Peter Delanoy and Nicholas Bayard, merchants and government officials, drafted or witnessed fifteen wills executed by Dutch colonists between 1669 and 1696. The ethnic Dutch therefore relied on only a few men to draft their wills. Bayard and Delanoy also served as official translators of Dutch documents into English. See, for example, the will of Christopher Hoogland and Catharina Cregiers. Their mutual will was drafted in the Dutch language by William Bogardus and translated into English by Peter Delanoy. See N.Y. Wills, 1st ser., no. 79, Mar. 12, 1676.
[19]N.Y. Wills, 1st. ser., no. 129.

By the mid-1690s, English legal procedure had supplanted Dutch notarial practice in New York City and the mid–Hudson Valley. Although Dutch notaries continued to keep official registers of documents in eighteenth-century Albany, their role in drafting documents diminished greatly. The notarial will had been the general rule before 1700, but it became the exception thereafter.[20] Anonymous scribes—whether legal professionals or laymen—assumed primary responsibility for drafting wills throughout the province. Although there is no obvious explanation for the demise of the notarial will, this change was probably linked to the death of Dutch officials from the New Netherland era. Younger men obviously looked to English rather than Dutch law as their model for drafting wills. The adoption of the English testament prepared the way for a more individualistic style of bequeathing property—one that was increasingly shaped by the testator's wishes irrespective of European tradition.

Dutch colonists in New York City adopted the English language in will writing during the same period when they adjusted to the English law of testaments. A considerable majority of all Dutch testators prepared wills in the Dutch language between 1664 and 1685 (see Table 1.1).[21] The transition to English as a legal language was quite pronounced by the late 1680s. Seventy-four percent of all wills prepared by Dutch colonists were written in English between 1686 and 1695. The use of English became nearly universal in New York City wills after 1695.

The number of wills prepared by Dutch colonists in New York City increased markedly during the late seventeenth century. While Dutch residents left only five wills between 1664 and 1675, they declared twenty-three testaments between 1676 and 1685, and forty-three between 1686 and 1695. This trend cannot be simply explained by an increase in the Dutch population since immigration to New York from Holland was negligible during this period. It seems that few, if any, Dutch colonists wished to risk preparing a will in the immediate aftermath of the English

[20]The notarial records of Albany County include sixty wills drafted between 1670 and 1765. Forty-six of these testaments (76.7 percent) were written between 1670 and 1710. Thirty-seven of all sixty wills were drafted between 1670 and 1694. See Pearson and Van Laer, *Early Records of Albany*, vols. 2–4: passim. A. J. F. Van Laer has also translated wills and notarial records (including marriage contracts, powers of attorney, and petitions) for Albany from 1665 to 1695 in the Dutch Settlers Society of Albany *Yearbook*. See vols. 6 (1930), 10 (1934), 13 (1937), and 14 (1938).

[21]A few English-language wills drafted before 1675 were undoubtedly translated from the Dutch though no evidence of the original can be found. See, for example, the mutual will of Sigismundus Lucas and his wife, Gertruta (Gertrude) Van Bulderen. This will was drafted by William Bogardus in New Orange (New York City) during the brief restoration of Dutch rule in 1673. An English copy of this will, but not the Dutch original, is extant. See N.Y. Wills, Liber 1:412, Sept. 17, 1673.

**Table 1.1** Language of Dutch colonists' wills,
New York City, 1664–1705

| Years | No. wills | No. wills in Dutch | % | No. wills in English | % |
|---|---|---|---|---|---|
| 1664–75 | 5 | 2 | 40.0 | 3 | 60.0 |
| 1676–85 | 23 | 18 | 78.3 | 5 | 21.7 |
| 1686–95 | 43 | 11 | 25.6 | 32 | 74.4 |
| 1696–1705 | 46 | 2 | 4.3 | 44 | 95.7 |

conquest. No Dutch colonists executed a testament in New York City from 1665 through 1668. The political situation was too unstable to allow Dutch burghers to have any confidence in the legal system. It took some ten to fifteen years for the Dutch to appreciate that they could prepare wills that preserved their own social customs under English rule.

In contrast to Manhattan, few Dutch colonists in the mid–Hudson River Valley declared wills in English until the 1750s. Consider, for example, the evidence from wills written in the predominantly Dutch communities of Kingston, Hurley, Marbletown, and Rochester Township, and the mostly French settlement of New Paltz. Between 1664 and 1725, fifty-one of all sixty-three Dutch testators in the five towns had their wills drafted in Dutch; more than three-fifths did so between 1726 and 1755 (see Table 1.2). The transition to English as the language of will writing occurred quite suddenly after that point. Seven-eighths of the ethnic Dutch prepared their wills in English between 1756 and 1775. French Huguenot wills in Ulster County indicate the complexity of social identity within early New York. Between 1664 and 1755, these colonists left ten wills in Dutch, eight in English, and five in French. Like the Dutch, they prepared the great majority of their testaments in English during the late colonial period.[22]

While nearly all New York City residents had their wills written in English by 1700, some colonists remained dependent on a legally trained official to draft their testaments in that language. Abraham Gouverneur, a merchant and native New Yorker of Dutch and French Huguenot origin, was the most prolific scribe in Manhattan during the early 1700s, witnessing forty-five city wills between 1690 and 1736. Since nearly all of these testaments bear an identical script, it seems probable that one man drafted them. Gouverneur himself generally signed as the third and last

[22]Twenty-two among twenty-five French colonists executed English-language wills between 1756 and 1775. Three testators prepared their wills in Dutch. Apparently only one Manhattan resident left a will in French. See N.Y. Wills, 1st. ser., no. 23, Mar. 9, 1695.

**Table 1.2** Language of Dutch colonists' wills,
Ulster County, 1664–1775

| Period | No. wills | No. wills in Dutch | % | No. wills in English | % |
|--------|-----------|--------------------|---|----------------------|---|
| 1664–95 | 32 | 24 | 75.0 | 8 | 25.0 |
| 1696–1725 | 31 | 27 | 87.1 | 4 | 12.9 |
| 1726–55 | 44 | 27 | 61.4 | 17 | 38.6 |
| 1756–75 | 48 | 6 | 12.5 | 42 | 87.5 |

witness, penning his impressive signature in an elegant and large hand. His major assets as a scribe were his legal knowledge and his fluency in Dutch, French, and English. In addition to serving as city recorder and counsel for some years, he was also deputy provincial secretary and an official translator of the Dutch and French languages. While he drafted wills exclusively in English, his clients were predominantly Dutch but also included a significant number of French and English colonists.[23]

One might assume that all persons who had their wills drafted in English could at least understand that language. They could then be assured that their oral declaration had been faithfully transcribed as it was read back to them. In at least one case, however, a New York City woman had a will written in English though she apparently understood only Dutch. Beginning in 1721, the Prerogative Court of New York inquired into the circumstances concerning the will of Cornelia De Peyster, a wealthy widow who had recently died. She had prepared her last will in 1699 and had later executed two codicils—all written in English—in 1711 and 1714.[24] One Mary Blood, an old acquaintance of the deceased, testified that De Peyster could conduct business in English only by relying on an interpreter: "Mrs Cornelia De Peyster did understand some English words and but few she could not understand whole discourse or not all of a whole sentence. . . . I was often called up to assist in the shop when any English people were there and us'd commonly to talk to them and interpret to her when none of her relations were there to interpret to her."[25]

[23]For biographical information on Gouverneur, see Paul M. Hamlin and Charles E. Baker, eds., *Supreme Court of Judicature of the Province of New York, 1691–1704*, 3 vols. (New York: New-York Historical Society, 1959), 3:334–35. Gouverneur's New York City clients included twenty-five Dutch, ten French, and ten English residents. Dutch-speaking legal advisers such as Gouverneur undoubtedly helped some Dutch colonists adjust to the English legal system. For additional evidence concerning this process see A. G. Roeber, "'The Origin of Whatever Is Not English among Us': The Dutch-Speaking and German-Speaking Peoples of Colonial British America," in Bernard Bailyn and Philip D. Morgan, eds., *Strangers within the Realm: Cultural Margins of the First British Empire* (Chapel Hill: University of North Carolina Press, 1991), 230.
[24]N.Y. Wills, no. 317, Feb. 19, 1699, and codicils.
[25]Ibid., testimony of Nov. 1, 1721.

Additional testimony further complicated the issue. Two New York attorneys identified the handwriting of the last codicil as the script of Jacob Regnier, a lawyer who had died several years prior to the hearing. Both men insisted that Regnier could not understand Dutch and had formerly admitted as much.[26] An incredible picture emerges from this testimony: a woman deficient in English dictating a codicil to any attorney ignorant of Dutch! De Peyster undoubtedly relied on an interpreter in executing her last testament.

Despite this testimony, Governor William Burnet personally admitted De Peyster's will to probate. Although no surviving record states the rationale for this decision, the governor was undoubtedly impressed by evidence that the controversial second codicil effected the widow's purpose of limiting her son-in-law's control of her grandchildren's inheritance.[27] She may not have been able to comprehend English, but she understood the terms of her will when she signed it. This case also indicates how colonial officials in an ethnically diverse society sometimes overlooked or ignored deviations from English legal practice that served the needs of the local populace.

Cornelia De Peyster was herself born in Holland, emigrated to New Amsterdam as a young girl, and married in that town in 1651.[28] Although she lived under English rule in New York for fifty years, she retained her native language and culture. Her grandson, Johannes, born in 1694, grew up in very different circumstances. In 1702, young Johannes accompanied his father, Johannes De Peyster, Sr., on a business trip to Boston. The father's letters to his brother, Abraham, the head of the New York family, are revealing about his son's education. Although Johannes wrote to his brother exclusively in Dutch, his letters proudly relate his son's progress in English:

> As for what YH [Your Honor] says about my son Johannes neither myself nor any one else speaks Dutch to him. Once in a while people called here who spoke Dutch to him. He answered them in English. English comes more fluently and easier to him than Dutch. YH would be surprised should you hear him converse in English. With God's help he will soon have mastered said language. He spells and reads fluently besides saying the English prayers and catechism. He is now standing here and kissing me for his Uncle, Mommie and Cousins, and says that when he understands his English and French he will pay a visit to his cousins. He has grown at least the width of a finger, since his arrival here. May God bless him further.[29]

[26]Ibid., testimony of David Jamison and Henry Wileman, esqs., Oct. 25, 1721.
[27]Ibid., testimony of Mary Blood, Nov. 1, 1721.
[28]Edwin R. Purple, *Contributions to the History of Ancient Families of New Amsterdam and New York* (New York: privately printed, 1881), 98.
[29]Johannes De Peyster to Abraham De Peyster, Feb. 23, 1703, Dingman Versteeg, trans., De Peyster Family Papers, 1:140–41, New-York Historical Society (hereafter NYHS).

When the boy's mother journeyed to Boston in June 1703, Johannes Sr. wrote to his brother that "she could not get a single Dutch word" out of the nine-year-old. Although she expressed anxiety about Johannes's neglect of Dutch, her husband still boasted of their son's ability to adopt English ways: "Our boy does not care for Jorke [New York]. He is entirely English and a Bostonian."[30] When the parents departed for New York in August 1703, they left their son in the care of an elderly couple who would continue to instruct him in the English and French languages. Although Johannes De Peyster, Sr., had once belonged to the predominantly Dutch Leislerian political faction, he realized that fluency in English was essential to his son's success in commerce or government. Considering his education, it is not surprising that Johannes Jr. adopted the name John in his adult life. He moved to Albany as a young man and began a distinguished career, serving successively as city recorder, mayor, member of the Provincial Assembly, surrogate of Albany County, and paymaster of New York forces during the revolutionary war. He died in 1789 at age ninety-five.[31]

By the 1740s, the use of the Dutch language had diminished appreciably in New York City. Cornelius Van Horne, a well-to-do merchant, wrote in June 1743 that "the Dutch tongue Declines fast amongst Us Especially with the young people. And all Affairs are transacted in English and that Language prevails Generally Amongst Us."[32] Since most burghers spoke English with considerable fluency, they could prepare wills without the assistance of interpreters. Dutch New Yorkers resembled other city residents in choosing scribes or notaries from a diverse group of attorneys or legally knowledgeable men. No single individual assumed such a major role in drafting testaments as Abraham Gouverneur or William Bogardus had previously done.

During the mid-1700s, several leading members of the New York bar became increasingly involved in the drafting of wills. Since these attorneys may have often composed wills without signing as witnesses, it is impossible to determine the precise number of persons whom they served. It is certain, however, that highly trained professionals drafted the wills of a broad spectrum of persons rather than confining their practice to the economic elite. The clients of John Chambers, Abraham Lodge, and Simon Johnson included a fairly even distribution of merchants, artisans or skilled tradesmen, and widows of varying means.[33]

[30]Ibid., June 14 and 28, 1703, 1:129, 173.
[31]Cuyler Reynolds, ed., *Albany Chronicles: A History of the City Arranged Chronologically . . . Addenda to Vol. 2, 1906* (Albany: J. B. Lyon, 1907), 204.
[32]Quoted in I. N. Phelps Stokes, *The Iconography of Manhattan Island*, 6 vols. (New York: R. H. Dodd, 1915–28), 4:576.
[33]These three attorneys witnessed the wills of seventeen merchants, twenty-seven artisans, and sixteen widows between 1720 and 1758.

Despite their growing role in drafting wills, attorneys still competed with persons who may have had some degree of legal knowledge but were by no means professionally trained. John Nathan Hutchins, a schoolmaster, signed his name as the last witness and apparent scribe of eleven wills executed between 1756 and 1774. The majority of his clients appear to have been drawn from the middling ranks of society: three shopkeepers, three artisans, two mariners, one laborer, and one merchant.

Although the use of scribes was common throughout the colonial period, a considerable number of merchants and other well-to-do persons were probably sufficiently acquainted with the law to be able to draft their own wills. A holographic testament, or one written in the testator's own hand, did not require the signature of any witnesses if it could be proved in court that the script was that of the deceased.[34] Sampson Simson, a Jewish merchant, was fully aware of this rule when he executed a will on July 30, 1773, before his brother Solomon alone. Although too ill to draft his testament, Simson summoned enough strength to pen a final paragraph that explained his course of action:

> I having intended to write this myself, but finding my self weak, desired my Brother to do it for me which he has done from my Mouth, and I having fully examined the same, do desire and order that it may pass and be held good and firm . . . as if it had been wrote every word and letter with my own hand and that it may require no other proof or authority than my hand and Seal hereunto Subscribed and fixed. . . .[35]

After Simson's death, his former business associates appeared before the Prerogative Court and testified that the final paragraph was indeed the "proper hand writing" of the decreased, "Their Cause of knowledge arising from having Several times Seen Said Sampson Simson write and sign his name, and each of these Deponents having often Seen Accoundts [sic] depending and settled with the said Sampson Simson in his life time."[36] The corroborative testimony of three witnesses and the testator's brother settled the issue, and Simson's will was probated without further delay.

Some persons lacked either sufficient knowledge to draft their own will or the resources to hire a scribe. As early as 1705, these testators

---

[34]Contrary to English legal practice, New York's Prerogative Court accepted the validity of holographic wills of real estate and not simply those of personal property. See Johnson, "Prerogative Court," 115–16.

[35]Leo Hershkowitz, ed., *Wills of Early New York Jews (1704–1799)* (New York: American Jewish Historical Society, 1967), 141–42.

[36]Ibid., probate Jan. 18, 1774.

might obtain a standardized, printed will from the Prerogative Office.[37] The testator had simply to enter his or her name at the top of the document, list the name of the principal beneficiary and executor in the body of the will, sign the testament, and obtain the signature of the necessary number of witnesses. An illiterate testator would of course require the assistance of someone to enter these facts. The single-page, printed will was used almost exclusively by common sailors who had few family ties and wished to leave all their property to a single person. The needs of the great majority of testators, including illiterates, could not be served by so simple a document.

If a person left more than one testament, courts recognized the validity only of a last will. Since nearly all recorded testaments were last wills, it is not possible to determine how many colonists composed other wills prior to their final testaments. We do know, however, that only 3 percent of all New York City wills included a codicil.[38] The small number of codicils suggests that the last testament was the sole testament in most cases. More than 70 percent of all codicils were executed by merchants, wealthy landowners, or the widows of these men. The urban elite confronted problems in conveying property that demanded both flexibility and legal precision. Samuel Bowne, a well-to-do merchant, prepared a will in 1771 that partitioned a large tract on the city's outskirts among several of his children. Thirteen years later, he added a codicil awarding an additional three hundred pounds to two children "if a street which fronts their lots . . . shall not be laid open within three years of my decease."[39] He anticipated that their inheritance would be of insufficient value unless adequate roads raised the value of the real estate. The wealthy were also careful to execute codicils that included their most recent purchases of land. This practice began to be used as colonists adjusted to the more technical aspects of English law during the mid-1700s. According to common law, a testator might devise or convey only those lands in his possession at the drafting of a will. He could not transfer a valid title to any subsequent acquisition of land unless those properties were specified in a new will or a codicil.[40] Thus Mary Alexander, the widow of a prominent attorney, executed a codicil in 1760 that granted her children all the real estate "that I have purchased or acquired since making my will." Her codicil was witnessed by William Livingston, one of New York's foremost lawyers.[41]

[37]See the will of Thomas Herrington, mariner, N.Y. Wills, 1st ser., no. 428, Dec. 24, 1705.

[38]Fifty-five wills among 1,572 New York City testaments included codicils between 1664 and 1775.

[39]N.Y. Wills, Liber 36:272–76, Nov. 5, 1771; codicil Jan. 4, 1784.

[40]Blackstone, *Commentaries* 1, bk. 2:378.

[41]N.Y. Wills, Liber 22:55–56, July 27, 1756, first codicil Feb. 29, 1758, second codicil Feb. 19, 1760.

PROBATE

The Duke's Laws of 1665 marked the first attempt to institute English law in New York. This code specified that the Court of Sessions or the Court of Assizes was to grant probate and to return all wills to the Office of Records in New York City for filing.[42] The Duke's Laws initially applied only to areas of English settlement—Long Island, Staten Island, and Westchester—and therefore implicitly recognized the validity of Dutch administration in other regions. Local courts exercised control over probate throughout the province during the period 1664–85; the wills of New York City residents came under the supervision of the Mayor's Court, a tribunal modeled closely on its Dutch predecessor, the Court of Burgomasters and Schepens.[43] While the Mayor's Court validated wills written according to Dutch law, it also established English procedures concerning probate. After a testator's decease, the subscribing witnesses to the will swore an oath in court that they judged the deceased to be of "sound mind and memory" when he had signed and declared his testament. (This procedure had not been necessary under Dutch law since a properly notarized will required no additional proof in court.) Magistrates throughout the province adopted the English method of taking witnesses' testimony by the early 1680s. It should be noted that colonial courts soon established a more liberal policy toward administering oaths than English tribunals did. Quakers were allowed to make a simple affirmation rather than a formal oath that would violate their religious principles. Jews customarily swore an oath on the Five Books of Moses rather than on the Christian Bible.[44]

The system of local control over probate continued until 1686 when New York became a royal province upon the accession of James II. The crown's instructions then empowered the governor to assume final authority over the probate of wills. The provincial assembly confirmed this power in 1692 "to the Governour or Such Person as he shall Delegate under the Seal of the Prerogative Office."[45] New York law thereafter distinguished between the *proof* and *probate* of wills. Inferior courts assisted in the proof of wills by recording the sworn testimony of witnesses and by administering oaths to executors. The Prerogative Court, a

---

[42]Lincoln, *Colonial Laws*, 1:8–11, 75, 83.

[43]Herbert Alan Johnson, "The Advent of Common Law in Colonial New York," in George Athan Billias, ed., *Selected Essays: Law and Authority in Colonial New York* (Barre, Mass.: Barre Publishers, 1965), 74–75, 80–83.

[44]Hamlin and Baker, *Supreme Court of Judicature*, 1:248; Hershkowitz, *Wills of Jews*, passim.

[45]For the 1686 royal instructions, see O'Callaghan, *Documents Relative to the Colonial History of New York*, 3:372. The statute of Nov. 11, 1692, is printed in Lincoln, *Colonial Laws*, 1:300–302.

branch of the provincial secretary's office, controlled probate, the legal validation of testaments. The statute of 1692 required that all wills concerning property in New York City or nearby counties be proved in Manhattan before the governor or his delegate. Witnesses to wills in the more remote counties were permitted to testify before the Court of Common Pleas in their particular area. Local justices then forwarded the wills and related documents to New York so that probate could be granted. The Courts of Common Pleas could themselves issue probate only for wills concerning estates valued at fifty pounds or less. During the eighteenth century, governors customarily appointed surrogates to administer the proof of wills in particular counties, including New York County comprising Manhattan Island.[46]

While local courts granted probate in most English colonies, the governor or his delegates controlled the validation of New York wills and also authorized interested parties to administer estates in cases of intestacy. A centralized system of probate encouraged the development of uniform legal practices within culturally diverse regions. The administrative reforms of the 1680s and 1690s coincided with the demise of both the Dutch notarial will and the mutual will drafted by husband and wife. Dutch colonists were undoubtedly cautious about preparing testaments that might be declared invalid by an English court. By 1700, they had adjusted to a new legal system without necessarily adopting English social customs.

### Preparation for Death

Men and women who declared wills confronted the basic human problem of providing for the living while themselves preparing for death. The will itself served as both a personal document and a legal instrument, using prescribed, almost ritualistic phrasing. Nearly all wills began with the words "In the Name of God Amen." A preamble then stated the testator's name, place of residence, and often his occupation. If a woman prepared a will, she identified herself by her marital status. Before disposing of any property, most testators referred to their physical condition, recognized their mortality, and declared their mental soundness to execute a will. They then bequeathed their souls to God and committed their bodies to the earth for a decent burial. These fundamental aspects of preparing a will differed little among diverse ethnic and social groups.

Although a testator had to be mentally competent, he or she did not

---

[46]Johnson, "Prerogative Court," 97–100.

**Table 1.3** Health of testators, New York City, 1664–1775

| Wills describing physical condition | Men | | Women | | All testators | |
|---|---|---|---|---|---|---|
| | N | % | N | % | N | % |
| In good health | 287 | 32.2 | 47 | 27.2 | 334 | 31.4 |
| Sick or weak | 589 | 66.0 | 113 | 65.3 | 702 | 65.9 |
| "Aged" | 16 | 1.8 | 13 | 7.5 | 29 | 2.7 |
| Total | 892 | 100 | 173 | 100 | 1065 | 100 |

necessarily need to be in good health. Some 1,593 men and women prepared wills in New York City between 1664 and 1775. About two-thirds of this entire group (1,065 persons) referred to their physical condition at the time that they declared their testaments. More than 65 percent of these 1,065 men and women described themselves as sick or weak; an additional 2.7 percent cited old age as a principal reason for declaring a will (see Table 1.3). Only 31 percent of the entire group stated that they were simply in good health. A slightly higher percentage of men than women were ill as they made their wills. Women were more likely than men to describe their condition as "aged," since they commonly prepared wills as elderly widows.[47]

New York City residents were apt to prepare wills when they confronted the risk of death for various reasons. Between 1664 and 1775, sixty-three men (4.7 percent of all male testators) declared a will just before departing on a voyage. These testators were mostly merchants and mariners who understood the perils of the sea. Their wills were especially numerous during wars in which New Yorkers boarded privateering ships against His Majesty's enemies.

Drafting a will in the face of death was a centuries-old practice in western Europe. In sixteenth- and seventeenth-century England, testators generally identified themselves as sick or weak as they settled their estates.[48] The Dutch too had similar motives for preparing testaments, though the decision might be prompted by either the husband's or wife's illness given the custom of shared marital responsibility over family property. For example, one Dutch couple, whose will was drafted in Holland prior to their arrival in New Netherland, acknowledged their course of action as being dictated by the wife's illness as well as by "the brevity of human life on this earth" which "is perishable like grass and

[47]See below, Appendix.
[48]R. C. Richardson, "Wills and Will-Makers in the Sixteenth and Seventeenth Centuries: Some Lancashire Evidence," *Local Population Studies* no. 9 (1972): 42.

hay, yea like a flower in the field."[49] While colonial New York wills were not usually written so poetically, their common allusions to mortality also had an immediate meaning given the poor health of many testators. For example, testators who identified themselves as "sick" or "weak" outnumbered the healthy by about three to one in rural Suffolk and Ulster counties.[50]

Because few death records for colonial New York have survived, it is not generally possible to determine the precise span between the drafting of a will and the testator's death. A useful though inexact measure of longevity is the interval between the preparation of the document and probate. (Not even this method yields comprehensive results since 6.2 percent of all recorded wills omit the month or year in which the documents were written or probated. It should also be noted that probate might sometimes be delayed for months or even years after a testator's death.) Notwithstanding these limitations in the historical record, a careful analysis of the available data yields some notable results. Many persons were quite close to death when they drafted their wills. Two-fifths of all wills were probated within one year after being written. Three-fifths were probated within two years. Only one-fourth were validated five or more years after being drafted (see Table 1.4). One might think that well-to-do New Yorkers would be especially careful to prepare their wills while in good health. Merchants and professional men, however, showed an even greater tendency than artisans or mariners to declare their testaments within a relatively short time before death.[51] There was little difference between the longevity of men and women after they executed a will. The most marked difference in longevity was between testators who described themselves as healthy and those who commented on being sick. Only 16 percent of the "healthy" had their wills

[49]See the will of Cornelis Jansen Pluvier and his wife, Geertruyd Andries, drafted in Holland in 1656 and recorded in New Amsterdam in 1661. The will is printed in Berthold Fernow, trans. and ed., *Minutes of the Orphanmasters Court of New Amsterdam, 1665–1663*, 2 vols. (New York: F. P. Harper, 1902–7), 1:199–201.

[50]In three Suffolk County towns (East Hampton, Southampton, and Southold) 557 men and women left wills between 1664 and 1775. While 333 were sick or weak, only 96 described their health as good. During this same period, 239 persons left wills in five Ulster County towns. While 117 referred to themselves as sick, only 35 stated that their health was good. The remaining testators in each county omitted any reference to their physical condition.

[51]Forty-six percent of merchants' wills (130 among 283 testaments) were probated within one year after being drafted. Forty percent of artisans' wills (124 among 306 testaments) and 34 percent of mariners' wills (88 of 256 testaments) fall within that same category. These data are based on all wills executed in New York City between 1664 and 1775. For the total number of wills by men within these groups, see Appendix.

**Table 1.4** Interval between the execution and probate of wills

| Period | 0–11 months | | 12–23 months | | 2–4 years | | 5–9 years | | 10–19 years | | 20 years or more | | Total | |
|---|---|---|---|---|---|---|---|---|---|---|---|---|---|---|
| | N* | % | N | % | N | % | N | % | N | % | N | % | N | % |
| 1664–95 | 43 | 44.3 | 16 | 16.5 | 6 | 6.2 | 16 | 16.5 | 9 | 9.3 | 7 | 7.2 | 97 | 100 |
| 1696–1725 | 131 | 42.7 | 62 | 20.2 | 39 | 12.7 | 41 | 13.3 | 26 | 8.5 | 8 | 2.6 | 307 | 100 |
| 1726–50 | 116 | 33.7 | 89 | 25.9 | 47 | 13.7 | 42 | 12.2 | 30 | 8.7 | 20 | 5.8 | 344 | 100 |
| 1751–75 | 306 | 42.1 | 139 | 19.1 | 102 | 14.0 | 71 | 9.8 | 91 | 12.5 | 17 | 2.3 | 726 | 99.8 |
| Entire period | 596 | 40.4 | 306 | 20.8 | 194 | 13.2 | 170 | 11.5 | 156 | 10.6 | 52 | 3.5 | 1474 | 100 |

*Each column indicates the number of cases that fell during a given interval.

probated within one year; at least 56 percent of the "sick" were dead within twelve months after declaring their wills.[52]

Most men and women spoke honestly and carefully of their physical condition as they drew up a testament. The traditional phrasing of wills reminds us that even healthy persons did not take their good fortune for granted. As one man declared in 1689: "I William Cox of the Citty of New Yorke merchant being of Sound and perfect health Memory and Understanding thanks be unto Almighty God for it and knowing the Frayletys of this Life that I must dye & not knowing how Soone have therefore made . . . this to be my Last will and Testament." Cox acted none too soon, for he was dead within two weeks, apparently drowned in the bay off Staten Island.[53]

Many New Yorkers put off the preparation of a will until they fell ill or felt some premonition of death. This tendency undoubtedly swelled the ranks of the intestate. James De Lancey, the lieutenant governor, neglected to declare a will before dying suddenly on July 30, 1760, at age fifty-seven. His failure to anticipate death is striking given his family obligations, his legal training, and his personal history of severe asthma attacks.[54] At least a few men escaped intestacy by declaring their wills at the last possible moment. Dennis Power, a ship captain, managed to dictate his last will to a lawyer but found himself too weak to sign the document when a friend returned to his bedside with the necessary number of witnesses. After Power's death, the Prerogative Court admitted the unsigned will to probate because the testator had made an oral declaration of intent before three persons.[55]

New York officials accepted the validity of nuncupative, or oral, wills executed under special circumstances. If a person became so ill that he was unable to prepare a written will, he might declare an oral testament before two or more witnesses. (The Prerogative Court did not enforce the three-witness requirement under the English Statute of Frauds of 1677.) As in England, an oral declaration had to be committed to writing within six days and presented for probate within six months. These requirements did not apply to oral testaments made by soldiers and

---

[52]Among 316 "healthy" testators, 50 (or 15.8 percent) had wills probated within one year after being drafted. Among 697 "sick" or "weak" testators, 392 (or 56.2 percent) prepared testaments that were probated within that same span. I have calculated the interval between the drafting and probate of wills declared by 1,013 of all 1,065 testators who described their physical condition.

[53]N.Y. Wills, 1st ser., no. 64, July 15, 1689.

[54]For a description of De Lancey's death, see William Smith, Jr., *The History of the Province of New York*, ed. Michael Kammen, 2 vols. (Cambridge, Mass.: Belknap Press, 1972), 2:244–45.

[55]N.Y. Wills, Liber 21:427–30, Oct. 10, 1759. The testator's name was also spelled Powers.

sailors in the king's service. Their wills were judged with special leniency given the circumstances of military life. By the early eighteenth century, New York magistrates accepted the common law rule that an oral will might bequeath personal property, but that it could not convey real estate. English law restricted the use of the oral testament because it was subject to fraud and error.[56]

Only fourteen residents of New York City declared oral testaments between 1664 and 1775. The great majority of colonists apparently regarded the nuncupative will as an unreliable and inadequate means of bequeathing property. How could they be certain that their last wishes would be faithfully committed to writing after they died? A nuncupative will was almost necessarily a deathbed testament—one composed hastily and under severe physical and mental stress.

The typical New York testator was physically ill but not quite on the verge of death. From 1664 through 1775, 21 percent (or 306) of 1,474 New York wills were probated less than six months after being drafted. Seventy-one (or less than 5 percent) were written and probated within the same month. New York testators settled their worldly affairs somewhat earlier than their counterparts in early modern England. W. K. Jordan, sampling English probate records between 1504 and 1517, found that a median span of only fifty-nine days elapsed between the drafting of a will and probate. This interval increased to four months in wills validated between 1617 and 1637. The historian Margaret Spufford concludes that deathbed testaments were commonplace in Cambridgeshire villages throughout the sixteenth and seventeenth centuries.[57]

Writing in 1590, Judge Henry Swinburne of York complained that too many Englishmen prepared wills in their final days. He attributed this practice to a popular superstition, especially strong among the "ruder and more ignorant people," that a man would hasten his own death by declaring a will while he was still in good health.[58] To execute a testament was somehow to tempt fate. It is likely that many New Yorkers held this belief during the colonial period. Doubtless some persons today still view the writing of a will with similar trepidation. In recent times, however, most men and women have drawn their testaments considerably in

---

[56]Johnson, "Prerogative Court," 116.

[57]W. K. Jordan, *Philanthropy in England, 1480–1660: A Study of the Changing Pattern of English Social Aspirations* (1959; rpt. New York: Russell Sage Foundation, 1964), 16–17; Margaret Spufford, *Contrasting Communities: English Villagers in the Sixteenth and Seventeenth Centuries* (Cambridge: Cambridge University Press, 1974), 321.

[58]Swinburne advised men to draft their wills while in good health so as to avoid the risks of either dying intestate or declaring an unreliable, oral testament. See *Treatise of Testaments*, 28.

advance of death. In one Ohio county during the mid-1960s, only 14.6 percent of 453 wills were probated within one year after being written. More than one-half of the testaments were probated at least five years after the date of drafting; 28.5 percent were probated after ten or more years.[59] The American will is now generally written in anticipation of death rather than in the face of death as was common in times past.

The writing of wills in early New York City lies partway between medieval European custom and present-day practice. As in earlier times, most colonial testators prepared spiritually for death by bequeathing their souls to God. The will's religious preamble lacked, however, the importance it possessed in medieval Europe. It was often phrased in a perfunctory manner that reflected custom as much as personal belief. By the mid-1700s, an increasing number of New York City testators began to dispense entirely with the bequest of the soul. By contrast, thirteenth-century Englishmen regarded the will as an essential vehicle for expressing their faith and assuring their salvation. Clerics urged that dying men bequeath money to the church before making their final confession. To refuse to declare a will was tantamount to rejecting the authority of the priesthood.[60] During the 1400s and early 1500s, English testators commonly bequeathed their souls to God, the Virgin Mary, and the saints; they also called for burial in the churchyard. In addition to charitable donations, many testators set aside sums for the performance of masses on behalf of themselves and their friends and relatives. English customs closely resembled the nature of will writing in medieval Italy.[61]

Some historians believe that the Reformation marked a crucial turning point in the long-term secularization of the will. Since Protestantism disparaged the deathbed rite of contrition, the testator could no longer hope to win salvation by granting alms to the poor or by offering one final prayer to God. The Christian's duty in leaving a will, wrote seventeenth-century Dutch ministers, was solely to "settle his house in order" before death and to prevent the outbreak of future disputes among his heirs.[62] Despite this fundamental shift in religious attitudes, the bequest

[59]Marvin B. Sussman, Judith N. Cates, and David T. Smith, *The Family and Inheritance* (New York: Russell Sage Foundation, 1970), 66–67.

[60]Michael Sheehan, *The Will in Medieval England* (Toronto: Pontifical Institute of Medieval Studies, 1963), 232–38.

[61]Holdsworth, *History of English Law*, 3:545–47; Spufford, *Contrasting Communities*, 335. For Italian wills of the twelfth and thirteenth centuries, see Steven Epstein, *Wills and Wealth in Medieval Genoa, 1150–1250* (Cambridge: Harvard University Press, 1984); Robert Brentano, *Rome before Avignon: A Social History of Thirteenth-Century Rome* (New York: Basic Books, 1974), chap. 7.

[62]Pim Den Boer, "Naar een geschiedenis van de dood: Mogelijkheden tot onderzoek naar de houding ten opzichte van de dode en de dood ten tijde van de Republiek,"

of the soul retained its position at the head of the will. Testators continued to seek a measure of spiritual assurance before death despite the notion that they could do nothing by themselves to further their own salvation.

Although the religious provisions of wills are a rich historical source, they also pose special difficulties in interpretation. Margaret Spufford, analyzing English villagers' wills of the sixteenth and seventeenth centuries, argues that scribes rather than the testators themselves were primarily responsible for phrasing the religious preamble. Unless a person had "abnormally strong convictions," she concludes, "he was unlikely to dictate the wording of the bequest."[63] He was instead apt to rely on the minister or educated layman who drew up the will. The testator's influence was largely negative—he might purposely avoid a scribe who held theological opinions opposed to his own. Although the wills of seventeenth-century English villagers reveal much about communal religious beliefs, they seldom permit us to enter directly into an individual's mind: "It is wrong for the historian to assume that if he takes a cross-section of four hundred and forty wills over a particular period, he is getting four hundred and forty different testators' religious opinions reflected."[64]

An examination of New York wills reveals many instances that support Spufford's generalizations. Abraham Gouverneur, one of the most active scribes during the early eighteenth century, expressed the beliefs of most of his clients through the following preamble:

> I bequeath my Soule after its departure out of this frail body into the Mercyful hands of the Most High God My Creator and Redeemer hoping and only trusting for Mercy and the Pardon of my Manyfold Sinns and Transgressions in and thro the meritorious death and Passion of the blessed Son of God Jesus Christ my Saviour and Redeemer and my body to the Earth there to be Decently Interred . . . in hopes of a blessed Resurrection at the Last Day.[65]

---

*Tijdschrift Voor Geschiedenis* 84 (1976): 161–201. For an analysis of the religious significance of the will in eighteenth-century France, see Michel Vovelle, *Piété baroque et déchristianisation en Provence au XVIII siècle: Les attitudes devant la mort d'après les clauses des testaments* (Paris: Plon, 1973).

[63]Spufford, *Contrasting Communities,* 333.

[64]Spufford, "The Scribes of Villagers' Wills in the Sixteenth and Seventeenth Centuries and Their Influence," *Local Population Studies* no. 7 (1971): 41. For two reviews of Spufford's work in the same journal, see "Wills and Their Scribes: A Communication from the Matlock Studies Population Group," no. 8 (1972): 55–57; R. C. Richardson, "Wills and Will-Makers," 33–40.

[65]See the wills of Johannes Hardenbrook, merchant; Peter Nagle, mariner; and Jacobus Vanderspiegel, silversmith. N.Y. Wills, 1st ser., no. 432, Sept. 12, 1702; no. 450, Nov. 30, 1711; and no. 469, Nov. 29, 1708.

Since this same preamble appears in several wills executed after Gouverneur's death, one suspects that the scribe may have copied rather than developed this particular formula.[66]

The use of a general formula does not itself indicate that the bequest of the soul was a purely ritualistic act that failed to engage the spirit of the ordinary person. A common prayer, after all, can be uttered with nearly as much intensity of feeling as a more spontaneous one. Only a small number of testators chose, however, to reveal the full depth of their personal feelings through their wills. Isaac Stoutenburgh, a carpenter, regarded the execution of his testament as the turning point in life when he might shift his gaze from material concerns to the preparation for the life hereafter:

> I pray God almighty for his grace to spend the rest of my days in his wholy fear and to be prepared for my Latter End and when it shall please his Infinite Wisdom to dissolve this frail Tabernacle by Death, I Recomend and frely bequeath my Soul unto my Creator to be disposed of not according to my deserts but according to the Infinite Riches of his free grace made manifest unto his world in the fulness of time by his son, Jesus Christ my Lord & Savior . . . author of my hope and Confidence.[67]

While some testaments assume the solemn and austere quality of a confession of faith, several wills betray only the peculiar preoccupations of their authors. St. George Talbot, a former vestryman of Trinity Church, recounted how "I did in the twenty first year of my Life devote myself to Celibacy, of which I never repented, Notwithstanding I have suffered great Affronts and scandalous, Base, vile & False Reports I do declare that I never knew any Woman carnally as men know their Wifes." The testator, now 103 years old but in "perfect health," bequeathed a substantial annuity to his housekeeper, Rachel Gould, "All on Condition that she . . . remain and continue single Chast & Virtuous, as she hath done more than twenty seven years past since I first became acquainted with her." Despite the highly unusual nature of this bequest, we have little reason to doubt Talbot's sincerity. He reserved most of his large estate for the support of several failing churches in England and for the benefit of the Society for the Propagation of the Gospel.[68]

Unlike these intensely personal statements, most preambles were phrased in doctrinally neutral language that nearly any Protestant might accept. One finds only a handful of testators who confidently identified

---

[66]See the wills of Jacobus Quick, cordwainer, and Jacobus Roosevelt, Jr. N.Y. Wills, Liber 14:156, Jan. 15, 1741; Liber 28:38, Jan. 16, 1771.

[67]N.Y. Wills, 1st ser., no. 462, Oct. 12, 1698.

[68]Ibid., Liber 26:68, May 11, 1765.

themselves as members of the "elect," that exclusive community that figured so prominently in the wills of seventeenth-century English Puritans.[69] It should be emphasized that laymen rather than ministers were almost entirely responsible for drafting New York City wills. This fact may help to explain the prosaic wording of many religious preambles. Laymen also assumed the predominant role as scribes in rural New York, particularly during the eighteenth century.

Even New York City Jews had little difficulty in adjusting to religious preambles phrased in general terms. Abraham De Lucena's will included one of the few preambles that bore a distinctively Jewish stamp: "I bequeath my Immortal Soul into the hands of the Almighty God of Israel my Creator Trusting in his Mercy for a pardon of All my Sins and hoping for a Joyful resurr[ection] to Life Eternal."[70] De Lucena's will expressed his Jewish faith even though it was witnessed by three Christians and possibly written by one of them, the attorney Frederick Van Cortlandt. Drafting a preamble was not simply a legalistic formality when conventional phrases were used. Although some Jewish wills include the phrase "Anno Domini," all were careful to avoid any direct mention of Jesus Christ.

Despite powerful continuities in the phrasing of wills, a significant number of New York City testators chose to dispense entirely with the religious preamble by the mid-eighteenth century. This trend, which developed during the 1740s, involved about one-fourth of all wills during the 1750s and more than one-third during the 1770s.[71] The failure of many testators to mention their spiritual needs does not necessarily indicate a diminution of religious feeling within the society as a whole. The gradual shift in the form of the will does, however, tell us that men and women were beginning to develop a new attitude toward the bequest of their material possessions. This act, which had for centuries been closely linked to the spiritual preparation for death, was slowly becoming a purely secular concern.

Further evidence of the secularization of the will lies in the nature of provisions concerning burial. The overwhelming majority of testators offered no specific instructions concerning their funerals, but simply requested that they be buried in a "decent" or "Christian" manner at the

---

[69]The phrasing of the Puritan will and the role of the clergy as scribes are analyzed in Richardson, "Wills and Will-Makers," 33–35. See also Spufford, *Contrasting Communities*, 320–44. For a New York will that uses the term "elect," see N.Y. Wills, 1st ser., no. 438, July 12, 1713 (will of Bartholomew Le Roux).

[70]Hershkowitz, *Wills of Jews*, 33, Feb. 12, 1716.

[71]Seventy-two New York City wills were probated from July 1771 through October 31, 1773. Twenty-seven (or 37.5 percent) of the wills omit the religious preamble.

discretion of their executors.[72] This formula, borrowed directly from seventeenth-century English practice, reflects the Protestant notion that elaborate burial rites were nothing but a popish superstition and could not possibly profit the soul. These ideas, which were also shared by French and Dutch Protestants, were in stark contrast to the prevalent attitudes toward the funeral in eighteenth-century France. The typical Catholic testator directed that he be buried in the churchyard and gave highly detailed instructions concerning his funeral, often requesting that orphans accompany the procession and offer their innocent prayers for the soul of the deceased.[73]

Although few testators left specific instructions concerning their burial, there is considerable evidence that the funeral had become an important social occasion by the beginning of the eighteenth century. Several surviving inventories of estates indicate that funerals sometimes consumed a large share of the personal estate of the deceased. The widow of Nicholas Garretse, a mariner, spent sixty pounds in funeral charges, about two-fifths of her husband's total holdings.[74] Although this level of expenditure was probably above average, it was not uncommon for the relatives of an artisan to use up more than 10 percent of the deceased's personal property for this purpose. Sarah Ewoutse, the widow of a bolter or miller, expended twelve pounds on her husband's funeral, almost one-sixth of his goods and credits. Like most executors, the widow devoted most of this money to the outfitting and entertainment of the mourners rather than the preparation of her husband's body for burial. Several friends and relatives of the deceased received gloves as a token of remembrance. Black silk and fine linens draped the coffin and perhaps provided the material for mourning cloaks and ribbons. After the burial, the mourners celebrated the memory of the departed by guzzling down one barrel of beer and one and a half gallons of rum, and consuming fifteen pounds of sugar. The widow also provided "one gross of pipes" and six pounds of tobacco for the smoking pleasure of participants. The charges for the burial itself were only fifteen shillings for the coffin and ten shillings for the bearing of the casket and the digging of the grave.[75]

[72]See the wills of James Neau, William Hamersley, and Peter Gibbons. N.Y. Wills, 1st ser., no. 453, Sept. 4, 1712; Liber 18:175, Aug. 3, 1752; Liber 28:164, Nov. 18, 1771.

[73]Den Boer, "Geschiedenis van de dood," 166–67, 172–75; Spufford, *Contrasting Communities*, 331.

[74]Court of Probates: Inventories and Accounts (hereafter N.Y. Inventories), 1666–1823, 2d ser., no. 113, Feb. 8, 1707, N.Y. Archives.

[75]Ibid., no. 98, Mar. 16, 1719. For an analysis of funerary rites in colonial New England, see David E. Stannard, *The Puritan Way of Death: A Study of Religion, Culture, and Social Change* (New York: Oxford University Press, 1977).

The funerals of wealthy merchants were distinguished from those of artisans by the more lavish scale of gifts and entertainment rather than by the nature of the ceremony itself. Benjamin D'Harriette, one of the few testators to leave behind specific instructions concerning his funeral, asked "to be decently buried by my Executors . . . in the same manner as my late dear wife was buried each of the persons who shall support my Paul to have a gold ring with a Scarf and a pair of Gloves And the Ministers and Doctors who shall be invited to, and attend my funeral each to have a gold Ring Scarfe and Gloves given to them."[76] The son and heir of Beatrix Ouzeel Cocq, a wealthy widow, spent the enormous sum of more than £100 on his mother's funeral, including £15 for wine, £2 for the making of sixteen gold rings, £7 for gloves, and £41 for "mourning cloth." The cost of the coffin clone amounted to nearly £5, and more than £3 were expended to meet the widow's desire to "be buried in the Dutch Reformed Church . . . upon my Brother Ouzeel van Swieten."[77]

The silence of most testators concerning their burial is in stark contrast to the often expensive and elaborate nature of funerals. The authors of wills were perhaps fully confident that their kin would not slight a ceremony so directly linked to the family's social status and dignity. Given their Protestant beliefs, most testators were also spared the fear that the neglect of funeral rites might imperil the salvation of their souls.

As in seventeenth-century Holland, New York's leading burghers attached a high degree of social prestige to being buried within the walls of the church. Judith Stuyvesant, the widow of New Netherland's most famous governor, composed a will in 1679 that offered her nephew Nicholas Bayard, his wife, and their children "A buryeing place in the Tombe or Vaught of my late deceased husband in ye Chappell or Church at my Bowrey And in case it should happen yt my sayd Church or Chappel did come to decay or for any other reason be demolished I doe hereby declare . . . yt of ye matterialls and rubbage of sch Chappell be made a building sufficient for a Cover upon ye sd Vaugvht." Five years after drafting this will, the widow attached a codicil that bequeathed the chapel to the overseers of the "Nether Dutch Church or Congregation of the Citty of New Yorke." Although the overseers were to enjoy complete freedom in using the building as they saw fit, the widow directed that they preserve the "tombe or vaught" under all circumstances.[78]

[76]N.Y. Wills, Liber 14:72, Apr. 3, 1741.
[77]N.Y. Inventories, 2d ser., no. 54, Sept. 20, 1711; N.Y. Wills, 1st ser., no. 482, Aug. 22, 1711.
[78]N.Y. Wills, Liber 19B:277–85, Jan. 29, 1679, first codicil Feb. 15, 1679, second codicil

During the mid-eighteenth century, wealthy New Yorkers might request to be buried in family vaults either on their own lands or within a churchyard. Frederick Philipse, one of the colony's largest landowners, directed that "my Body . . . be Buried with Great Decency but with no Ostentation in the Family Vault at the upper Mill."[79] The owners of vaults within Trinity churchyard held the power to convey these structures to their descendants in much the same manner as they would transmit other forms of real estate. Anne Waddell, executing a will in 1773, expressed her desire "to be buried in my Vault in Trinity Church Yard" and granted that chamber "to my Children to be held by them as tenants in Common each one part thereof."[80]

While some of New York's wealthiest families sought to preserve their privacy even in death, other groups expressed a more communal notion of burial. One Joshua Isaacs spoke for many of his co-religionists when he requested to "be buryed in Our Jews burying Ground among my relations and friends."[81] Once located outside the city walls, the Jewish cemetery in Chatham Square is today the oldest remaining graveyard from Manhattan's colonial past.

---

Dec. 1, 1684. For a discussion of burial customs in seventeenth-century Holland, see Den Boer, "Geschiedenis van de dood," 177–81.

[79] N.Y. Wills, Liber 18:1, June 6, 1751, codicil July 22, 1751.

[80] Ibid., Liber 28:479, Mar. 29, 1773.

[81] Hershkowitz, *Wills of Jews*, 69, July 13, 1744. See David de Sola Pool, *Portraits Etched in Stone: Early Jewish Settlers, 1682–1831* (New York: Columbia University Press, 1952).

# Chapter 2

# Marriage and Inheritance in New Netherland

The social experience of married women in early New York was profoundly influenced by the province's Dutch past. The Dutch *huysvrouw* (housewife) in New Amsterdam had far more control of property than the English goodwife in either Boston or Jamestown. Since brides and bridegrooms in New Netherland typically combined all their possessions into a jointly owned estate, they frequently developed and expressed a sense of reciprocal rights and responsibilities. Wives not only contributed to the family's earnings by engaging in commerce with their husbands' consent, but they also joined their spouses in disposing of property by last will and testament. The jointly written or mutual will generally allowed the surviving spouse—whether husband or wife—to receive the same rights to the family estate. Children usually inherited an equal share of property irrespective of their sex.

The transmission of Dutch law to New Netherland was complicated by the mixed character of the colonial population. Nearly half of all European immigrants during the 1640s came from areas outside the Dutch republic, primarily from Germany, Wallonia, and Scandinavia. Settlers from the Netherlands alone arrived from a wide diversity of regions—from the urban centers of Holland to rural villages in Gelderland.[1] The meaning of "custom" was therefore bound to be quite different in New Netherland than it was in Europe. In the Old World, "custom" referred to those social practices that were so long established in particular locales

---

[1] See Oliver A. Rink, *Holland on the Hudson: An Economic and Social History of Dutch New York* (Ithaca: Cornell University Press, 1986), chap. 6. David Steven Cohen, "How Dutch Were the Dutch of New Netherland?" *New York History* 62 (1981): 43–60.

that they had become law. The maintenance of traditional ways depended on a correspondence between legal institutions and communal values or norms.[2] New Netherland was a new and quite primitive colony that could not simply duplicate Dutch customs all at once. It was not until the 1650s, for example, that public officials in New Amsterdam effectively began to enforce Dutch laws regarding inheritance and orphaned children's property rights.

The assimilation of non-Dutch settlers within the Dutch population occurred gradually during the years prior to the English conquest. Germans, Scandinavians, and Walloons commonly intermarried with Dutch colonists, adopted the Dutch language, and grew accustomed to laws administered by Dutch court officials and notaries. The process of assimilation was eased by the fact that many non-Dutch settlers emigrated from regions whose legal traditions closely resembled those of Holland. These men and women readily accepted the custom of community property within marriage—the notion that marital property was part of a family estate, not simply the husband's wealth. Dutch customs of marriage and inheritance endured beyond the fall of New Netherland because they embodied pervasive social attitudes and practices.

## MARRIED WOMEN'S LEGAL STATUS IN THE NETHERLANDS

The concept of female subordination within marriage was basic to all western European societies in the seventeenth century, and the Netherlands was no exception. According to Roman-Dutch law, women lost their independent status upon marriage—a situation existing in theory if not quite in fact. Single women of full legal age could act independently in legal proceedings, but wives lacked this privilege. As soon as wedding vows were exchanged, the husband acquired the power of guardianship over his wife and obtained control of her property. The law recognized all married women, whatever their age, as minors who owed obedience to their spouses. They could therefore act neither as plaintiffs nor as defendants without their husbands' assistance or authorization. Their right to enter contracts was extremely limited unless they had their spouses' approval.[3]

[2]See, for example, Emmanuel Le Roy Ladurie, "Family Structures and Inheritance Customs in Sixteenth-Century France," in Jack Goody, Joan Thirsk, and E. P. Thompson, eds., *Family and Inheritance: Rural Society in Western Europe, 1200–1800* (Cambridge: Cambridge University Press, 1978), 37–70.

[3]Hugo Grotius (Huig de Groot), *The Jurisprudence of Holland*, ed. and trans. Robert Warden Lee, 2d. ed., 2 vols. (1953; rpt. Aalen, W. Ger.: Scientia Verlag, 1977), 63–71.

If these legal rules had been narrowly implemented, Dutch women would have been little better than servants. This was by no means the case. Dutch women often exercised powers over family property that belied their status as minors. It is significant that married women's legal capacity expanded as Dutch society became increasingly commercial during the late Middle Ages. Women's economic role grew sufficiently important that female traders were permitted to enter binding contracts in numerous circumstances. By the seventeenth century, a wife's contracts were considered valid whenever she traded with her spouse's permission, acted as his agent, or engaged in business pertaining to her household responsibilities. She might also obtain freedom to contract by an antenuptial agreement negotiated with her husband just before marriage.[4]

Women frequently exercised these legal rights and therefore assumed a significant economic role in seventeenth-century Holland. English visitors to the Netherlands marveled at the superior business skills of Dutch *vrouwen* compared with their own countrywomen. One Englishman noted that burghers could "hold on [to] their trades to their dying days, knowing the capacity of their wives to get in their estates and carry on their trades after their deaths."[5] The Dutchwoman's business skills promoted the family's prosperity rather than posing a risk to the children's inheritance.

Married women's legal status mirrored their position in Dutch society. A woman was not considered to be her husband's equal in power or rights. She was, however, a partner rather than a servant within marriage. Jacob Cats, the author of many popular books on domestic morality, described the ideal marriage as a partnership "in care and in joy / in bustle and in rest / in loss and in gain / in recreation and in work / in risk and in fortune." Success in marriage depended on mutual affection and a proper division of labor. Cats urged each spouse to accept his or her appointed tasks: "So you, industrious husband, go to earn your living / While you, O young wife, tend to your household."[6] This advice seems to have been generally observed, but not in as strict a manner as Cats desired. Women's role as housekeepers often required that they actively

---

[4]Grotius, *Jurisprudence of Holland*, 1:29–31; R. W. Lee, *An Introduction to Roman-Dutch Law*, 5th ed. (1953; rpt. Oxford: Oxford University Press, 1961), 64–66.

[5]Josiah Child, *A New Discourse of Trade . . .* , 5th ed. (Glasgow: R. and A. Foulis, 1751), 3. (This book was first published in London in 1693.) B. A. Holderness, "Widows in Pre-Industrial Society: An Essay upon Their Economic Functions," in Richard M. Smith, ed., *Land, Kinship, and Life-Cycle* (Cambridge: Cambridge University Press, 1984), 423, 427.

[6]Quoted in Simon Schama, *The Embarrassment of Riches: An Interpretation of Dutch Culture in the Golden Age* (New York: Knopf, 1987), 400.

assist their husbands in contributing to the family's wealth. Popular attitudes toward women's social role lagged somewhat behind economic realities.

## COMMUNITY PROPERTY

Historians of the family distinguish between two general systems of property relations that governed marriage in medieval and early modern Europe. The first—called community property—provided that bridegroom and bride combine their resources into a common fund during wedlock. The second mandated that each party retain distinct rights to any real or personal property brought by either spouse to the marriage. These two systems represented opposite ends on a spectrum. Married persons in certain regions customarily held some possessions in common while maintaining separate title to other goods.[7]

The custom of community property in the Netherlands was derived from Germanic traditions dating back to the early Middle Ages. Saxon and Frisian law initially limited the common estate to goods acquired during marriage. By the sixteenth century, the practice of "universal community" (*algeheele gemeenschap*) prevailed in most Dutch provinces. According to this custom, community property comprised nearly all possessions, including goods held at marriage as well as postnuptial gains. Excepted were only lands held under feudal tenure, property held as a trust, and gifts or legacies intended for one spouse alone.[8]

The practice of "universal community" in western Europe appears to have first arisen in urban areas such as Holland associated with a strong market economy. Family wealth in towns depended on the cash and movable goods that both bride and bridegroom contributed to the marriage. These funds financed the pursuit of trade and the growth of commercial farming in outlying rural districts.[9] Community property in the seventeenth-century Netherlands represented a partnership in profit and loss. Husband and wife assumed joint responsibility for each other's assets and liabilities. As one Dutch jurist explained: "Die den man of de vrouw trouwt, trouwt ook de schulden" (The person who weds also marries the debts).[10]

[7]David Sabean, "Aspects of Kinship Behavior and Property in Rural Western Europe before 1800," in Goody, Thirsk, and Thompson, *Family and Inheritance*, 105. W. S. Holdsworth, *A History of English Law*, 3d ed. rewritten, 13 vols. (Boston: Little, Brown, 1922–52), 3:521–22.

[8]J. W. Wessels, *History of the Roman-Dutch Law* (Grahamstown, Cape Colony: African Book Co., 1908), 454–56. Grotius, *Jurisprudence of Holland*, 1:121–23.

[9]Sabean, "Kinship and Property," 107–8.

[10]Quoted in Lee, *Roman-Dutch Law*, 69.

It should be noted that community property was an equal partnership only in a limited sense. Husbands had primary responsibility and legal power in managing the family estate. Inequality within marriage was counterbalanced by reciprocal rights during widowhood. If either husband or wife died intestate, the couple's jointly owned property was divided into two equal shares: one-half to the survivor of the marriage, the other half to the deceased spouse's heirs. This method of division reflected the principle that both parties had contributed equal amounts to their common estate.[11]

Despite the custom of community property within marriage, the law allowed betrothed couples to circumvent this rule at their discretion. By executing an antenuptial contract, men and women could choose either to maintain separate ownership of their possessions or to share only certain types of property within marriage. Although such agreements did not necessarily have to be put in writing, they were not considered legally binding unless they were made before two competent witnesses. If no contract was made, community property necessarily applied in both first marriages and subsequent unions.[12]

Betrothed couples among the Dutch gentry commonly executed antenuptial contracts during the sixteenth and seventeenth centuries. These agreements served familial interests, not merely the needs of the individuals to be wed. The bridegroom and bride therefore relied on their fathers or closest male kin to negotiate the contract with them. Mothers might assume the parental role in case of a father's death. Both families pledged a certain amount of property to the support of the marriage and also arranged the disposition of property in case of death. If the husband died first, his wife could expect to receive her clothing, jewelry, and the gifts bestowed upon her by the groom at their wedding. She also generally acquired a life-interest (*lijftocht*) in half of the family estate; the other half was reserved for the couple's children. If a husband survived his wife, he might acquire a similar life-interest as well as the use of certain personal possessions such as clothing. Any acquisitions during marriage would be counted as part of the family estate, and these goods would be divided equally between the survivor and the deceased spouse's heirs.[13]

In 1625 the directors of the Dutch West India Company ordered that all marriage contracts in New Netherland be written according to the law

[11]Grotius, *Jurisprudence of Holland*, 1:123.
[12]Ibid., 1:125–27.
[13]Sherrin Marshall, *The Dutch Gentry, 1500–1650: Family, Faith, and Fortune* (New York: Greenwood, 1987), 38–41. The custom of community property was also widespread in early modern Germany. See A. G. Roeber, "The Origins and Transfer of German-American Concepts of Property and Inheritance," *Perspectives in American History*, new ser., 3 (1987): 122, 128–29, 134.

of Holland and Zeeland.[14] As in Holland, contracts were not considered legally binding unless executed before a court secretary or a notary public. Public officials in New Amsterdam recorded six prenuptial agreements between 1639 and 1664. Five are found in the notarial records of Fort Orange (located on the future site of Albany) for the period from 1655 to the English conquest; these records include wills and related documents executed by residents of the surrounding community of Beverwyck and nearby Rensselaerswyck.[15] The small number of contracts indicates that most Dutch colonists accepted the common law rule of community property. Unlike gentry families in the Netherlands, the great majority of settlers along the Hudson had little reason to bother with complex antenuptial agreements. Men and women could combine their modest possessions into a joint estate without worrying about the succession to ancestral family lands or about protecting the interests of the lineage if the couple had no children.

Although few in number, marriage contracts are revealing about colonial family life, particularly remarriage. Nine of all eleven antenuptial agreements recorded in New Netherland involved at least one widowed parent with children by a previous union. Whereas brides and bridegrooms in Dutch gentry families were obliged to protect the interests of the lineage before a first marriage, colonists felt little need to enter marriage contracts unless the rights of their own children were at stake. Betrothed persons in New Netherland seem to have negotiated for themselves since their contracts do not list the names of parents or kin as was the case in the Old World.[16] While a few colonial brides bargained with the assistance of their own chosen guardians, none apparently relied on their blood relations.

Marriage contracts in New Netherland recognized reciprocity as the common basis of property relations between husband and wife. In July 1643, for example, Brant Peelen and Marritje Pieters signed an antenuptial agreement before the provincial secretary in New Amsterdam and decided to hold their possessions in common, "as no inventory is

[14]Arnold J. F. Van Laer, ed. and trans., *Documents Relating to New Netherland 1624–1626 in the Henry E. Huntington Library* (San Marino, Calif.: Henry E. Huntington Library and Art Gallery, 1924), 113–14.

[15]Berthold Fernow, ed. and trans., *Minutes of the Orphanmasters Court of New Amsterdam, 1655–1663*, 2 vols. (New York: F. P. Harper, 1902–7), 2:40–42; Jonathan Pearson and Arnold J. F. Van Laer, eds., and trans., *Early Records of the City and County of Albany and Colony of Rensselaerswyck*, 4 vols. (Albany: University of the State of New York, 1869–1919), 1:311, 321, 327–28; 3:273–74, 285; Arnold J. F. Van Laer, trans., Kenneth Scott and Kenn Stryker-Rodda, eds., *Register of the Provincial Secretary, 1638–1660*, New York Historical Manuscripts: Dutch (hereafter cited as N.Y. MSS Dutch), 3 vols. (Baltimore: Genealogical Publishing Co., 1974), 1:212–14, 313–15; 2:144–47, 230; 3:362–64.

[16]Marshall, *The Dutch Gentry*, 38.

made on either side and the property on both sides is accepted as of the same value." The bridegroom signed this agreement for himself while the bride acted with her chosen guardian, one Jan Schepmoes.[17]

As a widow, Marritje Pieters followed the Dutch tradition of signing the contract with her maiden surname or patronymic. Dutch women retained this symbolic link to their paternal lineage irrespective of the number of times they wed. Though a wife might be subordinate to her husband, her identity was distinct from his. Children in gentry families assumed their father's surname while lesser folk usually made do with a patronymic. Marritje Pieters was Marritje, daughter of Pieter Claesen (himself the son of Claes). Her fiancé's use of the surname Peelen suggests that he may have been of higher social origin than she was. He signed their marriage contract while she could only make her mark beside her name.[18]

Since Peelen and Pieters both had children by previous marriages, they needed to settle their heirs' existing property rights before establishing a new family estate. Peelen therefore pledged a certain sum of money to satisfy his children's maternal inheritance while Pieters offered payment for her offspring's patrimony. The heirs were to receive these legacies immediately if they were adults; minors were to inherit upon attaining their majority.

Marriage contracts in New Netherland served several related purposes—to establish the property rights of husband and wife, to settle children's inheritance by previous marriages, to specify the care of minor children, and to determine the succession to the new family estate. Since Marritje Pieters had one young daughter, Aeltje, who required special care, both the mother and stepfather promised to maintain the girl at their joint expense. They were to clothe her, send her to school, and see that she learned "reading, writing, and a good handicraft"—in sum, to act "in such manner as honest parents ought and should do and they are bound to do before God and men."[19] The Pieters-Peelen marriage contract followed customary practice by requiring the education of children and by reminding parents of their moral responsibilities. Such provisions were especially important to young children who fell under a stepparent's control. Though Marritje Pieters allowed her new husband the temporary use of her children's property, she insisted that he pay 5 percent interest to the heirs if he employed the principal for more than four years. This rather unusual provision indi-

[17]Scott and Stryker-Rodda, *Register of the Provincial Secretary,* 2:144–46.
[18]Ibid.
[19]Ibid.

cates that the widow was as determined to protect her own children's inheritance as to please her spouse.

Finally, Peelen and Pieters provided for the succession to their common properties. When either party died, the surviving spouse was to retain possession of the entire family estate. Because married persons regarded their obligations to each other as taking precedence over all other claims of inheritance, they often postponed the division of property until both spouses had died. Dutch customary law dictated the final succession to the Pieters-Peelen estate. One-half of all community property was to pass to Marritje Pieters's lineal descendants, that is, her children; the other half was to fall to Brant Peelen's side of the family. Children within each branch were to inherit equal shares of the inheritance irrespective of their sex.[20]

Few betrothed couples chose to limit community property to any appreciable extent. Men and women seem to have taken this step only if their wealth at marriage was markedly unequal. In these cases, the parties might restrict the family estate to a community of profit and loss—gains and debts contracted during marriage. Each spouse would retain separate responsibility for antenuptial assets and liabilities.[21]

Husbands and wives worked together to contribute to the family estate. Men were the chief breadwinners as merchants, artisans, farmers, or laborers. Women's lives centered on the domestic sphere but were not limited to it. Married women commonly assisted their husbands in business and sometimes traded on their own accounts. A few women were leading merchants whose ventures reached beyond their communities, even to Europe in some cases.[22] A far greater number of female colonists were petty traders dealing exclusively with local shops and markets.

Because husbands and wives often collaborated in business matters, either spouse might represent the couple's interests in legal proceedings. Women in both New Amsterdam and smaller towns often acted as plaintiffs or defendants in suits concerning the recovery of debts. In 1663, for example, New Amsterdam's magistrates considered 195 debt cases. Women—including wives, widows, and unmarried females—participated in 51 (or 26.1 percent) of these disputes. Thirty-eight suits were directly related to women's own business activities. In 13 cases, wives served as their husbands' legal representatives. In the village of Wilt-

[20]Ibid.

[21]See, for example, the contract between Isaac Grevenraet and Maritie Jans in Fernow, *Minutes of the Orphanmasters*, 2:40–42.

[22]See the brief account of Margaret Hardenbroeck's life in Linda Briggs Biemer, *Women and Property in Colonial New York: The Transition from Dutch to English Law, 1643–1727* (Ann Arbor: UMI Research Press, 1983), 33–44.

wyck, located near modern Kingston, women were plaintiffs or defendants in 31 (or 16 percent) of 193 suits for debt from 1661 through 1663.[23]

Because Dutch court officials regarded women's involvement in commerce as a routine matter, they only occasionally recorded the marital status of female litigants in their registers. One cannot therefore determine the exact frequency with which single women, wives, and widows appeared before the magistrates. It is apparent, however, that married women constituted a significant proportion of all female plaintiffs and defendants. Female traders were by no means confined to widows who carried on their deceased husbands' business. At least eight wives and six widows were among the twenty-seven New Amsterdam women who either sued or were sued for debt in 1663. Twenty female litigants in Wiltwyck during the years 1661–63 included at least seven married women and one widow.[24]

Nearly all women acted alone in court whether initiating or defending a suit. Only one woman, a widow, was assisted by a male relative in all the debt cases adjudicated in New Amsterdam in 1663. It should also be emphasized that women were nearly as likely to sue men as men were to sue women. There was little difference between the success of male and female creditors in recovering debts from persons of the other sex.[25]

Husband and wife were legally responsible for each other's debts whenever sharing property in common. This liability extended to widowhood except under special circumstances. A Dutch widow might escape responsibility for her deceased spouse's economic misfortunes or failures by renouncing any potential benefit from the family estate just prior to her husband's burial. Placing her housekeys on his coffin and walking out of the funeral chamber in borrowed clothing, she thereby surrendered all claim to marital property and protected her future earnings and assets from his creditors. Widows in numerous areas within seventeenth-century Germany as well as Holland commonly invoked this privilege.[26]

[23]For court cases, see Berthold Fernow, ed., *The Records of New Amsterdam from 1653 to 1674*, 7 vols. (New York, Knickerbocker Press, 1897); Dingman Versteeg, trans., and Kenneth Scott and Kenn Stryker-Rodda, eds., *Kingston Papers*, N.Y. MSS Dutch, 2 vols. (Baltimore: Genealogical Publishing Co., 1976). The court records of Kingston began on July 12, 1661, with the establishment of a municipal tribunal.

[24]The number of female litigants is smaller than the number of court cases because several women were parties to more than one suit.

[25]Maria Verlett, assisted by her brother pltf. v/s Jan Janszen de Jongh, Aug. 8, 1663. Fernow, *Records of New Amsterdam*, 4:284–85. Men initiated twenty suits against women while women brought eighteen suits against men in 1663. Thirteen male plaintiffs and ten female plaintiffs won their suits against persons of the other sex.

[26]Grotius, *Jurisprudence of Holland*, 1:122–23; Lee, *Roman-Dutch Law*, 70–71.

It should be noted that not all widows were eligible to free themselves from their husbands' debts. Women necessarily assumed liability if they had previously assisted their spouses in buying or selling merchandise. A wife's involvement in the family business therefore determined her legal rights and responsibilities during widowhood.

Unfortunately, some poor men's widows could not free themselves from the grasp of creditors without risking the surrender of prized possessions, including family heirlooms. On September 10, 1664, Anneke Ryzens, the widow of Salomon Lachaire, appeared with her new fiancé, Willem Doeckles, before the burgomasters and schepens (presiding officers of the municipal court) of New Amsterdam. Both the bride and the bridegroom renounced any interest in Lachaire's insolvent estate and asked to be released from paying his debts. In the symbolic language used in court, Anneke Ryzens declared her readiness to "push it" (i.e., her late husband's property) away "with the foot." Before his goods were sold for the benefit of creditors, however, she requested to be allowed to retain certain items: a picture of herself and her deceased husband; a gown that had belonged to her before marriage; a bed; and four shifts, three skirts, and a cap purchased during widowhood.[27]

The settlement of this case rested on the new husband's willingness to help his wife, but not to be financially ruined by her. Though Doeckles consented to assume the liabilities that his wife had accumulated during widowhood, he refused to accept any responsibility for the debts that she had contracted during her former marriage. The magistrates therefore allowed Anneke Ryzens to keep a petticoat and gown that she had been forced to pawn during widowhood but ordered her to relinquish all the property shared in common with her late spouse, evidently including the couple's portrait among the goods to be sold at auction.[28]

A widow had to petition the magistrates soon after her husband's death if she wished to be released from paying his creditors. In the absence of death records, one cannot determine precisely how much time a woman had to lodge this request. If she delayed too long, however, financial ruin could await her. In May 1663, Johannes Van Der Meulen presented a claim against Pietertje Jans, a widow, for her failure to meet payments on a mortgage. Only one week later, the widow asked the burgomasters and schepens to free her of any responsibility for her late husband's insolvent estate.[29] The court stated that it could do nothing in this case because Jans had not petitioned within sufficient time after her spouse's death. (Though it is not clear when the husband had

[27]Fernow, *Records of New Amsterdam,* 5:108–9, 114.
[28]Ibid., 123, 127–29. The final settlement of this case was reached on Sept. 27, 1664.
[29]Ibid., 4:238, 243, 251.

died, his name last appears in court records of New Amsterdam on June 2, 1662, almost one year before the magistrates denied the widow's request.)[30] Three days after the decision, Johannes Van Der Meulen moved to collect his debt by obtaining a court order authorizing the sale of Pietertje Jans's house and lot within fourteen days.[31]

The widow soon found herself in court again, charged this time with slander rather than the nonpayment of debts. Shortly after her house had been sold, she rushed to Van Der Meulen's home, probably in order to give him a tongue-lashing. Finding only his son in the vicinity, she ran out into the street and cried out against the magistrates who had auctioned her house for less than one-half of the price at which it had been offered for sale: "Ye despoilers, ye bloodsuckers . . . ye have not sold, but given away my house." Called before the burgomasters and schepens to answer for this slander, she was released after being warned not to utter such "blasphemies" again.[32] The court expressed no sympathy for this widow who had neglected to avail herself of her legal rights soon after her spouse's death.

Few widows, in fact, took advantage of the opportunity to avoid paying their late husbands' debts. Only five petitions of this type are recorded in the minutes of the Court of Burgomasters and Schepens of New Amsterdam between 1653 and 1664. Since many women engaged in commerce with their husbands, they were not legally eligible to escape responsibility for their spouses' debts. In assuming their deceased partners' liabilities, widows also gained the right to inherit their lawful share of the family estate.

## The Mutual Will and the Laws of Succession

In addition to sharing economic responsibility with their husbands, married women also exercised the right to determine the succession to the family estate. According to seventeenth-century Dutch law, either the husband or wife could declare a will disposing of his (or her) half of their common property. Both parties could, moreover, join in preparing a mutual will that directed the course of inheritance if either spouse happened to die.[33] The drafting of this type of testament required the cooperation of both husband and wife from beginning to end. A married couple might appear before a notary public to have their final

---

[30]Fernow, *Minutes of the Orphanmasters*, 2:140.
[31]Fernow, *Records of New Amsterdam*, 5:241.
[32]Ibid., 262–63.
[33]Grotius, *Jurisprudence of Holland*, 1:138–39; Lee, *Roman-Dutch Law*, 363, 390.

wishes recorded if either spouse fell sick and felt a premonition of death. The form of the mutual will itself indicates that husband and wife shared responsibility for their family's well-being. Notaries drafted the testament in the names of both parties. Each spouse endorsed the will by signing it or by making his or her mark at the document's end.[34]

The drafting of mutual wills in New Netherland was very similar to the execution of testaments in the Netherlands and Germany during the sixteenth and seventeenth centuries. Nearly all wills began with a preamble expressing the emotional bond between husband and wife. As a Dutch couple declared in 1617: "We make this [document] each of us of our own free will and without the influence of another, out of the greatest affection and matrimonial love which each of this couple bears towards the other."[35] One sixteenth-century German diary provides a rare glimpse into the family politics that influenced the writing of wills in both the Old World and the New. Hermann von Weinsberg of Cologne and his wife, Weisgin Ripgin, discussed the preparation of a testament over a four-month period before their will was finally notarized in 1549. While the husband, a lawyer and merchant, proposed drafts of the will, his wife scrutinized each point and convinced him to alter the document to meet her approval. Von Weinsberg noted in his diary that he could not overlook his wife's wishes since she was "clever and understanding enough."[36]

Although the husband was the head of the Dutch colonial family, he seldom bequeathed property without his wife's cooperation. The legal records of New Amsterdam and the Fort Orange (Albany) region include thirty-five wills made by married or betrothed men between 1638 and 1664. Husbands and wives jointly prepared twenty-two of these testaments. Eight betrothed couples—seven of which included at least one widowed party—executed their own mutual wills in order to secure their rights within a new marriage.[37] Only five married men therefore acted alone in bequeathing property during the entire period of Dutch rule. Three of these testators composed wills hastily after being wounded, perhaps in Indian warfare.[38] They prepared their own testa-

[34]See, for example, the will of Eldert Gerbertsen Cruyff and Tryntie Jans in Pearson and Van Laer, *Early Records of Albany*, 3:219–20.

[35]Cited by Sherrin Marshall Wyntjes, "Survivors and Status: Widowhood and Family in the Early Modern Netherlands," *Journal of Family History* 7 (1982): 400.

[36]Cited by Steven Ozment, *When Fathers Ruled: Family Life in Reformation Europe* (Cambridge: Harvard University Press, 1983), 74–75.

[37]Nineteen of the thirty mutual wills were left by residents of New Amsterdam; eleven were prepared by colonists in Beverwyck or Rensselaerswyck. The New Amsterdam wills include three documents drafted in Holland but subsequently recorded in Manhattan after the testators emigrated to New Netherland.

[38]Scott and Stryker-Rodda, *Register of the Provincial Secretary*, 2:130, 204–5, 311–12.

ments out of necessity rather than because of any desire to exclude their spouses.

Wives were even less likely than their husbands to declare a will apart from a spouse. Only one married woman apparently dictated her own testament in New Netherland. In March 1661 Geertje Broeders, lying sick at home in New Amsterdam, dictated a will while her husband, Bartholdus Maen, was away on a voyage to Holland. While Broeders appointed her spouse as her principal heir, she asked him to share authority over their infant son with two male guardians. After returning to Manhattan, Maen was apparently dissatisfied with his wife's independent action. The couple therefore executed a mutual will that annulled Broeders's testament just two months after the original document had been drafted. The new will effected a compromise between each spouse's concerns: the wife's need to provide for her infant son if she predeceased her spouse, and the husband's desire to be in sole control of the child during widowhood. Although Maen had vetoed his wife's testament, he still needed her consent in arranging a settlement of the estate.[39]

Twenty-two of the mutual wills written in New Netherland provide at least some information about the testators' place of origin. Among the thirty-five men and women whose native region is known, twenty-eight were born in the Netherlands. Three testators were from Denmark, two from Flanders, one from Germany, and one was born in New Netherland. It is striking that four of the non-Dutch settlers were married to colonists from the Netherlands. The use of the mutual will in New Netherland was almost entirely the result of the transmission of Dutch law and social customs to the province.

Although far more married persons wrote mutual wills than executed their own testaments, both groups represented only a minority among all colonists. This generalization even applies to the last decade of Dutch rule—a period during which eighteen of the thirty mutual wills were drafted. The small number of wills might indicate that most colonists were content to abide by the laws of intestacy. This hypothesis cannot be proved, however, because New Netherland lacked sufficient legal institutions to enforce a particular system of intestate succession, especially before 1650. It is also possible that some early wills may have been destroyed or lost, or even returned to the Netherlands with family or government papers. The extant colonial records, however, probably include most testaments since legal documents had to be recorded with

[39]Edmund B. O'Callaghan, trans., and Kenneth Scott and Kenn Stryker-Rodda, eds., *The Register of Salomon Lachaire Notary Public of New Amsterdam, 1661–1662*, N.Y. MSS Dutch (Baltimore: Genealogical Publishing Co., 1978), 23–24, 48–49.

local notaries or court officials in order to convey a valid title to property.

Dutch customs of inheritance were based on the principle that both husbands and wives contributed equal amounts to their common property. If either spouse died intestate, the family estate was divided into two equal shares—one-half fell to the surviving spouse; the remainder passed to the heirs of the deceased, relatives by ties of blood. The latter apportioned their share among each other according to the statutes and customs that governed inheritance in their town or region within the Netherlands. Despite local variations, Roman-Dutch law adhered to certain general principles. Children obtained the right to inherit their deceased parent's property before any other group of heirs. Males and females (related in the same degree to the deceased) received equal shares of property within each category of beneficiaries, whether these were children, parents, siblings, or more distant kin.[40]

Although testators in seventeenth-century Holland might circumvent the rules of intestate succession, their freedom to bequeath property was limited by Roman-Dutch law. If a deceased parent left behind more than four children, the latter had to inherit collectively at least one-half of the estate. If four or fewer children survived, they had to receive collectively one-third (or more) of all property. If a child had died, his lawful issue were entitled to receive his share instead. If no lineal descendants remained, the next lawful heirs acquired the right to at least one-fourth of the estate. This guaranteed portion of property, called the *legitim* or legitimate share, protected heirs against testators who might disregard or shortchange their familial obligations. Although parents could lawfully disinherit disobedient children, they had to institute all their offspring as beneficiaries under normal circumstances. Not a single instance of disinheritance is recorded in any New Netherland wills, and only one case records even the threat of this punishment.[41]

When married couples wrote mutual wills in New Netherland, they tended to follow the main principles of Dutch law while bequeathing property according to their individual needs and desires. These testators generally avoided the simple division of their possessions into two fractional shares—one-half to the widowed party, one-half to the deceased spouse's heirs. They preferred instead to allow the surviving spouse to maintain control of the family estate while buying out the interests of children or kin through cash payments. Mutual wills often freed the widowed party of the legal obligation to take an inventory of the estate

[40]Grotius, *Jurisprudence of Holland,* 1:192–213; Lee, *Roman-Dutch Law,* 395–400.

[41]Grotius, *Jurisprudence of Holland,* 1:142–47; Lee, *Roman-Dutch Law,* 368. For the threat of disinheritance, see Fernow, *Minutes of the Orphanmasters,* 2:22–23.

or to account in court to relatives for the administration of property. The surviving spouse's authority over family affairs remained paramount during widowhood. Testators tended, however, to restrict a widowed parent's control of property upon remarriage in order to protect their children's inheritance.

The succession to property reflected the Dutch notion of marriage as a partnership between two distinct lineages. While husband and wife possessed an equal claim to their common estate, each spouse's kin inherited property from their own side of the family. Testators departed from the rule only when they wished to bestow special favor on their in-laws or to punish their own blood relations. One married couple in New Amsterdam ordered that their property pass to the wife's relatives alone if their children died during their minority. Their will excluded the husband's kin from any benefit "because he [i.e., the testator] has never received any kindness or help from them, although they might and could have done it."[42]

A few childless couples regarded the marital bond as so important that they virtually ignored their legal obligations to their kin. Gerard Swart, a *schout* (or principal judicial officer) of Rensselaerswyck, and his wife, Anthonia Van Ryswyck, appointed the widowed spouse as the heir to their entire estate in "this country or in the Fatherland." The couple requested only that the survivor of the marriage select a "token of remembrance" at his "pleasure and discretion" for the deceased spouse's nearest kin.[43] This will indicates that even a government official believed that he and his wife could circumvent the strict requirements of Dutch law by writing a will. The informal nature of the colonial legal system allowed testators to exercise greater discretionary power over the family estate in New Netherland than testators possessed in Holland. The physical distance separating the Old World from the New also lessened the possibility that relatives in the fatherland might pursue a claim to the property of their kin across the ocean.

According to the laws of succession in seventeenth-century Holland, kin acquired property only from deceased relatives who left behind no lineal descendants, children or grandchildren. Testators in New Netherland followed this pattern with one notable exception—they often included their stepchildren as well as their own offspring as heirs. Eldert Gerbertsen Cruyff and his wife, Tryntie Jans, prepared a mutual will in Beverwyck in 1663 that followed a typical pattern—the survivor of the

---

[42]See the will of Daniel Letsco and Anna Claes Croesens recorded on December 26, 1661, in Fernow, *Minutes of the Orphanmasters*, 1:216–19.

[43]Pearson and Van Laer, *Early Records of Albany*, 3:138–39.

marriage was named as the heir to all property that the first dying might leave behind. This bequest conformed to the Dutch custom of *boedelhouderschap*, the retention of the *boedel* or the estate by a widowed parent who had minor children.[44] In this case, the surviving spouse incurred the responsibility of caring for the wife's son by a previous marriage. Since this child had not yet received his paternal inheritance, his mother and stepfather promised to pay him 150 guilders in beaver skins as he attained his majority. They also required the widowed party to transfer one-half of their common property to him as his rightful share of the family estate. In addition to obtaining his inheritance as he came of age, the boy was also to be awarded a gift at the widowed spouse's discretion. He obtained the same privileges from his stepfather and mother that he might have received had he been the child of their marriage. If he survived both testators, he was to inherit all their property.[45] Cruyff may have been especially generous to his stepson because he had no child of his own. His will was an exception to the legal principle allowing children to inherit property exclusively from their own parents.

## THE ORPHAN MASTERS COURT AND
## THE GUARDIANSHIP OF CHILDREN

Because married persons in the seventeenth-century Netherlands customarily held their property in common, their children could expect to inherit equal shares of the family estate from both parents. Under this system of bilateral inheritance, the succession to property usually occurred in several stages. If one parent died, his or her offspring gained title to one-half of the family estate; they acquired the remainder upon the widowed party's death. If the children were minors, however, the surviving parent usually retained possession of this inheritance. Children acquired control of property upon attaining their majority—the onset of their twenty-fifth year. The age of dependency lasted remarkably long during an era in which the average human life span was all too brief. Once men married, however, they were no longer considered to be minors even if they were below full legal age. Women's position was less enviable since they came under their husbands' guardianship no matter what their own age.[46]

Under the Dutch custom of *boedelhouderschap*, widowed parents maintained provisional control over their children's inheritance. Dutch law

---

[44]Grotius, *Jurisprudence of Holland*, 1:126–29; Lee, *Roman-Dutch Law*, 95–96.
[45]Pearson and Van Laer, *Early Records of Albany*, 3:219–20.
[46]Grotius, *Jurisprudence of Holland*, 1:28–29, 34–35.

established several safeguards to protect the minors' interest in their deceased father's or mother's property. While the widowed parent assumed liability for all the losses that might befall the estate, he or she had to assign one-half of the profits to the children's inheritance.[47] Dutch law considered children to be orphans if either their father or mother died during their minority. Though widowed parents maintained their personal authority over orphaned children, they could administer their property only if appointed as guardian by the deceased parent's will or by a court. This rule applied to fathers as well as mothers.

Roman-Dutch law reflected the notion that widowed parents should not be entrusted with sole control over their children's inheritance. As early as the mid-fifteenth century, special courts known as the Orphan Chambers arose in Dutch towns in order to protect the interests of minors who had lost either parent. Although magistrates generally appointed the widowed parent as guardian, they also selected at least two additional overseers from among the orphans' nearest and oldest male kin. If no relatives were available to serve, the court chose two respectable men within the community. The responsibility of guardianship was so important in seventeenth-century Holland that men could be imprisoned if they refused this office without just cause.[48]

Guardians assumed several important responsibilities under Roman-Dutch law. They were required to take an inventory of the estate they administered and to present it before the Orphan Chamber. If the widowed parent balked at performing this obligation, the children's other guardians could demand his or her cooperation. Once the inventory was executed, the surviving parent and overseers arranged a settlement of the estate. Although a widowed parent usually retained custody of the orphaned children, the parent's control over their inheritance was restricted. The other guardians customarily represented their wards in legal actions, supervised their maintenance and education, and invested the proceeds of the estate for the minors' benefit. They also protected the children's property rights if the widowed parent remarried or died. In addition to assuming these obligations, they had to render annual or periodic accounts to the Orphan Chamber for their administration of the inheritance. They acted as the court's surrogates in all matters relating to the welfare of orphaned children.[49]

If parents wished to control completely the selection of their children's guardians, they could do so by writing a will. In a will parents could lawfully appoint overseers according to their own preference and could

[47]Ibid., 1:126–29.
[48]Ibid., 1:34–39, 2:38–39; Lee, *Roman-Dutch Law*, 99–101.
[49]Grotius, *Jurisprudence of Holland*, 1:42–49.

even exclude the Orphan Chamber from interfering in their family affairs. After the testator's death, the widowed parent customarily exhibited the will before the judicial authorities. If the testament included the proper legal formula, the magistrates could do little more for the moment than have the document recorded in the court register. Testators in seventeenth-century Holland commonly evaded the Orphan Chamber's jurisdiction by utilizing this loophole. The court reserved, however, the right to act on the children's behalf if need required.[50]

Until the mid-1650s, New Netherland lacked any legal institutions that could assume a similar role to the Orphan Chambers in Holland. In 1640, the West India Company instructed the director-general and council of the province to take cognizance of all matters pertaining to the affairs of widows and orphans.[51] Public officials seldom became directly involved, however, in the appointment of guardians or in the settlement of estates. Before 1650 the provincial secretary recorded only nine contracts governing the relationship between widowed parents and their orphaned children.[52] The care of orphans depended therefore almost entirely on the children's parents or kin. If the minors had no relatives, the deacons of the Reformed church provided for their welfare. This system of guardianship proved inadequate to the colony's growing population, particularly in New Amsterdam. The leading municipal officials, the burgomasters and schepens, therefore assumed responsibility for the support of widows and orphans in 1653. An increase in cases before the magistrates soon led to the establishment of a separate Court of Orphan Masters in 1655. The director-general and council chose two men to head this tribunal from among four nominees proposed by the burgomasters and schepens.[53] Although New Amsterdam was the only town in the colony to maintain an Orphan Masters Court, at least one other settlement had public officials charged with a similar responsibility. Two Orphan Masters served Beverwyck as early as 1657.[54]

---

[50]Ibid., 1:44–45; Lee, *Roman-Dutch Law*, 101.

[51]Edmund B. O'Callaghan, ed., *Documents Relative to the Colonial History of the State of New York*, 15 vols. (Albany: Weed, Parsons, 1856–87), 1:123, 405.

[52]See Scott and Stryker-Rodda, *Register of the Provincial Secretary*, 1:12–13, 2:42–43, 48–49, 83–84, 115–16, 144–45, 432–33; 3:155–56.

[53]Fernow, *Minutes of the Orphanmasters*, vi–viii. Although the compound form "orphanmasters" is used in the book's title, the word is properly divided into its component parts in the text. While the extant court minutes end in 1668, only one case is included in the official record after December 1666. In this chapter I analyze the Orphan Masters Court from 1655 through the English conquest of New Netherland. For the final volume of court minutes, see Edmund B. O'Callaghan, trans., and Kenn Stryker-Rodda and Kenneth Scott, eds., *The Minutes of the Orphanmasters of New Amsterdam, 1663–1668* (Baltimore: Genealogical Publishing Co., 1976).

[54]See Pearson and Van Laer, *Early Records of Albany*, 1:25–26.

As in Holland, the Orphan Masters of New Amsterdam supervised the care of minor children through the appointment of guardians. The court might even rely on the orphans' kin in Holland to serve as overseers if the children were left without parents or relatives in the colony.[55] Although a few orphaned children were sent back to their relatives in the Old World, a far greater number remained in New Amsterdam. The Orphan Masters commonly provided for these children by hiring them out or by apprenticing them to skilled craftsmen. In some cases, the court simply ratified an agreement that had already been reached privately between an orphaned child and an employer. In July 1664, one David Wessels, a turner, appeared before the magistrates with Claes Gerritsen, a thirteen-year-old orphan. After explaining that the boy's father had died five months previously, the craftsman requested that the minor reside with him and learn his trade. Since young Claes consented to this proposal, the Orphan Masters ordered that he be bound to Wessels for a five-year term. In return for obtaining the boy's services, the turner was to provide him with food and clothing and to fit him out with "a decent Sunday and working day suit" at the end of the apprenticeship. Significantly, the master was not allowed to apply Claes's small inheritance toward the costs of maintenance. The Orphan Masters directed the secretary of the court to take an inventory of the deceased father's goods and to keep them in a sealed box for the boy's future use.[56]

If a child lost either father or mother, the Orphan Masters consulted the surviving parent before deciding on the appointment of guardians. Unlike some courts in Holland, the magistrates never formally designated a widowed father or mother as one of the children's overseers. In November 1655, the court summoned one Maria Varleth after her husband, Johannes Van Beeck, had been killed by the Indians. Although allowed some freedom of choice, the widow declined to suggest any possible guardians for her infant daughter and rejected several proposals by the Orphan Masters. After waiting just one week for Varleth to reach a decision, the tribunal put forward its own nominees: Joost Van Beeck, the deceased man's brother, and Nicholas Varleth, the widow's brother. Since Van Beeck asked to be excused from this duty and the widow also objected to his selection, the Orphan Masters decided to replace him with two disinterested men.[57] The consent of both sides of the family was important in settling the deceased man's estate. The court

[55]Fernow, *Minutes of the Orphanmasters*, 1:15–19, 21–22.
[56]O'Callaghan, *Orphanmasters, 1663–1668*, 12.
[57]Fernow, *Minutes of the Orphanmasters*, 1:3, 6–7, 11–12.

therefore attempted to appoint guardians who would be acceptable to Maria Varleth as well as to her late husband's relatives. The choice of impartial men lessened the possibility that the widow or her brother might deprive the child of her paternal inheritance.

Although the Orphan Masters seem to have preferred that kin serve as the guardians of orphaned children, the court minutes seldom specify any degree of relationship between the overseers and their wards. It is therefore likely that the magistrates commonly appointed guardians from outside the family circle. In a community of immigrants, the care of orphans apparently depended as much on the cooperation of neighbors as on kinship. The employment of disinterested men as overseers attests to the strength of communal ties in New Amsterdam during the 1650s and 1660s. According to Dutch law, guardians were entitled to be reimbursed for their costs but not to profit from their services. Although the Orphan Masters of New Amsterdam may have followed a similar rule, the court minutes include little evidence on this point.[58]

Guardians protected the rights of minor children by appealing to the Orphan Masters in cases of parental wrongdoing. Govert Loockermans, guardian of the motherless children of Jacob Van Couwenhoven, presented a complaint against the orphans' father in June 1656. The overseer maintained that Van Couwenhoven was tampering with his children's inheritance by selling and appropriating the clothing and jewelry they had acquired from their deceased mother. Judging this complaint to be reasonable, the court granted the guardian's request that the orphans' personal property be deposited with their grandmother. Van Couwenhoven soon had to answer again for his conduct toward his minor children. Having overextended his brewery, he sought to mortgage certain properties in order to obtain some desperately needed funds. The children's guardians feared that these business dealings might once again jeopardize the orphans' maternal inheritance. After briefly considering the complaint, the Orphan Masters ordered Van Couwenhoven to furnish the guardians with "a correct account and statement of his property, including debts and credits." This record was intended to ensure that the children's inheritance would be kept separate from their father's estate. The brewer was compelled to offer his person and property as security for the execution of the court order.[59]

The Orphan Masters occasionally encountered resistance from widowed parents who wished to raise their children by themselves. The case

[58]Grotius, *Jurisprudence of Holland*, 1:46, 47.
[59]Fernow, *Minutes of the Orphanmasters*, 1:20–21, 26–27. For a brief description of Van Couwenhoven's business dealings, see J. H. Innes, *New Amsterdam and Its People* (New York: Charles Scribner's Sons, 1902), 144–49.

of one widow, Geertje Hendricks, illustrates the uneasy, sometimes combative relationship between public supervision and parental control. Called before the Orphan Masters in February 1658, Hendricks was asked to display an inventory of the estate of her late husband, Andries Hoppe. The widow refused, however, to produce the record, citing the opinion of the notary Mattheus De Vos "that as long as she does not marry again, she need not report to the Orphans Chamber." The court responded sharply, informing the widow "that it was her duty to do it according to the customs of our Fatherland." Hendricks remained defiant, answering sarcastically that "she does not intend to do it and the Orphan Masters may do, [sic] what they please." Rejecting the widow's argument, the officials then summoned two men who had been appointed as her children's guardians before her husband's death. Appearing in court one week later, the widow and overseers reported that they had accounted for all the deceased man's debts and credits. Geertje Hendricks still refused, however, to assign her children's paternal inheritance. "Why," she pleaded, "should that be done before she marries again?" Told that she *must* do it, she answered, "Must is force."[60] Compelled by the Orphan Masters, the widow proceeded to negotiate with the guardians and produced an agreement within three weeks.

Although Geertje Hendricks lost this battle with the court, her complaint was not without some substance. The Orphan Masters generally exercised closer supervision over surviving parents who decided to remarry than over those who remained widowed, particularly if the latter had little property. In April 1663, one Lysbedt Ackermans appeared before the court soon after her husband died. After the magistrates ordered her to take an inventory of the deceased man's estate, the widow replied that she had only a few household goods, some of which she had to sell occasionally simply to procure food for her children. The Orphan Masters therefore allowed her to go home, guaranteeing that she would not be summoned again unless she remarried, "provided she does her duty by the children."[61] Because of the estate's small size, the court did not even insist on the customary procedure that guardians be appointed for the orphans. As one might expect, the magistrates directed more attention to children who inherited property than to those who received little, if anything, from their parents.

From 1655 through 1664, the Orphan Masters of New Amsterdam intervened in fifty-four instances in which children had lost only one of their parents. In thirty-two (or 59.3 percent) of these cases, the court

---

[60]Fernow, *Minutes of the Orphanmasters,* 1:75, 77, 82.
[61]Ibid., 1:242.

ordered the orphans' guardians and widowed parent to settle either the minors' paternal or maternal inheritance. This legal procedure required that the surviving father or mother pledge to pay a cash sum to the children as they came of age or married. The Orphan Masters ordered that a settlement of the estate be made wherever they believed that the minors needed special protection. More than two-thirds of these court rulings (twenty-two of thirty-two cases) were issued after a widowed parent had become engaged to remarry.

The Orphan Masters might learn of the marriage plans of widowed parents through the banns published by the Reformed church. According to a Dutch custom adopted in New Netherland, all betrothed couples had to request their ministers or magistrates to give public notice of an intended marriage in church or in the town hall on three successive Sundays or market days before the wedding.[62] In March 1657, the Orphan Masters of New Amsterdam summoned one Madaleen Dircks into court after being apprised that her marriage banns had just been published. Although the magistrates had already appointed guardians over the widow's infant daughter, they had not yet required that the orphan's paternal inheritance be assigned. The court now ordered, however, that Dircks "should not be allowed to marry, before she made a settlement on her child."[63] This she subsequently did.

Whenever a settlement of an estate concerned the interests of minor children, this procedure had to be approved by the Orphan Masters or by other judicial officials before it could be put into effect. The widowed parent and the children's guardians therefore appeared before the court in order to complete an agreement. After the secretary of the court or a notary public recorded the proceedings, all the interested parties and at least two witnesses signed the contract. If the agreement was made prior to a widow's remarriage, her betrothed often assisted her. If the widow had no immediate plans to wed again, she usually selected two men as her guardians in executing the contract.[64]

Before the mid-1650s, the legal records of New Netherland include only a handful of agreements concluded between widowed parents and their children's guardians. The small number of these contracts indicates that the deceased person's relatives, not public officials, determined whether a formal settlement of the estate occurred. This situation changed considerably as the colony's legal institutions became more similar to the mature system of law in the Netherlands. The adoption of

[62]Edmund B. O'Callaghan, ed., *Laws and Ordinances of New Netherland* (Albany: Weed, Parsons, 1868), 152–53, 328: Lee, *Roman-Dutch Law,* 61.
[63]Fernow, *Minutes of the Orphanmasters,* 1:4–5, 7–8, 29–31.
[64]Ibid., 39–41.

Dutch judicial practices was most advanced in New Amsterdam, but it was also evident in Beverwyck and Rensselaerswyck in the early 1660s. During the period of Dutch rule, the notarial records of these communities include eleven agreements concluded between widowed parents and their children's guardians. Though these records begin in 1656, all eleven contracts were executed between 1662 and 1664. Either the Orphan Masters of Beverwyck or the sheriff of Rensselaerswyck supervised these contracts as official witnesses.[65]

The growing effectiveness of legal institutions in New Netherland was especially beneficial to orphaned children because of the frequency of remarriage among their parents. During the last four years of Dutch rule (1661–64), ninety-six couples were wed in the Reformed church in New Amsterdam. In at least thirty cases (31.2 percent), either the bridegroom or bride had been widowed previously. In ten additional cases (10.4 percent), both parties had been widowed.[66] These statistics indicate that the premature death of either spouse frequently severed marriages in seventeenth-century New Amsterdam. The maintenance of family stability in these circumstances depended on the formation of new two-parent households through remarriage. The Orphan Masters and other judicial officials ensured that this essential process protected rather than jeopardized the minor children's property rights and welfare.

Whether executed in Beverwyck or in New Amsterdam, the settlement of estates followed a nearly identical pattern. The widowed parent retained custody of his or her orphaned children after remarriage but assumed a new series of legal obligations toward them. Although maintaining possession of the minors' property, he or she had to give security to pay their inheritance as they came of age or married. Because remarrying parents faced conflicts between new and old family loyalties, they had to promise to fulfill responsibilities that previously had required only limited public supervision. These duties included seeing that their sons and daughters were taught to read and write and to acquire a useful occupation. Isaac Grevenraet, a wealthy merchant in New Amsterdam, pledged soon after his remarriage to maintain his two children "in eating, drinking, clothes, woolen and linen, stockings and shoes, lodging and accommodation [and] to provide [for] them in sickness and in health." He also agreed with the minors' guardians to have

[65]Pearson and Van Laer, *Early Records of Albany,* 3:283–85.
[66]The records for this four-year period have been analyzed because they include ample information concerning the marital status of bridegrooms and brides. The records of the 1650s are less complete. See "Records of the Reformed Dutch Church—Marriages," *New York Genealogical and Biographical Record* 6 (1875).

them instructed in "the Christian prayer, Our Father, the Ten Com-
mandments, which are a rule of Christian Life, and furthermore in all
virtue . . . to teach and direct them as an honest father is bound to do."
In addition to guaranteeing his children's care, Grevenraet pledged to
pay their maternal inheritance as they attained their majority. Finally, he
satisfied the court's demands by offering his three houses in New
Amsterdam as security for payment.[67]

After a settlement of an estate had been reached, the children's guardians often deposited their inheritance with the Orphan Masters. The
court then placed the money out at interest in order to obtain funds for
the minors' maintenance and education. During the 1660s, the magistrates were able to make loans to reliable borrowers such as the municipal government and the Reformed church at an annual rate of 10 percent. While a surviving parent might apply the interest toward the
children's immediate support, he or she was not allowed to control the
principal sum.[68] This method of investment reduced the parent's financial burden without diminishing the child's inheritance.

The care of orphaned children required the cooperation of step-
parents as well as the supervision of public officials. Since spouses generally held their property in common, they tended to share responsibility
for each other's children by previous marriages. The right to benefit
from a new family estate entailed the assumption of parental duties. In
September 1662, Jacob Gevick and Geertruy Barents Van Dwingeloo, a
widow with two young daughters, executed a marriage contract in Beverwyck. Although the bridegroom was from Mecklenburgh in Germany
and the bride was from Holland, they agreed to hold their property in
common "according to the laws of our Fatherland [i.e., the Nether-
lands]." Both parties also pledged to bring up the widow's children "in
the fear of the Lord" and to maintain them until they married or attained their majority. The orphans gained the right to inherit property
from both their former family and their new one. Before their mother
wed again, she reserved one-half of her estate from her first marriage
for their paternal inheritance. If she died without having any children
by her new spouse, her offspring were guaranteed one-half of all properties owned jointly by their mother *and* stepfather. They were also to
acquire exclusive title to their mother's clothing, gold rings, and silver
ornaments after her death. The contract offered the orphans nearly the
identical share of property from their mother's second marriage as from
her first. Finally, both Geertruy Barents and her future husband put

[67]O'Callaghan, *Orphanmasters, 1663–1668*, 2–3.
[68]Ibid., 13, 18.

their marks to this agreement executed before one of the Orphan Masters of Beverwyck.[69]

As in the Old World, parents in New Netherland held the right to exclude the jurisdiction of the Orphan Masters by including a prohibitory clause in their wills. Between 1654 and 1664, eleven testaments written in the colony specifically referred to minor children. Six of these wills, all left by residents of New Amsterdam, barred the Orphan Masters or other public officials from assuming any role in the settlement of the estate. Although only a small minority of colonists refused to accept the court's rulings, their testaments are important to our understanding of popular attitudes toward inheritance and family life. When husbands and wives bequeathed property, they tended to fulfill their parental obligations while allowing the widowed spouse to maintain nearly undisputed control of the estate. Their wills attest to the strength of the marital bond within the Dutch colonial family.

Testators excluded the jurisdiction of the Orphan Masters not in order to defraud their children but because they wished to benefit the widowed spouse. Juriaen Blanck and Tryntie Klaessen prepared a mutual will in New Amsterdam in 1662 that named the surviving spouse as the heir to all their property. In addition to freeing the widowed party of the obligation to take an inventory of the estate, they also prohibited the Orphan Masters from supervising their children's care. The widowed parent assumed sole responsibility for maintaining and educating their children, including the wife's son by a previous marriage, until they married or attained their majority. Although Blanck and Klaessen offered certain benefits to their children, they left the surviving spouse in control of most of their property. The will directed that the orphans receive their "legitimate share" of their deceased parent's estate as they came of age—the minimal bequest required by Dutch law. The testators also released the widowed parent from paying a specific sum of money to the children as a marriage portion or gift. The widow or widower simply had to give them an amount that he or she judged to be fair "in conscience and equity." The children had to wait until both parents had died before acquiring the greater part of the family estate.[70]

Although Juriaen Blanck and Tryntie Klaessen allowed almost unlimited power to each other during widowhood, they severely restricted the survivor's authority upon remarriage. Before the widowed person wed again, he or she was to execute a properly notarized document that assigned one-half of the deceased parent's estate to the children. The

[69]Pearson and Van Laer, *Early Records of Albany,* 1:311.
[70]Fernow, *Minutes of the Orphanmasters,* 2:19–23.

testators refused, however, to permit the Orphan Masters any role in the children's care even if the surviving parent remarried. They authorized the widowed party to act as principal overseer and to select co-guardians of his or her own free choice. They thereby protected their children's interests without allowing public officials to supervise the appointment of guardians or the settlement of the estate.[71]

If either parent died without choosing guardians for the minor children, the widowed parent still might do so. In February 1663, Cornelis Langevelt and his wife, Marritje Jans Joncke, declared a will that allowed the survivor of their marriage to retain possession of all their property during widowhood. In addition to excluding the Orphan Masters, the couple authorized the widowed spouse to maintain sole control over their two sons and their yet unborn child. Ten days later Langevelt was dead, and Marritje Jans Joncke summoned a notary to her house in New Amsterdam in order to dictate her own final wishes. Since she "was now in childbed and sick abed of children's pocks," she appointed two men as guardians for her three children, including her newborn daughter, "in case God takes her through this illness into his eternal kingdom." Her deed authorized the overseers to administer all the property left behind by herself and her husband for the children's benefit. Although the widow obviously cared greatly for her children's welfare, she still excluded the Orphan Masters from interfering in her family affairs. She may have believed that guardians would assume their responsibilities only if freed from public supervision. In case one overseer died, she directed the other to name a successor. Her deed provides yet another example of popular distrust of judicial authority.[72]

New Netherland was not the only mainland colony in North America to establish orphans' courts during the seventeenth century. Among the English colonies, Maryland and Virginia developed the most effective legal institutions of this type. The high rate of death in Chesapeake society required that county courts assume a major role in the protection of orphans' rights. In one Virginia county, nearly one-fourth of all children lost one or both parents by their fifth birthday; almost three-fourths suffered the same loss before they either obtained age twenty-one or married. In both Chesapeake colonies, the justices of the county courts designated special days for an "Orphan's Court," or they impaneled juries each year to inquire into the affairs of orphans. Like the Orphan Masters in New Amsterdam, the magistrates supervised the

[71]Ibid.
[72]Ibid., 1:239–40; 2:34, 36–37. Langevelt was also known as Van Langevelde.

appointment of guardians and the posting of bond by the children's overseers.[73]

Despite similarities in legal practice, however, the protection of orphans' rights differed significantly in the Chesapeake colonies and New Netherland. In Maryland and Virginia, men appointed overseers by wills made without their wives' participation and could thereby exclude their spouses from guardianship. In accordance with English common law, courts regarded minors as orphans only if the father had died since children usually inherited from him alone. Public officials protected the minors' interests if the father died intestate by requiring widowed mothers to post bond, find sufficient sureties, and account in court for their management of the orphans' estate. The justices seldom intervened on behalf of minors who remained in their father's custody, and they rarely appointed men as guardians if the mother was still alive. In New Netherland, however, children inherited equal shares of the family estate from their father and mother. The Orphan Masters therefore provided the same type of care for children who had lost either parent. Unlike the county courts in the Chesapeake colonies, Dutch colonial magistrates customarily appointed guardians for minors who remained in a widowed parent's household. This was indeed a striking degree of public intervention in family affairs.

By the time of the English conquest of New Netherland, the Orphan Masters had become important public officials in New Amsterdam and in the smaller community of Beverwyck. Their rulings governed non-Dutch colonists as well as emigrants from the Netherlands. The Dutch authorities did not, however, attempt to impose their laws of inheritance on English settlements either on Long Island or to the east of the Hudson River. The weakness of provincial government dictated a policy of toleration in regions outside the major centers of Dutch population.

Although the Orphan Masters encountered some opposition to their rulings in New Amsterdam, few colonists availed themselves of their lawful right to exclude the court's jurisdiction by writing a will. Many settlers seem to have regarded inheritance as a social process outside their individual control. During the entire period of Dutch rule, only thirty-seven wills of Manhattan residents were recorded in colonial registers. A substantial majority of settlers apparently accepted that fact that

[73]Lois Green Carr, "The Development of the Maryland Orphan's Court, 1654–1715," in Aubrey C. Land, Lois Green Carr, and Edward C. Papenfuse, eds., *Law, Society, and Politics in Early Maryland* (Baltimore: Johns Hopkins University Press, 1977), 41–62; Darrett B. Rutman and Anita H. Rutman, " 'Now-Wives and Sons-in-Law': Parental Death in a Seventeenth-Century Virginia County," in Thad W. Tate and David L. Ammerman, eds., *The Chesapeake in the Seventeenth Century: Essays on Anglo-American Society and Politics* (New York: Norton, 1979), 153–82.

certain rules of inheritance would be applied even if they died intestate. Testators themselves bequeathed property according to their individual preferences while following several major principles of Dutch law—the transfer of family property to the widowed spouse, the settlement of the estate upon the widowed parent's remarriage or death, and the equal division of property among sons and daughters. It is striking that married couples adopted the same procedures in bequeathing property as the Orphan Masters Court applied in cases of intestacy.

The Dutch custom of community property within marriage influenced nearly all aspects of inheritance in New Netherland. Since husband and wife shared their property in common, each spouse held an equal claim to the family estate. Rather than being an exclusively male concern, the preparation of wills depended on the cooperation of both parties to the marriage. The authors of mutual wills usually transferred control of the estate to the widowed spouse and ordered the survivor to buy out the claims of the deceased spouse's children or nearest blood relations. The custom of *boedelhouderschap* allowed a widowed parent to retain possession of the children's inheritance during their minority. Before remarrying, however, he or she had to arrange a settlement of the estate with the children's guardians. The Dutch system of inheritance rested on a finely attuned balance between the authority of widowed parents and the rights of children. The adoption of English law in New York after 1664 was gradually to upset this equilibrium by undermining the legal institutions that had governed family life during the final decade of Dutch rule. The institution of English law would lead eventually to a decline in the widow's authority over property, a greater emphasis on children's material advancement, and a weakening of public supervision of family relations.

# Chapter 3

# From Husbands to Their Wives: Widows' Property Rights under English Rule

Dutch assimilation of English law in seventeenth-century New York City was a gradual, rather unsystematic process. Many burghers maintained their distinctive social traditions while outwardly conforming to English legal procedures. The custom of community property within marriage, for example, endured beyond the demise of the mutual will. Though husbands assumed sole authority over bequeathing marital property, they continued to respect their wives' rights to the family estate. From the 1660s through the 1710s, Dutchmen throughout the province followed the same basic pattern in preparing their wills—the postponement of their children's inheritance until their widows' remarriage or death.

It is not surprising that many seventeenth-century wills—even some testaments not written by Dutchmen—often reflected Dutch rather than English customs. Many men who prepared testaments in the late 1600s were longtime residents of Manhattan who had lived there under Dutch rule. Though these persons might be French, German, or Scandinavian in origin, they tended to bequeath property just as the ethnic Dutch did. English immigrants to seventeenth-century New York frequently adopted Dutch customs as they adjusted to living in a predominantly Dutch city. Ethnic assimilation was therefore a complex process within an unstable, pluralistic society.

Since few immigrants from the Netherlands came to New York after the English conquest, Dutchmen who wished to prosper in eighteenth-century Manhattan had to accommodate themselves to a growing British presence.[1] Many burghers who prepared wills after 1720 had grown up in Dutch-speaking households but had also acquired familiarity with English ways over many years. Their wills show some Dutch influence, but they also reflect a growing trend of Anglicization. These men increasingly abandoned the custom of community property and accepted the English notion that they owned property apart from their wives. This change is apparent in wills written in the rural Hudson Valley as well as in New York City. Anglicization was most pronounced among the urban mercantile elite, but it was not limited to that group alone.

Colonial New York City wills reveal a gradual shift in how men reconciled competing family interests, particularly their wives' and children's needs. This problem is so fundamental that it needs to be examined apart from other domestic concerns, such as the property rights of kin. During the seventeenth century, most male heads of households valued their widows' authority as parents above their children's interests as heirs. By the 1750s, however, widowed mothers within most occupational and ethnic groups tended to receive a quite limited degree of power over their husbands' estates. Though testators provided amply for their wives' material needs, they restricted their control of property. The widow's loss of authority often increased her children's opportunities for advancement. Sons and daughters in the late colonial era frequently received a major portion of their patrimony before their widowed mother's death.

## Colonial Women and English Property Law

It is well known that the English common law severely restricted married women's property rights in the seventeenth and eighteenth centuries. According to common law, a married woman was classified as a feme covert—a person completely dependent on her husband's will and authority. She could not enter contracts, convey property, or act as a legal guardian or administrator without her spouse. Though a single woman might independently represent her own legal interests, a married woman could not do so under most circumstances. Sir William Blackstone thus defined the status of feme covert:

> By marriage, the husband and wife are one person in law: That is, the very being or legal existence of the woman is suspended during the marriage, or at least is incorporated and consolidated into that of the husband; under whose wing, protection, and *cover*, she performs everything; and is

[1]See Appendix.

therefore in our law-french a *feme-covert* . . . under the protection of her husband, her *baron* or lord; and her condition during her marriage is called her *coverture*.[2]

Not all women in England or its American colonies were subject to common law restrictions. Equity law, administered by Chancery courts, mitigated the severity of common law by judging women's legal status with respect to abstract principles of justice as well as custom. The English Court of Chancery from the late 1500s through the 1700s developed a body of law that allowed married women to control property much more fully than was generally permissible according to common law. Equity law recognized numerous instances in which a wife might benefit from a separate estate independently of her husband. Through the creation of a marriage settlement, she might own, manage, convey, and devise property as if she were single.[3]

The historian Marylynn Salmon has emphasized the diversity of early American law concerning women's property rights. She argues that married women's legal status was most favorable in those colonies that closely duplicated English law, particularly those jurisdictions that recognized the distinction between common law and equity. Female property rights generally received greater respect in the southern colonies than in New England. Chancery courts in Maryland, Virginia, and South Carolina acknowledged a married woman's right to a separate estate created through equitable procedures. Common law courts in these colonies enforced the English rule requiring a wife's express consent to her spouse's conveyance of real estate. When southern law diverged from English practice, it generally aimed to protect rather than to restrict women's property rights.[4]

In contrast to the South, Massachusetts and Connecticut applied English law in a manner that tended to enhance the husband's authority over his wife. Neither colony ever established a Chancery court and neither countenanced separate estates for married women, at least during the eighteenth century. New England magistrates ignored or rejected certain common law procedures intended to protect a married woman's interest in her own real estate. Salmon attributes the distinctive character of New England law to two major forces. First, Puritan ide-

[2]Sir William Blackstone, *Commentaries on the Laws of England,* ed. James DeWitt Andrews, 4th ed., 2 vols. (Chicago: Callaghan and Co., 1899), 1, bk. 1:442.

[3]W. S. Holdsworth, *A History of English Law,* 3d ed. rewritten, 13 vols. (Boston: Little, Brown, 1922–52), 5:310–15.

[4]Marylynn Salmon, *Women and the Law of Property in Early America* (Chapel Hill: University of North Carolina Press, 1986).

ology influenced courts and legislative assemblies to favor patriarchal authority. Second, colonists adopted a simplified version of English law because they regarded legal complexity as either unnecessary or undesirable. Both these trends generally worked against women's interests. It should be noted, however, that Puritan departure from English law benefited wives in at least one area. Women in eighteenth-century Massachusetts might obtain a divorce if they were either treated cruelly or deserted by their husbands. Their counterparts in New York or the South might only gain separation from bed and board (without the right to remarry) for these abuses.[5]

Salmon presents a definite contrast between women's legal status in eighteenth-century New England and the southern colonies. Her valuable study is, however, only somewhat useful in placing New York within the context of early American law. By the early eighteenth century, the province's formal legal institutions increasingly reflected English practice—a trend that was to diminish women's property rights during widowhood. Though wives had been subordinate to their husbands in Dutch colonial society, both parties held the same rights of succession to the family estate. This notion of reciprocity weakened as Dutch colonists assimilated English customs of marriage and inheritance.

## THE ENGLISH COMMON LAW BACKGROUND
## TO NEW YORK LAW

Though married women had limited legal powers, they had important rights in both Roman-Dutch and English law. In seventeenth-century Holland and England, it was customary for both bride and bridegroom to contribute some form of material wealth to their union. The particular manner of holding property within marriage determined each spouse's rights during widowhood.

The historical origins of distinctive Dutch and English marital customs can be traced back to the medieval era. Some regions in the Netherlands recognized community property between spouses by the late fourteenth century, if not earlier.[6] By contrast, the development of English law after the Norman conquest ran counter to the notion of a conjugal estate. By the year 1200, the succession to personal property had become a separate legal process from the inheritance of land. The interests of the lineage within feudalism demanded that husband and wife retain dis-

---

[5] Ibid.

[6] J. W. Wessels, *A History of the Roman-Dutch Law* (Grahamstown, Cape Colony: African Book Co., 1908), 454–56.

tinct claims to any lands that either spouse brought to marriage or that might come to either party during wedlock. Marital customs that originated among the Norman ruling class eventually became part of English common law. It is not unusual in English history, as Frederick Pollock and Frederic William Maitland have written, that "law for the great becomes the law for all."[7]

During the late seventeenth century, common law principles came to define married women's property rights in colonial New York. According to this legal system, a man acquired ownership of his bride's personal property as soon as the couple wed. While he controlled these possessions in a nearly absolute manner, he exercised a form of guardianship over his spouse's real estate. Though he could not lawfully alienate her lands without her consent, he might appropriate all the income and rent from such property to his own use. Once the couple had their first child, he was allowed by custom (the curtesy of England) to retain this proprietary interest throughout life even if his wife predeceased him or if the child died. Her heirs acquired title to the land only after she and her husband had died.[8]

English common law severely restricted a married woman's capacity to prepare a last will and testament. Because a husband was the sole owner of personal property within marriage, his wife might bequeath movable goods only with his permission. She was prohibited from devising real estate by will either by herself or with her husband. Common law courts denied the married woman this power for two principal reasons. First, the law regarded her as a dependent person who had no identity apart from her husband. Second, courts feared that a man might dictate his wife's will to benefit himself to her heirs' disadvantage. A married woman's power to will property was contrary to the orderly descent of land at common law.[9]

The adoption of English law in colonial New York virtually deprived married women of any direct role over the bequest of property. Only six wives in New York City prepared wills from 1700 to 1775. Married women's wills were also a rarity in rural areas of the province.

The writing of wills has long rested upon the notion that the individual property holder has personal interests distinct from his family's needs. Freedom to bequeath property is potentially the power to alienate

---

[7]Sir Frederick Pollock and Frederic William Maitland, *The History of English Law before the Time of Edward I,* 2 vols. (Cambridge: Cambridge University Press, 1895), 2:397–400.

[8]Holdsworth, *History of English Law,* 3:185–89, 523–27. Blackstone, *Commentaries* 1, bk. 1:444–45.

[9]After 1700, only one married woman's will in New York City devised real estate. See N.Y. Wills, Liber 17:142–46, Aug. 30, 1748.

wealth from one's spouse and kin. Ancient Germanic peoples lacked any concept of the will because they regarded property as being basically subject to communal control. The idea that social custom, not choice, should determine the descent of property is reflected in an old Dutch maxim "that a person cannot name an heir" (*dat men niet een erfgenaem kan aanwijzen*). The right to make a will in Holland originated during the medieval era under the influence of the church and Roman law.[10] In Anglo-Saxon England, men first obtained authority to bequeath those goods that were most nearly their own property, notably their personal equipment such as swords and ornaments. After the Norman conquest, it became generally permissible for a man to grant a limited portion of his personal estate by last will and testament. Englishmen commonly referred to this share of goods as the "dead man's part"—possessions that were usually assigned to the church for the benefit of the deceased person's soul. An individual's power of bequest depended on the extent of his family responsibilities. If he had a wife and child, he could lawfully dispose of no more than one-third of his personal property. One-third necessarily passed to the wife while the remainder fell to the children. A testator might grant up to one-half of all movable goods if he had only a wife or child.[11] It should be noted that the bequest of movable goods gained acceptance long before the devise or conveyance of real estate by will. The performance of feudal obligations depended on the descent of land according to customary rules rather than individual choice. It was not until 1540 that English landholders first obtained statutory authority to make a will devising real estate.[12]

Englishmen gained greater freedom to bequeath personal property as their wives' legal powers contracted. Common law courts during the late Middle Ages restricted a married woman's right to prepare a will for either secular or religious purposes. A widower might choose to have his deceased spouse's testament voided even if he had previously allowed her to execute the document. Her testament was subject to his veto unless he consented to its probate. As the concept of family property eroded, husbands gained greater individual control over the succession to wealth. By the fifteenth century, Englishmen in many regions could bequeath all their movables in almost any manner that they wished. A testator could therefore deny his widow any personal property except her paraphernalia—clothing, jewelry, and personal ornaments appro-

[10]A. S. de Blécourt, *Kort Begrip van het Oud-Vaderlands Burgelijk Recht,* ed. H. F. W. D. Fischer (Groningen: J. B. Wolters, 1950), 330.

[11]Michael Sheehan, *The Will in Medieval England: From the Conversion of the Anglo-Saxons to the End of the Thirteenth Century* (Toronto: Pontifical Institute of Medieval Studies, 1963), 16–19, 83, 306; Pollock and Maitland, *History of English Law,* 2:312–28, 346–54.

[12]Holdsworth, *History of English Law,* 7:362–66.

priate to her social status. Only certain areas—notably York, Wales, and London—continued to guarantee widows and children a definite share of personal property regardless of the deceased man's will. Parliament abolished these local customs in 1693, 1696, and 1725.[13]

Once English law became instituted in colonial New York, a man had great latitude in bequeathing his personal estate. The widow's right to her deceased husband's movable goods was legally secure only in cases of intestacy. If a man died without leaving a will, the Duke's Laws of 1665 guaranteed his widow one-third of his personal estate after the payment of debts and funeral charges.[14] The English Statute of Distributions, passed by Parliament in 1670, eventually became the rule of intestate succession in eighteenth-century New York. Colonial courts adopted this statute by 1754, and the provincial assembly enacted it into law in 1774.[15] The Statute of Distributions reflected the ancient English notion that a widow ought to receive a lesser share of her husband's personal estate if he left behind any children than if he had none. The widow's share was one-third in the former case (two-thirds going to the children), but one-half of all movables in the latter. The deceased man's kin acquired the other half of the property if there were no surviving children.[16]

The widow's rights to her husband's real estate in English common law can be traced to the marital customs of the late Anglo-Saxon and early Norman periods. At a couple's marriage, it was customary for a freeman to endow his bride with a gift of land or money for her use during widowhood. Standing at the church door, the bridegroom pronounced the ritual words: "Wyth yis ryng I wedde ye, and wyth yis gold and sylvere I honoure ye, and wyth my gyfts I dow ye."[17] During the twelfth century, a husband was allowed to endow his wife with no more than one-third of his lands, but he might grant her a lesser portion if he pleased. If no specific donation were made, the common law provided the widow with one-third of her husband's lands at the time of the engagement. Should the bridegroom own no land, a pledge of goods, chattels, or money might suffice to exclude the wife's claim to any realty that he subsequently acquired. A widow was entitled under the Magna

---

[13]Ibid., 3:543–45, 550–56.

[14]Charles Z. Lincoln, comp., *The Colonial Laws of the State of New York*, 5 vols. (Albany: J. B. Lyon, 1894), 1:9–10.

[15]Ibid., 5:616–17. Herbert Alan Johnson, "English Statutes in Colonial New York," *New York History* 58 (1977): 277–96.

[16]Blackstone, *Commentaries* 1, bk. 2:516.

[17]Cited in Cicely Howell, "Peasant Inheritance Customs in the Midlands, 1280–1700," in Jack Goody, Joan Thirsk, and E. P. Thompson, eds., *Family and Inheritance: Rural Society in Western Europe 1200–1800* (Cambridge: Cambridge University Press, 1976), 144.

Carta to receive her assigned gift or dower within forty days after her husband's death. During this period, called the *quarantine*, she was allowed to remain in her husband's principal house. Apart from the protection offered by common law, the widow had by custom in many parts of England the right of "free bench"—the privilege of remaining at home and using part of her deceased spouse's estate, often on condition that she did not remarry.[18]

The widow's dower eventually became fixed at one-third of all lands and tenements, including houses and other buildings, that her husband had possessed during their marriage. Her "thirds" ceased to be tied to a wedding gift and instead became a general estate or right to property. A widow's claim to her deceased husband's real estate was fundamentally different from her title to his personal property. While she acquired absolute ownership of a portion of movable goods, her dower amounted only to a life-interest. She was entitled to receive the rent or income from realty, but she was not permitted to sell or otherwise dispose of the estate itself, which passed automatically to her husband's heirs upon her death. These basic legal principles, with some variation, applied in all English colonies in North America.[19]

New York law concerning dower was ambiguous at the outset of English rule in the province. The Duke's Laws defined the widow's property rights in negative rather than positive terms. This code simply stated that a married woman would forfeit her "dowry," presumably her dower, if she deserted her husband and refused to return to him upon legal complaint.[20] The Charter of Liberties of 1683 guaranteed a widow's right to one-third of all lands her husband had possessed during wedlock, unless she had received a lesser portion before marriage.[21] This definition of dower agreed with the Magna Carta rather than contemporary English law in that it omitted any mention of tenements, that is, houses and other buildings. It is unclear whether this discrepancy reflected any conscious intent to restrict widows' property rights. The legislators' limited knowledge may have instead been responsible for their reliance on an archaic custom. In any case, the charter had little impact on provincial law because it was revoked by James II in 1686 for political reasons.

The adoption of English common law procedures was not uniform in

    [18]Pollock and Maitland, *History of English Law*, 2:418–22. For additional discussion of free bench, see E. P. Thompson, "The Grid of Inheritance: A Comment," in Goody, Thirsk, and Thompson, *Family and Inheritance*, 349–55.

    [19]Holdsworth, *History of English Law*, 3:189–95. Blackstone, *Commentaries* 1, bk. 2:129–40; Salmon, *Women and the Law of Property*, 142–47.

    [20]Lincoln, *Colonial Laws*, 1:32.

    [21]Ibid., 1:114–15.

eighteenth-century New York. Manhattan residents generally observed the custom by which men secured their wives' approval when selling or mortgaging land.[22] According to English practice, a married woman's consent depended on her being privately examined before magistrates. She could not be assumed to yield her "thirds" voluntarily if her husband were present during the hearing. City magistrates commonly registered married women's renunciations of dower rights, but officials in rural areas seldom did so. Dutch and English yeomen in outlying regions apparently had little use for English legal procedures that protected their widows' property rights at their own expense or inconvenience.[23]

By the mid-1700s, New York City residents closely observed some finer points of English property law. For example, a testator could not arbitrarily deprive his widow of her "thirds" by last will and testament. If he desired to circumvent dower, he had to offer his spouse a generous bequest in lieu of her lawful claim. A widow was then still free either to accept the legacy or insist on receiving dower.[24] Men were therefore restricted in their capacity to devise real estate, though they had nearly absolute freedom to bequeath personal property. A married woman's future security during widowhood limited her husband's control of land, the social basis of wealth and prestige.

## MARRIAGE CONTRACTS AND SETTLEMENTS

New York magistrates recognized certain procedures by which a married woman might retain separate control of property within marriage, including the right to prepare a will. During the late seventeenth century, a simple antenuptial contract between husband and wife might suffice for this purpose. Elbert Elbertz Stoothoff and the widow Sara Roelofs agreed before their marriage in Manhattan's Dutch church in 1683

> that the aforesaid bridegroom, for the support and maintenance of this marriage and to the advantage of the family, shall bring in such goods as he, the party appearing by the blessing of God, has acquired, nothing

---

[22]See, for example, New York City, Office of the City Register, Conveyance Libers-Microfiche, Liber 31:513–15. This reference is to a deed executed by a Dutch burgher and his wife on Nov. 9, 1702.

[23]This generalization is based on an analysis of Suffolk and Ulster County deeds. See Deed Books A–C, Suffolk County Courthouse, Riverhead, N.Y., and Deed Books AA–GG, Ulster County Courthouse, Kingston, N.Y.

[24]Richard B. Morris, *Studies in the History of American Law*, 2d ed. (1930; rpt. New York: Octagon Books, 1964), 157–58.

thereof being reserved, but shall have no common ownership, in the estate
and property of the aforesaid future bride, and shall also bring in whatever he shall obtain and acquire hereafter; and that the future bride, for
the support and maintenance of this marriage, shall not bring in anything,
but that she, with her two children, Rachael and Anna, shall be cared for
and supported out of the estate and property of her future bridegroom as
to board and clothing, as is otherwise honorable and fitting. Wherefore it
is provided . . . that she shall hold and control her goods separately, either
by herself or others; and dispose thereof as she shall see fit, without the
future bridegroom having or claiming any guardianship, power or administration over the property of the future bride, against her will or desire . . . inasmuch as all community of debts and property between the two
aforesaid parties is most expressly prohibited and excluded hereby.[25]

This extraordinary document demonstrates the power that some
women held in determining the terms of marriage. Stoothoff was willing
to pledge his entire property to the support of his wife and her children
without acquiring the use of any part of her estate. Though similar
agreements were executed in seventeenth-century New England and
Maryland,[26] the Roelofs-Stoothoff contract was designed to meet a
uniquely Dutch problem. Rather than circumvent English common law,
Roelofs protected herself against the possibility of community property
within marriage—the usual arrangement under Dutch customary law.
Although marrying in 1683, Roelofs and Stoothoff evidently considered
themselves to be still subject to Dutch rather than English custom.

Still, how can one explain Stoothoff's decision to wed on terms so
unmistakably favorable to his wife? Both were well advanced in age,
having been born in the Netherlands, arrived in New Amsterdam at an
early age, and first wed during the 1640s. By the time Sara Roelofs
married Stoothoff, she was the widow of two distinguished men: the
city's leading physician, Hans Kierstede, and a well-to-do merchant,
Cornelius Van Borsum. Having prospered during these marriages, she
would eventually leave five black slaves and one Indian servant to her
heirs.[27] Elbert Stoothoff, a farmer from neighboring Kings County, was
willing to concede much in order to advance his social status through
marriage.[28] His wife would also profit from her new spouse. Roelofs

[25]Cited in Morris, *Studies in American Law,* 136–37.

[26]Ibid., 135–38.

[27]Court of Probates: Inventories and Accounts, 1666–1823, 1st ser., no. 103, Apr. 10,
1694, N.Y. Archives. For information about Kierstede, see J. H. Innes, *New Amsterdam and
Its People* (New York: Charles Scribner's Sons, 1902), 45–46. Van Borsum was listed among
the city's wealthiest inhabitants in 1674. See the tax list in Edmund B. O'Callaghan, ed.,
*Documents Relative to the Colonial History of the State of New York,* 15 vols. (Albany: Weed,
Parsons, 1856–87), 2:699–700.

[28]Elbert Elbertz Stoothoff was prosperous but not among the wealthiest farmers in his

desired a husband who would assist her in maintaining herself and her family, but would threaten neither her own freedom nor the security of her children. She would acquire certain benefits from remarriage but would retain the privileges of a single woman, including the power to own property and to dispose of her entire estate as she pleased. This tenaciously independent woman was to outlive her third husband and to compose her own will just before her death in 1693.[29]

By the late 1690s, Dutch colonists in New York had begun to execute antenuptial contracts with reference to English law rather than Netherlandish custom. On September 23, 1697, Shuardt (Sioert) Olphardt and Heilkea Clopper, a blacksmith's widow, agreed to marry while retaining separate control over all property acquired before their wedding. The bridegroom confirmed his bride's right to declare her own last will and testament during the marriage "in as Large & ample Manner as if the said Hielkea was then feme Sole and unmarried." Olphardt and Clopper guaranteed each other a certain share of property depending on which party survived his or her partner. If Clopper died first, her husband was to enjoy a life estate in her house and lot in Maiden Lane within the city. If she survived her husband, however, she was to receive £150 from his estate "in full recompense & Satisfaction . . . of her dower & thirds at the Common Law."[30] By agreeing to accept this cash sum, Clopper relinquished all other claim to her spouse's estate. Her marriage contract was similar to an English jointure—a legal agreement offering a married woman a fixed amount of property during widowhood instead of her common law right.[31]

Heilkea Clopper executed this contract as an elderly widow who was less interested in benefiting from her second husband's property than in controlling her own estate as she pleased. Her last will, executed three years after she married her second husband, remained faithful to a Dutch will that she had drafted with her first spouse thirty-one years previously.[32] Though Clopper apparently could not write her own name, she was a shrewd woman who understood the importance of respecting provincial law. She relied on William Huddlestone, an attorney who had recently emigrated from England, in drafting her last will and testament.[33]

---

village. See the 1683 rate list of Amesfort (New Amersfoort) in Edmund B. O'Callaghan, *The Documentary History of the State of New York,* 4 vols. (Albany: Weed, Parsons, 1849–51), 2:495–97.

[29] N.Y. Wills, 1st ser., no. 157, July 29, 1693.

[30] Ibid., Liber 1:362–65.

[31] Salmon, *Women and the Law of Property,* 86–87, 146.

[32] N.Y. Wills, Liber 3–4:442–44, Sept. 10, 1669.

[33] Ibid., Liber 1:363, Oct. 14, 1700.

By the mid-1700s, married women could no longer retain separate ownership of property through a simple antenuptial contract. The wholesale adoption of English legal institutions necessitated more complex procedures in order to achieve this goal. Rather than execute a marriage settlement by herself, a woman had to rely on male trustees while negotiating with her future husband. In 1755, for example, Margareta Van Beverhoudt, the widow of a wealthy merchant in the Dutch West Indies, agreed to marry Nicholas Bayard, a third-generation New Yorker and a prominent trader. The bride had inherited a substantial estate from her deceased spouse and therefore wished to retain the right to bequeath property to her three orphaned children. As part of her marriage settlement, she conveyed her entire estate to a kinsman in trust for her own use until the wedding, and then for the use of her husband and his heirs. The contract itself assumed the form of an indenture tripartite, a complex agreement by which Nicholas Bayard was to acquire the use of his wife's property while she and her children retained an equitable interest in part of the estate. He entered a dual obligation to his spouse and her trustee that she be allowed to bequeath £2,400 to her three children at any time during the marriage.[34] When Margareta Van Beverhoudt prepared a will three years later, her husband confirmed her testament by a legal instrument drafted at the same time. A married woman in mid-eighteenth-century New York City could not be too careful in preparing a will given the highly unusual and questionable nature of her action. The provincial Court of Chancery subsequently upheld Van Beverhoudt's testament because her marriage settlement respected English equitable procedures.[35] As in the southern colonies, a married woman's separate control of property came to depend on the creation of a trust estate.[36]

Though the nature of marriage settlements changed over time, one fact remained constant: only a small minority of strong-minded women negotiated contracts allowing them independent control of property during marriage. It seems that not even widows, the persons most likely to enter such agreements, were apt to do so before they wed. Though the precise number of antenuptial contracts cannot be determined, it is probable that they governed less than 1 percent of all marriages during the entire period of English rule. Very few references to marriage contracts or settlements appear in probate records—a likely source of infor-

[34]Nicholas Bayard Papers, New-York Historical Society, New York City (hereafter cited as NYHS).

[35]Nicholas Bayard, Heir and Executor of Nicholas Bayard, deceased vs. Barent Van Beure et al. (June 1772). See John Tabor Kempe Papers, NYHS.

[36]Salmon, *Women and the Law of Property*, 88–119.

mation about such agreements.[37] Testators seem to have felt bound to mention antenuptial contracts if those documents influenced the bequest of property within their families. Thus Abraham Santford, a merchant, ordered in his will that a marriage contract with his second and present spouse be honored. If a widow's support was established by contract before marriage, she was legally bound to accept her assigned income or property instead of dower or any other right to her deceased husband's estate.[38]

Given a lack of documentary evidence about personal motives, one can only speculate why so few women asserted their right to retain separate ownership of property within marriage. In the case of first marriages, brides may have had little chance to protect themselves from an unscrupulous, tyrannical, or careless husband. By agreeing to marry, women in New Netherland implicitly expressed trust in their spouses to administer all common property in the family's interest. After the adoption of English law in the late 1600s, wives were in an even more dependent position within the family since all their personal property came under their husbands' ownership. Few young women had any real estate, and they were therefore often powerless with respect to property. While most brides may have been willing to defer to their future husbands, few men were willing to relinquish control over goods that their wives brought to the marriage or might acquire during it. If no marriage contract was executed, the husband would possess the same power over his wife's assets whether either party was entering a first or subsequent marriage.

A woman's ability to establish separate control of property through an antenuptial agreement depended ultimately on her future husband's consent. The unequal balance of power between spouses partly explains why few women insisted on retaining separate control of property before marrying. By implicitly accepting her husband's authority over property, a woman also gained certain rights to his estate if she outlived him. While a widow who remarried accepted a certain degree of risk for herself and any children by previous spouses, she might also acquire benefits from a new husband. If her family prospered, she would gain an increased level of support should she be widowed again. If her husband were cruel or improvident, however, she might be left destitute. Feme covert status offered little protection to colonial women whose husbands were abusive or irresponsible.[39]

[37]Only seventeen marriage contracts or settlements are referred to in New York City wills executed between 1664 and 1775.
[38]For Santford's will, see N.Y. Wills, Liber 16:124–25, Aug. 3, 1742. English law on this subject is discussed in Salmon, *Women and the Law of Property*, 145.
[39]Salmon, *Women and the Law of Property*, 15.

Marriage settlements were less common among prominent New York families than among the English gentry or the South Carolina planter elite. In eighteenth-century England, these complex legal contracts served primarily to guarantee a bride's future support during widowhood rather than to allow her independent control of property within marriage. The married woman's "pin-money" compensated her for the loss of common law rights but was incidental to the trust's major purpose—the descent of land to the male heir.[40] South Carolina marriage settlements were especially important in protecting a married woman's property in slaves. By means of a trust created before marriage, she might retain ownership of blacks independently of her husband. Even if her spouse died insolvent, his creditors could not then seize control of her property. The right to dispose of blacks was important both to women who had inherited slaves from their own kin and to widows who had acquired them from their late husbands.[41] It is ironic that South Carolina women exploited their rights under equity law for the purpose of maintaining their command of slaves. While New York women seem to have been resigned to male control of their property, many Carolina wives clung tenaciously to legal privileges that set them above the blacks who served them.

New York court records support Marylynn Salmon's conclusion that the law of separate estates was of greater theoretical importance than practical significance during the colonial era.[42] Equity law influenced nineteenth-century reforms in the area of married women's property rights. Common law rules—though not adopted completely—were fundamental to white women's daily lives. Early New York society may have been dominated by a landholding and mercantile elite, but it was decidedly middle class in its marital customs.

## THE DECLINE OF THE MUTUAL WILL

Dutch assimilation of English common law is evident in the decline of the mutual will. From 1660 through 1679, eighteen married men of

---

[40]Lloyd Bonfield, "Marriage Settlements, 1660–1740: The Adoption of the Strict Settlement in Kent and Northamptonshire," in R. B. Outhwaite, ed., *Marriage and Society: Studies in the Social History of Marriage* (New York: St. Martin's, 1981), 105–6.

[41]Marylynn Salmon has analyzed 638 marriage settlements executed in South Carolina between 1730 and 1830. Though South Carolina settlements far exceeded the number of New York contracts, they still governed only 1–2 percent of all marriages between 1785 and 1810. See Salmon, "Women and the Law of Property in South Carolina: The Evidence from Marriage Settlements, 1730 to 1830," *William and Mary Quarterly*, 3rd ser., 39 (1982): 655–85.

[42]Salmon, *Women and the Law of Property*, 83.

**Table 3.1** Mutual wills executed by Dutch colonists in New York City*

| | | Wills drafted by married persons | | | |
| | | Husband and wife | | Husband alone | |
| Period | N | N | % | N | % |
|---|---|---|---|---|---|
| 1660–69 | 10 | 8 | 80.0 | 2 | 20.0 |
| 1670–79 | 8 | 7 | 87.5 | 1 | 12.5 |
| 1680–89 | 28 | 10 | 35.7 | 18 | 64.3 |
| 1690–99 | 29 | 2 | 6.9 | 27 | 93.1 |
| Entire period | 75 | 27 | 36.0 | 48 | 64.0 |

*Only one case has been found in which a non-Dutch colonist in New York City drafted such a document. Testators have been classified by ethnic groups through an analysis of surnames.

Dutch origin prepared wills in Manhattan; fifteen of these husbands executed mutual testaments with their wives. During the next decade (1680–89), twenty-eight married men of Dutch ancestry left wills, and eighteen of them (64 percent of the entire group) acted without their wives' participation (see Table 3.1). The use of the mutual will declined sharply during the mid-1680s and soon became a thing of the past. The last will of this type in New York City was drafted in 1693.[43]

The decline of the mutual will was even more sudden in the mid–Hudson River Valley than in Manhattan. Between 1664 and 1683, twenty-four men in Kingston and nearby towns (communities that were soon to be part of Ulster County) executed wills. Eighteen of these testators—fifteen Dutchmen and three Huguenots—declared mutual wills. Not a single mutual will was drafted in these towns after 1683.[44] The demise of the mutual will in Ulster County occurred at the same time that the English governor asserted his control over the local judicial system. This policy may have led some colonists to doubt whether public officials would sanction Dutch legal procedures that were at variance with English law.[45]

By 1700 a mere handful of married couples prepared mutual wills in

[43]See the will of Martin Janse Meijer and his wife, Hendrickje. N.Y. Wills, 1st ser., no. 408, Mar. 1693.

[44]Gustave Anjou, ed., *Ulster County, N.Y. Probate Records* (1906; rpt. Baltimore: Genealogical Publishing Co., 1975). The use of the mutual will in Albany County declined sharply after 1695. See Jonathan Pearson and Arnold J. F. Van Laer, trans. and eds., *Early Records of the City and County of Albany and County of Rensselaerswyck*, 4 vols. (Albany: University of the State of New York, 1869–1919). See also Court of Probates, Wills, New York State Archives, Albany.

[45]Robert C. Ritchie, *The Duke's Province: A Study of New York Politics and Society, 1664–1691* (Chapel Hill: University of North Carolina Press, 1977), 182.

colonial New York. The transition from Dutch to English testamentary practice occurred at roughly the same time throughout the province. It is striking that the mutual will disappeared from use without being declared invalid by either provincial statute or court decision. There is no evidence that judicial officials ever refused to probate such a will. Indeed, the Prerogative Court—acting directly under the governor's authority—admitted an Albany County joint testament to probate as late as 1766.[46] Since Dutch colonists themselves abandoned the mutual will without public comment or protest, their precise motives for adopting English legal practice cannot be determined. It seems likely, however, that Dutch settlers shifted their mode of preparing wills for two principal reasons. First, they wished to execute legal documents that would pass any potential court challenge. Second, husbands may have readily adopted English usage because it allowed them sole authority over the disposition of family property. Why should their wives participate in preparing a will if their express consent was legally questionable rather than necessary? Considering women's subordinate social position, they had little choice but to accept their loss of power.

Dutch colonists began to utilize English naming practices as they adopted the English form of will. Men who executed their own testaments in the 1680s usually referred to their wives by first name only. They no longer followed the traditional Dutch custom of identifying a married woman by her maiden surname or patronymic.[47] This trend was at first limited to men's wills alone. Women who prepared mutual wills with their husbands continued to sign those documents, or have them inscribed, with their names at birth. Widows of Dutch descent also identified themselves in this manner in nearly all wills drafted before 1695. The use of the English style of surnames became nearly universal in legal documents after this point. Wives adopted their current spouse's name while widows referred to themselves by their most recent husband's surname.[48] This shift in married women's social identity paralleled their increasing dependence under New York law.

---

[46]N.Y. Wills, Liber 26:83–84, May 4, 1764. The will of Jurian Hogan and his wife, Maria, was proved in Albany on May 27, 1766, and confirmed in New York City on Nov. 18, 1767.

[47]See, for example, the Dutch-language will of Nicholas de Puis who left "mijn huysvrouw Catalina de Puis" in control of the family estate during widowhood. N.Y. Wills, Liber 3–4:281, Oct. 13, 1685.

[48]See, for example, the will of Mary (Varlet) Teller, a widow who wrote her will using her third husband's surname. N.Y. Wills, 1st ser., no. 178, Nov. 1701. For the traditional use of the wife's maiden name, see the mutual will of Evert Wessels and Jannetie Claes, N.Y. Wills, 1st ser., no. 109, Nov. 1, 1683. See also the will of Elizabeth Grevenraet, a woman who survived three husbands. N.Y. Wills, Liber 3–4:79–80, July 4, 1684.

## THE BEQUEST OF PROPERTY IN DUTCH HOUSEHOLDS, 1664–95

Irrespective of provincial law, Dutch burghers and yeomen in seventeenth-century New York retained the traditional notion of community property within marriage. Though men might prepare their own testaments, they viewed themselves and their wives as custodians of a family estate. Husbands generally directed that their spouses maintain provisional possession of nearly all their real estate as well as personal property during widowhood. Men followed this basic procedure, moreover, whether they composed a joint testament or executed their own will.

Dutchmen viewed the widow's control of the family estate as even more important than the transfer of property to their children. These testators therefore tended to postpone the younger generation's inheritance until the spouse's remarriage or death. Between 1664 and 1695, forty-four Dutchmen in New York City named both a wife and at least one child in their wills. Thirty (or 68 percent) of these fathers allowed their wives to possess either all or nearly all of their property *throughout* widowhood (even *after* all the children were of age). Eight testators (or 18 percent of the group) offered their spouses one-half of the family estate—a share in accordance with the Dutch custom of community property. It should be noted that men were even more likely to grant all their real estate than their personal property for the widow's support (see Table 3.2). Though children might receive a cash legacy or certain movable goods upon attaining adulthood, their widowed mothers maintained control over the family estate as a whole.

Dutch colonists in early New York wrote wills that were quite consistent with biblical notions of parental authority: "As long as thou livest

**Table 3.2** Property bequeathed by Dutch colonists to their wives, 1664–95

| | N* | All | | One-half | | Other part | |
|---|---|---|---|---|---|---|---|
| | | N | % | N | % | N | % |
| Estate as a whole | 44 | 30 | 68.2 | 8 | 18.2 | 6 | 13.6 |
| Real estate | 44 | 34 | 77.3 | 8 | 18.2 | 2 | 4.5 |
| Personal estate | 43 | 30 | 69.8 | 8 | 18.6 | 5 | 11.6 |

*All of the wills considered here were left by married men who had at least one child. I have categorized bequests in this chapter according to the wife's share of the estate throughout her widowhood, and not simply before the testator's children came of age. (A widow's share is therefore marked as "part" instead of "all" if she received temporary possession of the whole but later had to yield most of her property prior to remarriage or death.) The categories "one-half" or "one-third" in the chapter include some cases in which the widow received additional property besides her basic fractional share.

and hast breath in thee, give not thyself over to any. For better it is that thy children should seek to thee, than that thou shouldest stand to their courtesy" (Ecclus. 33:20–21). Such advice reflected prevalent social attitudes in early modern Europe. As the English essayist Richard Steele noted: "Old people are commonly despised especially when they are not supported with good estates." However, he who "hath [an] estate of his own to maintain himself and to pleasure his children, oh, then he is had in estimation, his age is honoured, his person is reverenced, his counsel is sought, his voice is obeyed."[49]

Dutchmen in late seventeenth-century New York were even more inclined than their predecessors in New Netherland to postpone their children's inheritance until the widow's death. While Dutch customary law restricted an individual's bequests in his heirs' interest, English law allowed the testator to dispose of his estate almost entirely as he pleased. Once freed of legal obligations to the next generation, men seldom required their wives to buy out the children's paternal inheritance for a fixed cash sum. Widows instead generally had the right to use all family property, including the authority to sell real estate, as long as they did not remarry. Men's trust in their wives was based on affection as well as respect. Hendrick Areson, a New York City mason, expressed his "Special Love and Affection towards my beloved Wife" by granting her the power during widowhood to dispose of his entire estate as her "owne free goods according to her pleasure."[50]

Viewing their wives as their immediate successors, men commonly freed them from the legal obligations of taking an inventory of the estate or accounting to public authorities for the management of property. Hendrick Van Borsum, a Manhattan carpenter, absolved his wife, Maria, from these responsibilities because he did "fully confide" that she "Shall not wrong my Children gotten with her but rather Shall indeavour all aid, assistance and benefitt of them."[51] Like the great majority of Dutch testators, Van Borsum protected his children's interests by specifying that they divide the estate equally among themselves after the widow's death. Maria Van Borsum gained the right to administer nearly all family property, but not the power to alter her deceased husband's will.

While conforming to a general pattern, the provisions of wills varied somewhat according to particular family circumstances. If the testator had been married only once, he was especially likely to grant possession

---

[49]Both the Bible and Steele are quoted in Keith Thomas, "Age and Authority in Early Modern England," *Proceedings of the British Academy* 62 (1976): 239, 247–48.

[50]N.Y. Wills, Liber 14A:41–42, Nov. 1, 1686. A wife's participation in drafting a will made it especially likely that she would receive the authority to sell real estate.

[51]Ibid., 1st ser., no. 82, Apr. 18, 1687.

of the entire estate (or nearly all property) to his spouse. A man usually left a major share of wealth to a second or third spouse if both parties had merged their property and had children together during marriage. Isaac Van Vleck, a well-to-do New York City brewer who married three times, bequeathed the use of one-half of his estate to his last wife, Cathalina, who had one child by him. He also appointed her sole executor and authorized her to give each of his five children a wedding gift "according to ye Condition of ye Estate, and according as they [i.e., the heirs] Shall behave them selfs, which I leave totaly to my said wife, forbidding my Children to Speake or doe anything against their mothers actions, being all left to her discretion." While supporting his wife's authority, Van Vleck named the children as his eventual heirs and safeguarded their rights if his widow remarried.[52]

Cathalina Van Vleck's command of family resources depended on her role as a "pious mother"—a parent who nourished the children and ensured that they learned reading, writing, and a useful trade. Lest the widow neglect these responsibilities or be unable to perform them, Van Vleck chose six male relatives to serve as the children's guardians.[53] These men were to assume authority over those offspring to whom they were kin by blood (see chart below). The testator's will implicitly expressed the notion that his estate had been formed through property contributed by his three wives as well as himself. He assigned an equal share of the patrimony to each child, but he also recognized that each heir had particular needs and claims depending upon maternal lineage.

### GUARDIANS OF VAN VLECK'S CHILDREN BY HIS THREE WIVES

| Wife | Guardians | Relation |
|---|---|---|
| Petronella Van Couwenhoven | Johannes V. Couwenhoven (brewer) | wife's brother |
| | Cornelius Plevier | husband of wife's sister |
| Cornelia Beekman | William Beekman (brewer) | wife's father |
| | Henry Beekman | wife's brother |
| Cathalina Delanoy | Abraham Delanoy | wife's brother |
| | Peter Delanoy (merchant) | wife's brother |

Seventeenth-century New York wills indicate that Dutch settlers were committed to three major principles concerning inheritance—the trans-

---

[52]Ibid., 1st ser., no. 138, Jan. 18, 1689.
[53]Ibid.

fer of the family estate to the widowed spouse, the division of community property upon remarriage, and the equal (or nearly equal) partition of property among children. It should be emphasized that Dutchmen adhered to these social customs whatever their particular occupational or economic status. City residents bequeathed property in nearly the same manner as yeomen did in rural Long Island or the Hudson Valley.[54] Men defined their wives' rights and responsibilities according to Dutch traditions even after adopting the English form of will.

## ETHNIC INFLUENCES IN SEVENTEENTH-CENTURY WILLS

Dutchmen in seventeenth-century New York bequeathed property according to a pattern substantially different from that of Englishmen in other colonies. In both New England and the Chesapeake, men's bequests to their wives were greatly influenced by the age, number, and sex of their children. Fathers with at least some minor children were most likely to grant a large share of the estate to their widows since the latter had crucial parental responsibilities. Men's generosity to their wives diminished if they had many children requiring support, or if they had any grown sons—the primary claimants to land.[55] This was not the case among Dutch households in either seventeenth-century Manhattan or rural areas of New York. The great majority of Dutch burghers and yeomen transferred the entire estate to their spouses throughout widowhood irrespective of the number of their children or the heirs' age or

[54]David E. Narrett, "Men's Wills and Women's Property Rights in Colonial New York," in Ronald Hoffman and Peter J. Albert, eds., *Women in the Age of the American Revolution* (Charlottesville: University Press of Virginia, 1989), 107–14. See also William John McLaughlin, "Dutch Rural New York: Community, Economy, and Family in Colonial Flatbush" (Ph.D. diss., Columbia University, 1981), chaps. 6–7.

[55]Kim Lacy Rogers, "Relicts of the New World: Conditions of Widowhood in Seventeenth Century New England," in Mary Kelley, ed., *Woman's Being, Woman's Place: Female Identity and Vocation in American History* (Boston: Hall, 1979), 26–52; Gloria L. Main, "Widows in Rural Massachusetts on the Eve of the Revolution," in Hoffman and Albert, *Women in the Age of the American Revolution*, 80–82, 89–90. See also in the same volume Lois Green Carr, "Inheritance in the Colonial Chesapeake," 171–74, 186–97; Lois Green Carr and Lorena S. Walsh, "The Planter's Wife: The Experience of White Women in Seventeenth-Century Maryland," *William and Mary Quarterly*, 3d ser., 34 (1977): 555–58. Eighteenth-century wills in several colonies also indicate that the widow's share depended on the age, number, and sex of children. In addition to the above studies, see Linda S. Speth, "More Than Her 'Thirds': Wives and Widows in Colonial Virginia," *Women and History* no. 4 (1982): 5–41; John E. Crowley, "Family Relations and Inheritance in Early South Carolina," *Histoire Sociale* 17 (1984): 35–57. For evidence from eighteenth-century Bucks County, Pennsylvania, see Carole Shammas, "Early American Women and Control over Capital," in Hoffman and Albert, *Women in the Age of the American Revolution*, 144–47.

sex. Unlike English colonists, the Dutch very seldom distinguished between the widow's right to property during her children's minority and after they came of age. She was the undisputed head of the family as long as she remained widowed.

Englishmen in Manhattan were less inclined than their Dutch counterparts to convey the entire estate to their wives. Twenty-four men of British origin mentioned a wife and at least one child in city wills drafted between 1664 and 1695. Eleven of these colonists bequeathed either provisional or unconditional control of all their property to their spouses. Englishmen were less careful than the Dutch to establish guidelines concerning the widow's management of the estate and their children's property rights. Unlike the Dutch, they seldom instructed their spouses on specific parental responsibilities, appointed guardians for their minor children, or mandated a settlement of the estate in case of the widow's remarriage. While the Englishman's widow might receive an ample share of her husband's property, the Dutch *huysvrouw* succeeded to the family estate as a whole.

At least some Britons in seventeenth-century America clearly preferred their own legal traditions to Dutch social practice. Henry Mackintosh, a well-traveled sugar planter who lived in the Dutch colony of Surinam, executed a marriage contract in Port Royal, Jamaica, in 1688 with Elizabeth Lehunt, a resident of that town. Openly declaring his aversion to community property, he took no chances that Dutch law would govern his family life upon his return to Surinam. The contract stated the bride's consent to abide by her spouse's "goodness and Generosity," and offered her no more than one-fourth of his estate if she survived him. Mackintosh declared his own will in 1690 while residing in New York City on business. Unfortunately, one cannot determine the precise portion of his estate that his wife received. After making some token bequests and conveying 100,000 pounds of sugar to his brother, he left her the remainder of his wealth.[56] Mackintosh may have provided generously for his wife, but he did not wish to be bound by any Dutch custom that obligated him to give at least one-half of family property to her.

Intermarriage helped to promote English assimilation of Dutch social customs in early New York. As the historian Joyce Goodfriend has written, marriages between Englishmen and Dutch women in the seventeenth century were far more common than unions between Dutch bur-

[56]William S. Pelletreau, ed., *Abstracts of Wills on File in the Surrogate's Office, City of New York, 1665–1801*, 17 vols., Collections of the New-York Historical Society (New York, 1893–1909), 1:178–79.

ghers and Englishwomen.[57] Because single men probably accounted for most early English immigrants, they necessarily had to look outside their own national group if they wished to broaden their opportunity to wed. Marriage to a Dutch woman might be especially appealing if she came from a well-established colonial family.

John Spratt's marriage to Maria De Peyster in 1687 indicates that British newcomers were apt to adopt Dutch social customs if they wed women of Dutch ancestry. While the bridegroom was an aspiring young trader from Sotland, the bride was the widow of a prosperous merchant, Paulus Schrick, and the daughter of Johannes De Peyster and Cornelia Lubberts, the heads of a prominent mercantile family. Prior to being wed in the Dutch Reformed church, the betrothed couple negotiated a marriage contract that adopted the Dutch custom of community property between spouses. John Spratt and Maria De Peyster Schrick excepted only one form of property from their jointly owned estate. If either husband or wife inherited any property, he or she was to acquire sole ownership of those assets. This provision applied to both parties, but it undoubtedly benefited the bride more than the bridegroom. While he was but a newcomer to the colony, she was an heir to the De Peyster family wealth. Finally, the marriage contract stipulated that the family estate was to be divided into two equal parts if either spouse died—one-half to the survivor; the other share to any children whom the couple might have.[58] This agreement was modeled on Dutch customs of inheritance even though it was negotiated twenty-three years after the English conquest.

It is not surprising that Dutch social customs influenced the descendants of several French Huguenot families living in colonial New York City. The Bayard family, for example, traced its Dutch origins to Balthazar Bayard, a professor at the Protestant University in Paris, who sought religious refuge in the Netherlands during the early seventeenth century. His son, Samuel, married Anna Stuyvesant and thereby became a brother-in-law to Pieter Stuyvesant, the future governor of New Netherland. The bonds between these Huguenot and Dutch families soon grew close as Pieter Stuyvesant wed Samuel Bayard's sister, Judith, shortly before being appointed to the governorship in 1645. When he left Holland for America two years later, he was accompanied by his sister Anna, now a widow, and her three sons, Balthazar, Nicholas, and Petrus Bayard. While Petrus eventually settled in New Jersey and Dela-

---

[57]Joyce Diane Goodfriend, "'Too Great a Mixture of Nations': The Development of New York City Society in the Seventeenth Century" (Ph.D. diss., UCLA, 1975), 203, 209.

[58]N.Y. Wills, Liber 5–6:134–36. For genealogical notes on the De Peyster family, see Edward R. Purple, *Contributions to the History of Ancient Families of New Amsterdam and New York* (New York: privately printed, 1881), 98.

ware, Balthazar and Nicholas married in the mid-1660s into prominent Dutch families in Manhattan.[59]

The Bayards were Dutch in their family affiliations but by no means steadfastly pro-Dutch in their political loyalties. Nicholas Bayard petitioned Governor Andros to respect Dutch civil rights in 1675, but he soon learned the importance of accommodation to English rule after being briefly imprisoned that year. He eventually became a leading opponent of the predominantly Dutch faction that seized control of the province in 1689 under Jacob Leisler's command. Condemned to prison by the rebels in 1690, he curried favor with the English by categorizing his enemies as "a parcel of ignorant and innocent people, almost none but of the Dutch nation."[60] Once restored to the Governor's Council, he seized upon his office as a means of amassing substantial land grants and acquiring other economic benefits. Men such as Bayard were well advised to exploit any momentary advantage for profit and revenge. When the Leislerians regained power in 1702, Bayard was arrested, tried, and sentenced to be hung for treason. He was saved from death only by a reprieve from England.[61]

Nicholas Bayard's and Jacob Leisler's mutual hostility was rooted in family politics as well as in their conflicting attitudes toward the English provincial government. Nicholas's elder brother, Balthazar, was married to Maria Loockermans, the daughter of a wealthy Dutch merchant in Manhattan by the name of Govert Loockermans. Loockermans died intestate in 1671, beginning one of the most prolonged inheritance disputes in early New York.[62] Because the deceased had had three wives during his lifetime, the settlement of his estate was especially difficult. It was further complicated by the fact that his third wife and widow, Mary Jansen, had a daughter named Elsie by a previous husband. Elsie just happened to be Jacob Leisler's wife. Jacob Leisler and Balthazar Bayard therefore had conflicting interests in the Loockermans-Jansen estate. Leisler's claim was through his wife, a principal beneficiary of Mary Jansen's will executed in 1677.[63] Bayard's claim was through his spouse, a child of Govert Loockermans's first marriage.

Because of gaps in the historical record, it is not possible to reconstruct

---

[59]Mrs. Anson Phelps Atterbury, *The Bayard Family* (Baltimore, 1928). See also Purple, *History of Ancient Families*, 39, 81n, 112–13.

[60]Quoted in Thomas J. Archdeacon, *New York City, 1664–1710: Conquest and Change* (Ithaca: Cornell University Press, 1976), 114. For Bayard's politics, see also Ritchie, *The Duke's Province*, 141–43, 180–81, 225, 229–30. A more recent contribution is Adrian Howe, "The Bayard Treason Trial: Dramatizing Dutch Politics in Early Eighteenth-Century New York City," *William and Mary Quarterly*, 3d ser., 47 (1990): 57–89.

[61]Archdeacon, *New York City, 1664–1710*, 124, 143.

[62]Pelletreau, *Abstracts of Wills*, 1:190–91. See also Purple, *History of Ancient Families*, 27–40.

[63]N.Y. Wills, Liber 1:239–42, May 7, 1679, codicil executed Nov. 1, 1677.

the course of litigation in this inheritance dispute. It is apparent, however, that the opposing parties argued strenuously over the precise bounds between Govert Loockermans's and Mary Jansen's estates. Jacob Leisler exploited his ties to his mother-in-law in order to gain control of most of the Loockermans family land in Manhattan following her death. Govert Loockermans's lineal descendants—heirs by his first and second wives—rejected Leisler's possession as unlawful.[64]

This controversy was eventually resolved on October 21, 1692, more than seventeen months after Leisler's rebellion was suppressed and the leader executed. The surviving parties then concluded an agreement that was not only written in the Dutch language but also drafted according to the Dutch custom of community property (*de hollantse costuym*) rather than provincial law. The Bayards might be avowedly pro-English in politics, but they finally agreed with Leisler's heirs that Dutch law was the proper basis for settling a dispute over inheritance. Both sides of the family agreed to treat Govert Loockermans's and Mary Jansen's possessions as forming a single estate that was to be appraised and then divided into two equal parts—one-half for Loockermans's descendants, the other half for Jansen's. Elsie Leisler, the rebel leader's widow, received one share. The remainder was to be distributed equally among three claimants: Govert Loockermans's son, Jacob; his daughter, Jannetie, widow of Hans Kierstede; and Balthazar Bayard, representing his wife, Maria, the deceased man's other daughter.[65]

Balthazar Bayard's own last will and testament, written in 1699, indicates the complexity of ethnic ties and loyalties in late seventeenth-century New York City. Although his forebears were French, he lived his adult years in a predominantly Dutch society that was under English rule. He bequeathed his property according to certain Dutch social customs while also being influenced by the colony's new legal institutions. His will allowed his wife to maintain possession of nearly his entire estate, including a brewery, during her widowhood. Because Bayard had already given wedding gifts of one hundred pounds each to his two eldest daughters, he offered similar sums to his other children. Apart from certain limited bequests, he postponed his children's inheritance until his wife's remarriage or death. If she wed again, her claim to the estate was restricted to her dower under New York law.[66] This last provision is significant because it suggests that Balthazar Bayard conceived of the family estate as being ultimately his own property. If he had fully

[64]Archdeacon, *New York City, 1664–1710*, 110–11.
[65]Legal Documents, no. 5810, Museum of the City of New York.
[66]Pelletreau, *Abstracts of Wills*, 1:416, Mar. 4, 1699.

respected the Dutch custom of community property, he would have allowed his wife one-half of all possessions upon remarriage. He instead adopted English law in this instance in order to protect his children's inheritance. Treating his wife's possessions as his own property, he even bequeathed all her clothing and jewelry to his daughters after her death.[67] Though he probably offered this bequest with his wife's consent, his action limited her legal authority during widowhood. Neither Balthazar nor Maria Bayard apparently had any knowledge of the English custom allowing a married woman to dispose freely of her own paraphernalia or personal effects after her husband's death. Considering the uncertainty of New York law, husband and wife chose wisely to bequeath these items through Balthazar's will alone.

Cultural assimilation in seventeenth-century New York City involved Africans as well as European colonists. New Amsterdam had at least some black inhabitants from the first decade of colonization and eventually became an important center in the Dutch West India Company's slave trade. By 1664 some seven hundred blacks lived in all New Netherland, nearly one-tenth of the colonial population.[68] Most Africans remained slaves throughout life, but some blacks obtained their freedom, acquired title to land, joined the Dutch Reformed church, and staked out an independent existence at the margins of colonial society. Solomon Pieters (also spelled Peters), a former slave, received a patent to a thirty-acre tract of land during Pieter Stuyvesant's governorship. Like other freedmen, he lived along the west side of the Bowery Road between modern-day Prince Street and Astor Place—an area that had been occupied by blacks as early as the 1630s.[69] He was married to Maria Antonia Portuguez, whose name suggests either Brazilian or Angolan ancestry. This couple had nine children baptized in the Dutch Reformed church between 1665 and 1685. Pieters's will, written in 1694, is the only extant testament prepared by a black man or woman in colonial New York City history. As a church member and landowner in the community for many years, he undoubtedly had acquired familiarity with Dutch social customs, including those concerning inheritance. He bequeathed his property in the typical Dutch fashion by postponing his children's inheritance until his widow's remarriage or death. If she wed again, she was to retain only one-half of the estate while the remainder was to be divided immediately among the couple's four sons and four daughters.

[67]Ibid.

[68]See Joyce D. Goodfriend, "Burghers and Blacks: The Evolution of a Slave Society at New Amsterdam," *New York History* 59 (1978): 125–43.

[69]See I. N. Phelps Stokes, *The Iconography of Manhattan Island, 1498–1909,* 6 vols. (New York: R. H. Dodd, 1915–28), 6:106–7, 123.

The testator allotted an equal share of property to each child except that his sons were to divide his farming tools, guns, and other arms among themselves while the daughters were to share the household goods. He also followed Dutch custom by offering his sons the right of first refusal to the estate—the option of purchasing the other heirs' claims to land. Recognized as a capable man throughout the city, Pieters put his mark to a will dictated in an authoritative manner. His apparent inability to write did not prevent him from controlling his family's resources as he thought fit.[70]

## THE DECLINE IN WIDOWS' PROPERTY RIGHTS, 1696–1775

Family life is generally one of the most stable areas of social behavior and one of the least subject to sudden or dramatic changes. There was no single point in eighteenth-century New York when Dutch social customs ceased to influence either inheritance or domestic relations. One can, however, identify a general period—from the 1720s to the 1770s—when wills indicate a shift in men's attitudes toward both property and their wives' role within the family. As Dutch New Yorkers assimilated English law and culture, they tended to develop a more pronounced sense of individual ownership of wealth. While most testators continued to provide generously for their wives, few husbands viewed their spouses as the successors to a jointly owned family estate. Men of Dutch origin increasingly showed the same general purpose in bequeathing property as other colonists did. A growing proportion of all fathers who left wills chose to restrict their wives' property rights and thereby to transfer a major share of wealth immediately upon death to their children. Men limited their spouses' share of the estate during widowhood for their children's benefit, but seldom for the advantage of other kin.

Most men of Dutch ancestry in mid-eighteenth-century New York City bequeathed property in a markedly different manner than had their fathers or grandfathers. This trend is especially apparent in wills left by individuals who had a wife and at least one child. Beginning in the late 1720s, a decreasing proportion of fathers in the Dutch community transferred all their property to their wives throughout widowhood (see Table 3.3). Seventy percent of Dutch heads of households had followed

[70]N.Y. Wills, 1st ser., no. 658, Nov. 30, 1694. Pieters's will was not proved or validated until June 11, 1724.

**Table 3.3** Property bequeathed by Dutch colonists to their wives

| Period | N* | All or nearly all | | Residual estate (after legacies)** | | One-half | | One-third | | Other part | |
|---|---|---|---|---|---|---|---|---|---|---|---|
| | | N | % | N | % | N | % | N | % | N | % |
| 1664–95 | 44 | 30 | 68.2 | 3 | 6.8 | 8 | 18.2 | 0 | 0 | 3 | 6.8 |
| 1696–1725 | 82 | 58 | 70.7 | 13 | 15.8 | 2 | 2.4 | 1 | 1.2 | 8 | 9.8 |
| 1726–50 | 72 | 43 | 59.7 | 4 | 5.6 | 2 | 2.8 | 5 | 6.9 | 18 | 25.0 |
| 1751–75 | 106 | 48 | 45.3 | 8 | 7.5 | 4 | 3.8 | 7 | 6.6 | 39 | 36.8 |
| Entire period | 304 | 179 | 58.9 | 28 | 9.2 | 16 | 5.3 | 13 | 4.3 | 68 | 22.4 |

*All wills considered here were left by married men who had at least one child.

**This column indicates cases in which the widow received the entire estate except for certain cash legacies to children. The residual estate usually amounted to a major portion of the deceased man's property.

this procedure in wills drafted from 1664 through 1725. During the late colonial era (1751–75), only 45 percent of testators within the same ethnic group granted the entire estate to their spouses. It is also significant that the widow's fractional share of the estate decreased over time. In the late 1600s, this portion of property commonly amounted to one-half of all family wealth. It might also be defined as the residual estate (all remaining property after the payment of cash legacies to the surviving children). The bequest of a half-share seldom occurred after 1700; the widow usually received a lesser proportion, especially after 1725. The bequest of the residual estate was quite common in the early 1700s, but it, too, was seldom used once men came to convey most of their wealth directly to their children.

Men within most ethnic groups tended to restrict their widows' share of the estate more sharply as the eighteenth century advanced. This trend was especially apparent among colonists of British descent (see Table 3.4). More than 40 percent of British fathers who left wills from 1664 through 1725 conveyed the entire estate (or nearly all property) to their spouses, but only 27 percent did so from 1751 through 1775.

Though eighteenth-century wills conform to a general pattern, the pace of social change was uneven. The city continued to absorb some European immigrants who maintained the traditional notion of family property. German colonists, for example, were strongly inclined to convey the use of the entire estate (or nearly all property) to their wives during widowhood. Thirteen among twenty-two testators of German ancestry followed this practice between 1751 and 1775—a far higher percentage than among Dutch burghers who were assimilated into English colonial society.

**Table 3.4** Property bequeathed by British colonists to their wives

| Period | N* | All or nearly all | | Residual estate (after legacies)** | | One-half | | One-third | | Other part | |
|---|---|---|---|---|---|---|---|---|---|---|---|
| | | N | % | N | % | N | % | N | % | N | % |
| 1664–95 | 24 | 11 | 45.8 | 1 | 4.2 | 3 | 12.5 | 2 | 8.3 | 7 | 29.2 |
| 1696–1725 | 56 | 24 | 42.9 | 3 | 5.4 | 5 | 8.9 | 5 | 8.9 | 19 | 33.9 |
| 1726–50 | 67 | 22 | 32.8 | 2 | 3.0 | 4 | 6.0 | 10 | 14.9 | 29 | 43.3 |
| 1751–75 | 135 | 36 | 26.7 | 5 | 3.7 | 7 | 5.2 | 21 | 15.5 | 66 | 48.9 |
| Entire period | 282 | 93 | 33.0 | 11 | 3.9 | 19 | 6.7 | 38 | 13.5 | 121 | 42.9 |

*All wills considered here were left by married men who had at least one child.

**This column indicates cases in which the widow received the entire estate except for certain cash legacies to children. The residual estate usually amounted to a major portion of the deceased man's property.

It is simpler to document statistical trends concerning the bequest of property than to explain the historical meaning of those patterns. One should note that a widow's share of her deceased husband's estate did not alone determine her material welfare or personal security within the family. A widow might be better equipped to provide for her needs if she obtained ownership of one-third of her spouse's property than if she held a passive interest in the estate as a whole. As discussed below, many widows obtained the use of wealth, especially real estate, without being permitted to sell or convey the property itself. These women might find it difficult to support themselves unless they were able to accumulate interest from capital sums or to earn rent income from housing or land.

Economic status, as well as ethnic background, was a major influence on the bequest of property in eighteenth-century New York City. In the absence of sufficient documentary evidence (in the form of inventories of estates or tax lists), one cannot determine the precise relationship between a man's wealth and his manner of preparing a will. It is unquestionable, however, that fathers within the most affluent occupational group were the most inclined to advance property directly to their children rather than to postpone inheritance until their widows' remarriage or death. Between 1664 and 1725, sixty-seven merchants named a wife and at least one child in their wills. Thirty (or 45 percent) of these men transferred all their property to their wives for the entire period of widowhood (see Table 3.5). This practice became very uncommon among New York traders who left wills during the mid-1700s. Between 1726 and 1775, ninety-nine merchants prepared testaments that referred to a spouse and at least one son or daughter, yet only nineteen (or 19 percent) allowed their wives to control the entire estate throughout widowhood.

**Table 3.5** Property bequeathed by merchants to their wives

| Period | N* | All or nearly all | | Residual estate (after legacies)** | | One-half | | One-third | | Other part | |
|---|---|---|---|---|---|---|---|---|---|---|---|
| | | N | % | N | % | N | % | N | % | N | % |
| 1664–95 | 19 | 9 | 47.4 | 1 | 5.3 | 3 | 15.8 | 2 | 10.5 | 4 | 21.0 |
| 1696–1725 | 48 | 21 | 43.7 | 4 | 8.3 | 3 | 6.2 | 7 | 14.6 | 13 | 27.1 |
| 1726–50 | 45 | 11 | 24.4 | 3 | 6.7 | 2 | 4.4 | 5 | 11.1 | 24 | 53.3 |
| 1751–75 | 54 | 8 | 14.8 | 6 | 11.1 | 3 | 5.6 | 5 | 9.3 | 32 | 59.2 |
| Entire period | 166 | 49 | 29.5 | 14 | 8.4 | 11 | 6.6 | 19 | 11.4 | 73 | 44.0 |

*All wills considered here were left by married men who had at least one child.

**This column indicates cases in which the widow received the entire estate except for certain cash legacies to children. The residual estate usually amounted to a major portion of the deceased man's property.

Artisans were less inclined to limit their wives' share of the estate than were merchants, especially in wills drafted before 1750. Between 1664 and 1750, ninety-nine craftsmen in New York City bequeathed property to a spouse and at least one child. Sixty-eight fathers (or 69 percent) within this group transferred all their property to their wives (see Table 3.6). This tendency declined appreciably in the late colonial era. From 1751 through 1775, only thirty-nine (or 45 percent) of eighty-seven artisans allowed their wives to control all property throughout widowhood when they also left behind a child or children.

Merchants were the most likely of all testators to restrict their wives' share of the estate, partly because they had the greatest degree of flexibility in bequeathing property. These men usually had enough wealth to satisfy their wives' needs by offering them either a fractional share of the

**Table 3.6** Property bequeathed by artisans to their wives

| Period | N* | All or nearly all | | Residual estate (after legacies)** | | One-half | | One-third | | Other part | |
|---|---|---|---|---|---|---|---|---|---|---|---|
| | | N | % | N | % | N | % | N | % | N | % |
| 1664–95 | 17 | 12 | 70.6 | 1 | 5.9 | 2 | 11.8 | 0 | 0 | 2 | 11.8 |
| 1696–1725 | 46 | 32 | 69.6 | 8 | 17.4 | 1 | 2.2 | 1 | 2.2 | 4 | 8.7 |
| 1726–50 | 36 | 24 | 66.7 | 2 | 5.5 | 2 | 5.5 | 3 | 8.3 | 5 | 13.9 |
| 1751–75 | 87 | 39 | 44.8 | 3 | 3.4 | 5 | 5.7 | 8 | 9.2 | 32 | 36.8 |
| Entire period | 186 | 107 | 57.5 | 14 | 7.5 | 10 | 5.4 | 12 | 6.4 | 43 | 23.1 |

*All wills considered here were left by married men who had at least one child.

**This column indicates cases in which the widow received the entire estate except for certain cash legacies to children. The residual estate usually amounted to a major portion of the deceased man's property.

estate or certain specific goods (instead of all property). Dutch traders, in particular, gained sufficient familiarity with English law during the early 1700s in order to adjust their bequests to meet their personal economic situation. Artisans with modest resources necessarily had greater difficulty in balancing their wives' security during widowhood with their children's economic needs. Faced with the question of how to distribute a comparatively modest estate, craftsmen would frequently place the wife's interest above their obligation to children.[71]

An analysis of wills indicates that certain ethnic traditions declined among the elite before they lost influence among men within the middling or lower social ranks. During the period 1664–1725, the great majority of Dutch colonists—whatever their occupational status—had granted possession of the entire estate (or nearly all of it) to their wives. Merchants of Dutch ancestry abandoned this practice in eighteenth-century wills to a far greater extent than did artisans. Between 1751 and 1775, only three among twenty-one merchants of Dutch background granted the estate as a whole to their wives; yet nineteen among thirty-one Dutch artisans did so during the same period. Dutch craftsmen, still influenced by their own ethnic traditions, were more likely than British artisans to convey all their property to their wives throughout widowhood.

Although the extent of Anglicization varied among distinct groups of burghers, nearly all Dutch colonists had assimilated certain English notions of property law by the 1720s. Consider, for example, widows' property rights upon remarriage. Dutchmen in seventeenth-century New York City had generally authorized their wives to assume absolute ownership of one-half of all family property if they wed again. This practice was fairly common until 1710, but thereafter it was seldom used. Not a single Dutch New Yorker after 1725 granted his wife a half share of the entire estate upon remarriage. The custom of community property within marriage had ceased to be strictly followed at this point since women were no longer being treated as co-owners of the family estate.

Dutch farmers in the rural Hudson Valley also altered their pattern of bequeathing property during this same period. Though many yeomen continued to entrust their widows with provisional control of the entire estate, they almost invariably restricted their spouses' rights upon remarriage. Most testators went so far as to deny their widows any property in that case.[72]

---

[71]See, for example, the wills of Abraham Alsteyn, bricklayer, and Jacob Kip, cordwainer. N.Y. Wills, Liber 18:245–47, Sept. 7, 1744: Liber 19:172–73, June 17, 1751.

[72]Narrett, "Men's Wills and Women's Property Rights," 112–13.

Most men of Dutch descent in eighteenth-century New York were quite selective in following Netherlandish customs of inheritance. This trend is apparent even among craftsmen and laborers who wed women of Dutch ancestry, and who probably had limited familiarity with English colonial culture. Albertus Clock, a shoemaker who was born in New Amsterdam in 1660, wrote a will at age fifty-nine that conveyed the use of nearly his entire estate to his wife, Tryntie, herself born in Manhattan in 1662. Though he postponed his children's inheritance in typical Dutch fashion, Clock restricted his wife's right upon remarriage in accordance with English custom—a life-interest in one-third of his real estate and ownership of one-third of his personal property.[73] Tryntie Clock was never to remarry, probably because of her advanced age as well as her limited legal rights during widowhood.

Testators increasingly restricted their wives' property rights upon remarriage according to their own personal needs rather than social tradition. New York wills in the mid-1700s indicate a variety of bequests to satisfy the widow's needs at that time: one-third of the estate, an equal portion of property with the children, an annuity or outright cash gift.[74] Many men simply granted the use of property during widowhood without indicating that their wives were to receive any goods or money upon remarriage. These testators apparently understood the legal principle that a widow could not sue for dower or any other right to her deceased husband's estate if she had initially accepted a bequest from his will.

Three generations of Verplanck family wills illustrate how changes in legal institutions and social attitudes affected widows' property rights from the 1680s to the 1750s. Gulian Verplanck, born in 1637 to Dutch immigrants in New Amsterdam, entered the local beaver trade as a young man, achieved wealth through overseas commercial ventures, and eventually acquired a tract of several thousand acres in the Hudson River Valley. His marriage to Hendrickje Wessels, the daughter of a notable female innkeeper, was instrumental to his economic success. When Verplanck fell ill in 1684, he and his spouse summoned a notary public to record their last will and testament in the Dutch language. Bequeathing their common estate according to Dutch custom, they appointed the survivor of the marriage as the immediate successor to all their property. The will appointed the widowed spouse as sole executor, authorizing that person to administer the estate without accounting to their children, kin, or public officials. If the survivor remarried, however, he or she was to set aside half of all property for the couple's five

[73] N.Y. Wills, 1st ser., no. 727, Oct. 1, 1719.
[74] See, for example, the wills of Gerrit Harsin, gunsmith; Gerardus Hardenbroeck, baker; and Peter Van Deursen, chandler. N.Y. Wills, Liber 19:75–77, May 15, 1753; Liber 23:533–34, June 26, 1755; Liber 26:313–14, Oct. 16, 1762.

children. These heirs, ranging in age from four to fourteen years old, were not offered any specific legacy prior to the widowed parent's death or remarriage. Since Hendrickje Wessels remarried just one year after Gulian Verplanck's death, she had to protect the children's patrimony in accordance with the mutual will. Though obligated to assign half of the estate to her offspring, she was directed not to transfer any share of this property until the youngest heir came of age.[75] Verplanck and Wessels viewed their own security and their children's maintenance as more important than the advancement of wealth to particular heirs. Like other Dutch parents in early Manhattan, they were not prepared to encourage individual success at the expense of family stability.

Samuel Verplanck, the couple's eldest son, composed his own will in 1698 when he was just twenty-eight years old. Though he utilized the English style of testament, he bequeathed his property in typical Dutch fashion. Postponing his children's inheritance, he granted the use of nearly the entire family estate to his wife during widowhood. Not having yet received his full inheritance, he allowed his spouse future possession of all property that he was entitled to receive from his deceased father as well as his mother who was still alive. Samuel died too young to become a wealthy man, but he left behind three children to benefit from his family's wealth after his wife's death.[76]

Samuel's eldest son, Gulian, was as successful in business as the paternal grandfather for whom he was named. Born in 1698, this fourth-generation Manhattanite cemented his fortune at age thirty-nine by marrying Mary Crommelin, the daughter of a wealthy merchant who specialized in commerce between New York and Holland. Gulian Verplanck prepared his own will in July 1750, only seventeenth months before his death. Unlike his father or grandfather, he restricted his wife's property rights and allowed his three children to receive much of their inheritance as soon as they attained adulthood. Rather than obtain command of a family estate, his widow received a sufficient amount of her husband's wealth to guarantee her comfort and security. She gained an annuity of two hundred pounds and the use of her clothing, all household furniture, plate, jewels, and the services of four slaves. These goods and chattels were to descend eventually to her children since the widow lacked any right to dispose of them. If she remarried, her husband limited her privileges to an annuity of twenty pounds and the income from a certain house throughout life. Gulian Verplanck ob-

---

[75]N.Y. Wills, 1st ser., no. 15, Apr. 22, 1684. For biographical information on the Verplanck family, see Robert W. July, *The Essential New Yorker: Gulian Crommelin Verplanck* (Durham: Duke University Press, 1951), 3–5.

[76]N.Y. Wills, Liber 5–6:295–96, Sept. 6, 1698.

viously regarded himself as the sole owner of his estate rather than as the custodian of community property. Though he appointed his widow to be one of his executors, he also asked his three brothers-in-law, all well-to-do merchants, to assume that office. Offering these men sixty pounds each for their trouble, he relied on them to assist his widow in administering a complex estate. Their responsibilities included the leasing of land to tenants, the payment of rent income to his heirs, and the division of property by lot among the children.[77]

Gulian Verplanck was not necessarily a more devoted father than his immediate ancestors, but he was more directly involved in managing his children's inheritance. Rather than entrust his widow with this task, he guaranteed each heir a substantial legacy: £1,000 to his son at age twenty-one and £2,500 to each of his two daughters when they married or attained their majority. The girls received larger cash sums to balance the value of the country estate inherited by their brother. Though his father and grandfather had ordered an equal division of property among all children, Gulian Verplanck placed special importance on the descent of land to his only son, Samuel. He even went so far as to devise real estate to Samuel "and the heirs of his body," thereby ensuring that certain properties remained within the family for at least two generations.[78] Verplanck's will was still influenced by certain Dutch traditions, but it also expressed the values of an aspiring English colonial gentleman.

Men asserted greater control over the process of inheritance by restricting their wives' discretionary power over real estate. By the mid-1700s, a sharply decreasing percentage of widows obtained the unrestricted right to sell all of a deceased spouse's realty (see Table 3.7). Whereas more than one-third of widows received such authority from 1664 through 1695, only 6 percent did so between 1751 and 1775. As men came to restrict their widows' control of property, they were increasingly likely to order the sale of all their real estate immediately upon death. Fifteen percent of testators adopted this course between 1751 and 1775. An additional 7 percent of fathers during this period denied their wives any claim to real estate assigned to their heirs. Though widows often retained the use of part of the estate, they seldom had any independent power to alienate or convey either houses or land. A woman during the late colonial era commonly served as one of her deceased husband's executors in selling real property, but she seldom had the power to decide this issue by herself.

[77]Ibid., Liber 18:68–75, July 5, 1750.
[78]Ibid.

**Table 3.7** Widow's discretionary power to sell real estate

| Period | N* | Widow can sell all | | Widow can sell part | | Occupy but not sell | | All real estate to be sold immediately | | Widow receives no real estate | |
|---|---|---|---|---|---|---|---|---|---|---|---|
| | | N | % | N | % | N | % | N | % | N | % |
| 1664–95 | 71 | 24 | 33.8 | 16 | 22.5 | 29 | 40.8 | 0 | 0 | 2 | 2.8 |
| 1696–1725 | 156 | 46 | 29.5 | 31 | 19.9 | 66 | 42.3 | 7 | 4.5 | 6 | 3.8 |
| 1726–50 | 162 | 14 | 8.6 | 29 | 17.9 | 93 | 57.4 | 18 | 11.1 | 8 | 4.9 |
| 1751–75 | 284 | 18 | 6.3 | 51 | 18.0 | 150 | 52.8 | 44 | 15.5 | 21 | 7.4 |
| Entire period | 673 | 102 | 15.2 | 127 | 18.9 | 338 | 50.2 | 69 | 10.2 | 37 | 5.5 |

*All wills considered here were left by married men who owned some real estate and had at least one child.

Some New Yorkers viewed the raising of capital sums for their heirs as so important that they ordered the sale of property even when that would disrupt existing living arrangements. Luke Benjamin Kierstede, a sailmaker who composed his last will and testament in 1760, requested that his only house be sold along with the rest of his possessions immediately upon death. Allowing his widow to claim one-third of the proceeds as her own property, he requested that the remainder be loaned out and the interest used for the maintenance of his young son and daughter. Each child was to receive an equal portion of the principal as soon as he or she reached age twenty-one. It is significant that Kierstede, a man of Dutch origin, was married to an Englishwoman by the name of Martha Sutton. He defined his wife's share of the estate according to English rather than Dutch custom.[79]

A few widows refused to accept restrictions on their power to sell real estate. Jeremiah Tothill, a wealthy merchant, wrote a will in 1705 that authorized his wife, Jane (or Janneke), to administer two city lots for two of their daughters until they reached their majority. Rather than simply hold the land in trust, however, the widow sold both lots for two hundred pounds. Having violated her deceased husband's instructions, this independent-minded woman of Dutch descent decided to execute her own will in order to explain and justify her actions. Maintaining that the lots were "for a long time of little value," she proudly declared that she had sold them for the "better augmentation" of the children's fortunes and had received "much more [money] than the same lotts were really worth." Despite her belief in the rightness of her conduct, Jane Tothill was also aware that her actions could be legally challenged. She there-

[79]Ibid., Liber 22:307, July 26, 1760.

fore executed a bond that secured the purchaser's claim at her own risk. This guarantee, a note for five hundred pounds, would indemnify the buyer in case her children should object to the sale and sue to recover the real estate under the terms of their father's will. Jane Tothill concluded her will by entreating her daughters to accept her judgment and by requesting that they release all claim to the purchaser of their lots. Should they refuse to abide by these terms, they would be absolutely "Debarred Divested and Deprived" of all rights to her estate.[80]

Despite Jane Tothill's forcefulness and independence, it is probable that only a few women actually attempted to alter the settlement of their late husbands' estates. In four cases, all dating between 1712 and 1721, widows successfully appealed to the General Assembly for permission to sell properties in which they held a life-interest. After living under the terms of her husband's will for about twenty-five years, one Elsie Bosch and her children complained of an intolerable situation. Although she possessed a life-interest in her husband's real estate, she could no longer derive any income from his one house:

> the said House is very old and Decayed, and . . . the Said Elsie [the widow] is not in a Capacity to repair the Same, and hath nothing Else left her to live upon, but the income or Rent of the Said House, which in the Condition it now is, is not tenantable, and therefore Humbly prayed that She might be Impowered to Sell and dispose of the Said House and Ground and During her life, enjoy the moneys arising thereby and What Shall be left at her Decease, Shall be divided amongst the Children and Grandchildren [heirs of her deceased husband].

Considering this request to be reasonable, the General Assembly agreed to all aspects of the petition.[81] Since only a handful of such appeals were made, however, it seems that most widows had to make do with income gained from renting rather than from selling part of their husbands' real estate.

Eighteenth-century New Yorkers became adept at limiting their wives' share of real estate while fulfilling their legal responsibilities. Testators achieved their goal by offering substantial bequests of personal property in lieu of dower, the widow's life-interest in one-third of her deceased husband's realty. Whereas very few men offered such legacies in wills before 1725, a steadily increasing percentage of men did so after that point (see Table 3.8). From 1751 to 1775, 284 freeholders mentioned a

---

[80]Ibid., 1st ser., no. 339, May 29, 1705; no. 648, June 23, 1720, codicil June 25, 1720.
[81]Lincoln, *Colonial Laws,* 2:36–38, bill passed July 27, 1721. For similar cases, see *Colonial Laws,* 1:1036–38; 2:14–15, 78–79.

**Table 3.8** Bequests that explicitly circumvented
widows' dower rights

| Period | Testators owning real estate | Bequests instead of dower | |
|---|---|---|---|
| | N* | N | % |
| 1664–95 | 71 | 0 | 0 |
| 1696–1725 | 156 | 4 | 2.6 |
| 1726–50 | 162 | 13 | 8.0 |
| 1751–75 | 284 | 62 | 21.8 |
| Entire period | 673 | 79 | 11.7 |

*All wills considered here were left by married men
who had at least one child.

wife and at least one child in their wills. More than one-fifth of these
men explicitly granted cash sums or other personal property in order to
circumvent dower. Merchants and wealthy professionals were more likely than artisans to follow this procedure because they had greater opportunity to use their real estate as a capital asset. They were also knowledgeable about legal stratagems that might enhance their own flexibility
in bequeathing property.

Although widows' suits for dower were very common in late colonial
Maryland and Virginia, there is almost no evidence of such cases in New
York. Many Chesapeake planters compelled their widows to sue for their
minimal lawful rights because they had offered less than dower in their
wills.[82] New York City testators were inclined to grant their widows a
generous portion of personal property so as to preclude any dower
claims. Their aim was not simply to restrict the widow's share, but to
encourage her to accept gifts of cash and movables instead of the use of
real estate. William Burling, a Quaker merchant, chose a typical means
of fulfilling his legal obligations in a will written in 1743. Ordering the
sale of his real estate in Queens and Westchester counties immediately
upon death, he divided the proceeds equally among his wife and five
children. He also offered his spouse the best bed in their home and
numerous household goods, including an entire tea service and six silver
spoons. If she declined these legacies and insisted on her dower rights,
however, she was to gain no more than the bed.[83]

Numerous men offered their wives a major portion of the estate even
when they assigned a specific sum of money to their children. John

[82]Carr, "Inheritance in the Colonial Chesapeake," 174–77. I have not found any suits
for dower in New York court records.
[83]N.Y. Wills, Liber 15:132–35, Sept. 9, 1743.

Amory, a wealthy ship captain of British descent, composed a will in 1757 that apportioned his estate fairly evenly between his wife, Mary, and the couple's only child, John. The testator granted each of them a cash legacy of five hundred pounds, one-half of his interest in a privateering ship, and one-half of all profits that might accrue from the battle cruise on which he was about to embark. The widow also obtained the use of the family home, two black slaves, all the household furniture that she might need, and the interest from a one-thousand-pound capital sum until her death or remarriage.[84]

In addition to bequeathing cash sums, wealthy men also tended to set aside particular household goods or personal effects as part of their wives' share. Widows were more likely to receive outright ownership of these possessions than simply the use of property. One Joshua Isaacs, a Jewish merchant, determined whether his wife would receive unrestricted control of household goods and plate according to the precise value of his estate. He granted her full ownership of these items if all his property at death was valued at £1250 or more. If the estate was of lesser value, she was to receive only provisional use during widowhood. Isaacs calculated his wife's legacy in light of the fact that he had already promised her five hundred pounds according to a marriage contract. His wife's privileges were to be increased in direct proportion to the value of his estate in order to satisfy her "thirds" under New York law. Isaacs reserved the bulk of his estate for his only child, Grace, as soon as she wed or came of age.[85]

A man commonly granted most household goods to his first wife, while reserving a portion of these items for a subsequent spouse. Testators often attached particular importance to silverplate since it was a major form of wealth in an economy lacking banks and other safe means of storing money. John Kelly, a leading attorney, acknowledged in his will of 1765 that his second wife, Mary, should receive all plate that she had brought to their marriage and that she had previously acquired from her two deceased husbands' wills.[86] Though Kelly might have lawfully bequeathed these items to his only daughter, he recognized that his widow had a special right to this property.

Although property was generally prized for its monetary value or practical utility, certain clothing or other objects acquired a unique personal significance. Consider, for example, three wills written by merchants of French, Dutch, and British descent. Peter Barberie bequeathed

---

[84]Ibid., Liber 23:540–43, Aug. 20, 1757; Liber 21:138, Oct. 20, 1758.

[85]Leo Hershkowitz, ed., *Wills of Early New York Jews (1704–1799)* (New York: American Jewish Historical Society, 1967), 69–70. Isaacs's will is dated July 14, 1744.

[86]N.Y. Wills, Liber 25:497–99, May 22, 1765.

his portrait to his spouse, while Dirck Brinckerhoff offered his wife a suit of mourning and "a piece of silver plate as she shall choose for a remembrance." James McEvers ordered his executors to "pay 20 guineas for a ring for my wife, as she shall direct, as a token of my unalterable regard and affection for her in my last moments."[87] Eighteenth-century men were not necessarily more devoted husbands than their forebears, but they adopted a more highly personal approach to the bequest of property.

Peter Schuyler openly expressed the implicit values of many wealthy New Yorkers in leaving his wife Mary a legacy of fifteen hundred pounds, her choice of two slaves, and "so much of my household furniture as will furnish one room in a Genteel manar."[88] The overriding aim of such men, whatever their ethnic background, was to advance a major portion of their estate to their children as soon as possible while enabling their widows to live as gentlewomen. Isaac Gomez, a Jewish merchant, allowed his wife, Deborah, the use of his house in Queen Street and an annuity of £150 during widowhood. The will also set aside certain possessions that would assure her comfortable support: "all my Furniture Plate and Jewels with as many of my Slaves as necessary to attend her." Having conveyed the remainder of his real and personal property to his only child, Gomez made certain that his will met all legal requirements: "It is my Will . . . that what I have herein given to my said Wife is and shall be in full Bar of Dower and Right of thirds in and to my Estate."[89]

## THE WIDOW'S APPOINTMENT AS EXECUTOR

The choice of executors reveals much about a man's confidence in his spouse's administrative abilities as well as his concern for the family's welfare. From 1664 through 1775, 874 married men left wills that appointed at least one executor of the estate, and more than four-fifths of them appointed their spouses (see Table 3.9). Though the widow's appointment as executor was the general rule throughout the colonial era, this practice became less common after 1750. More than one-fourth of all husbands who left wills from 1751 through 1775 declined to name their wives as executors. Because these individuals came from diverse ethnic and occupational backgrounds, their decisions cannot be at-

[87]Ibid., 1st ser., no. 789, Mar. 18, 1725; Liber 30:49–53, July 2, 1772; Liber 26:385–87, Aug. 12, 1768, codicil dated Sept. 4, 1768.
[88]Ibid., Liber 23:341–43, Mar. 21, 1761.
[89]Hershkowitz, *Wills of Jews*, 129–30, Feb. 16, 1769.

**Table 3.9** Appointment of widows as executors

| Period | N* | Appointed | | Not appointed | |
|---|---|---|---|---|---|
| | | N | % | N | % |
| 1664–95 | 74 | 63 | 85.1 | 11 | 14.9 |
| 1696–1725 | 205 | 175 | 85.4 | 30 | 14.6 |
| 1726–50 | 202 | 175 | 86.6 | 27 | 13.4 |
| 1751–75 | 393 | 292 | 74.3 | 101 | 25.7 |
| Entire period | 874 | 705 | 80.7 | 169 | 19.3 |

*This table considers all married men's wills in which at least one executor was appointed.

tributed to Anglicization or to any other clearly identifiable process of social change. It should be emphasized, however, that only a minority of men during the late colonial era lacked sufficient trust in their wives' business skills to appoint them as executors.

While widows usually served as executors of their husbands' wills, the nature of their appointment changed significantly during the colonial era. More than three-fourths of husbands who left wills between 1664 and 1695 named their wives as sole executor (see Table 3.10). This practice declined sharply during the eighteenth century, particularly after 1725. Fifty-six percent of husbands appointed their spouses as sole executor between 1696 and 1725, 31 percent did so over the next quarter-century, and only 24 percent between 1751 and 1775.

Eighteenth-century city residents increasingly nominated several executors as a policy of social insurance, in case one appointee declined the responsibility or died. Prior to the mid-1700s, most testators failed to take such precautions. They often imposed the burden of sole executorship upon their wives without adequately preparing for contingencies such as a widow's death, remarriage, or illness. Dutch colonists

**Table 3.10** Appointment of widows as executors by their husbands

| Period | N* | Sole executor | | Co-executor | | Not appointed | |
|---|---|---|---|---|---|---|---|
| | | N | % | N | % | N | % |
| 1664–95 | 74 | 56 | 75.7 | 7 | 9.4 | 11 | 14.9 |
| 1696–1725 | 205 | 114 | 55.6 | 61 | 29.8 | 30 | 14.6 |
| 1726–50 | 202 | 62 | 30.7 | 113 | 55.9 | 27 | 13.4 |
| 1751–75 | 393 | 94 | 23.9 | 198 | 50.4 | 101 | 25.7 |
| Entire period | 874 | 326 | 37.3 | 379 | 43.4 | 169 | 19.3 |

alone tended to anticipate these problems in wills written from the 1660s through the 1710s by frequently appointing guardians for underage children even when selecting their spouses as sole executor.

Merchants were in the forefront of nearly all changes concerning inheritance and family life in eighteenth-century New York, and the appointment of executors was no exception. Whereas seventeenth-century merchants usually selected their wives as sole executor, subsequent generations increasingly named at least one other executor to assist a spouse (see Table 3.11). During 1751–75, two-thirds of this occupational group adopted the latter course. A growing number of merchants excluded their spouses from any role in the settlement of the estate. Between 1751 and 1775, 24 percent of merchants declined to name their spouses as executors; only 9 percent chose the widow alone.

Mariners were the only group of testators during the mid-eighteenth century who tended to appoint their spouses as sole executor (see Table 3.11). Fifty-eight married seamen left wills between 1751 and 1775, and thirty-three of them (or 57 percent) named their spouses as sole executor. Mariners' choice of executors was based on the size of their estates and the extent of their social and family ties. Because many common sailors had few relatives in New York, they necessarily relied on their wives to administer their modest estates. Ship captains who were heads of households usually appointed several executors just as merchants did.

Many wives undoubtedly were appointed executors because they were knowledgeable about family finances and business. Unfortunately, court records and other sources provide little evidence concerning married women's participation in trade after the English conquest. Whereas New Amsterdam *vrouwen* commonly prosecuted or defended suits for debt, very few married women did so after the mid-1670s.[90] Wives continued to be active in the retailing of goods in both shop and marketplace, but they had little role in the legal settlement of business disputes. Few New Yorkers seem to have qualified as feme sole traders—married women whose independent commercial dealings entitled them to execute contracts and to sue or be sued as if they were single. Those few wives who became involved in debt litigation nearly always acted with their spouses' assistance or as their agents.[91]

[90]This generalization is based on a survey of the Mayor's Court minutes, microfilm in the Paul Klapper Library, Queens College, City University of New York.

[91]For the legal status of feme sole traders, see Salmon, *Women and the Law of Property,* 44–57. My conclusions concerning married women's participation in trade agree with Linda Biemer's. See Linda Briggs Biemer, *Women and Property in Colonial New York: The Transition from Dutch to English Law, 1643–1727* (Ann Arbor: UMI Research Press, 1983), 43, 56, appendix B.

**Table 3.11** Frequency of husbands' appointment of their widows as executors, by husband's occupation

| | N | Sole executor | | Co-executor | | Not appointed | |
|---|---|---|---|---|---|---|---|
| | | N | % | N | % | N | % |
| **1664–95** | | | | | | | |
| Artisans | 16 | 11 | 68.7 | 2 | 12.5 | 3 | 18.7 |
| Laborers | 1 | 1 | 100 | 0 | 0 | 0 | 0 |
| Mariners | 7 | 5 | 71.4 | 1 | 14.3 | 1 | 14.3 |
| Merchants | 19 | 15 | 78.9 | 3 | 15.8 | 1 | 5.3 |
| Processors of food and drink | 3 | 2 | 66.7 | 0 | 0 | 1 | 33.3 |
| Professionals | 4 | 3 | 75.0 | 0 | 0 | 1 | 25.0 |
| Shopkeepers | 4 | 3 | 75.0 | 1 | 25.0 | 0 | 0 |
| **1696–1725** | | | | | | | |
| Artisans | 53 | 31 | 58.5 | 18 | 34.0 | 4 | 7.5 |
| Laborers | 4 | 3 | 75.0 | 0 | 0 | 1 | 25.0 |
| Mariners | 27 | 15 | 55.6 | 6 | 22.2 | 6 | 22.2 |
| Merchants | 59 | 27 | 45.8 | 20 | 33.9 | 12 | 20.3 |
| Processors of food and drink | 4 | 3 | 75.0 | 0 | 0 | 1 | 25.0 |
| Professionals | 19 | 14 | 73.7 | 3 | 15.8 | 2 | 10.5 |
| Shopkeepers | 8 | 3 | 37.5 | 5 | 63.5 | 0 | 0 |
| **1726–50** | | | | | | | |
| Artisans | 49 | 19 | 38.8 | 26 | 53.1 | 4 | 8.2 |
| Laborers | 7 | 3 | 42.9 | 4 | 57.1 | 0 | 0 |
| Mariners | 26 | 11 | 42.3 | 15 | 57.7 | 0 | 0 |
| Merchants | 52 | 9 | 17.3 | 34 | 65.4 | 9 | 17.3 |
| Processors of food and drink | 14 | 4 | 28.6 | 5 | 35.7 | 5 | 35.7 |
| Professionals | 15 | 5 | 33.3 | 9 | 60.0 | 1 | 6.7 |
| Shopkeepers | 15 | 5 | 33.3 | 10 | 66.7 | 0 | 0 |
| **1751–75** | | | | | | | |
| Artisans | 117 | 28 | 23.9 | 57 | 48.7 | 32 | 27.3 |
| Laborers | 23 | 4 | 17.4 | 11 | 47.8 | 8 | 34.8 |
| Mariners | 58 | 33 | 56.9 | 17 | 29.3 | 8 | 13.8 |
| Merchants | 67 | 6 | 8.9 | 45 | 67.2 | 16 | 23.9 |
| Processors of food and drink | 20 | 3 | 15.0 | 10 | 50.0 | 7 | 35.0 |
| Professionals | 30 | 3 | 10.0 | 21 | 70.0 | 6 | 20.0 |
| Shopkeepers | 30 | 8 | 26.7 | 18 | 60.0 | 4 | 13.3 |

A widow's appointment as executor did not itself determine whether she would maintain her deceased husband's business or enter into commerce. She herself had to decide this issue based on her own needs and abilities, her legal rights to property, and her particular family circumstances. The historian Jean P. Jordan has identified 106 women who were merchants in New York City from 1660 to 1775. While these traders' marital status cannot always be determined, widows undoubtedly accounted for the great majority of the entire group. ( Jordan identifies only six "spinsters" and three married women who operated as independent traders).[92] At least 31 among all 106 female merchants engaged in business after being appointed an executor of a deceased spouse's estate. Other widows entered business without any official sanction for their management of family resources. These women seem to have been mainly small traders who assumed control of their deceased husbands' property entirely of their own accord.

Widows of Dutch ancestry were especially inclined to engage in trade during the early 1700s because they grew up in a culture that valued female competence and business acumen. Gertrude Van Cortlandt, widow of a wealthy merchant and landowner, entered international commerce soon after her husband, Stephanus, died in 1700. Though her own widowed mother was still in business at that time, it is remarkable that Gertrude Van Cortlandt, herself forty-six years old and the mother of eleven children, found sufficient time for her various responsibilities. Appointed as her deceased spouse's sole executor, she held the right to manage the income from his entire personal estate and most of his lands during widowhood.[93] Her control of family resources was based on her personal authority as well as her legal rights under Stephanus Van Cortlandt's will. Sparring with the provincial government, she refused for some years to yield official tax records in her family's keeping because she claimed that the colony owed money to her late husband.[94]

Her attitude toward her own children was equally strong-willed and exacting. Composing a will in 1718 at age sixty-four, she recounted her business dealings since her husband's death. In addition to augmenting family wealth by purchasing land and acquiring mortgages and bonds, she had also settled the estate of her deceased son, Johannes, himself a father. Since she had previously loaned him money and later overpaid the value of his estate to satisfy creditors, she now ordered that the balance of his account be awarded to her other heirs rather than to his children.[95] She thereby guaranteed that her deceased son's debts would not diminish her surviving children's inheritance. Gertrude Van Cortlandt was obviously an active manager of family wealth rather than the passive beneficiary of interest income. It should be mentioned that this

[92]Jean P. Jordan, "Women Merchants in Colonial New York," *New York History* 58 (1977): 412–38.

[93]For Stephanus Van Cortlandt's will, see Wills, document 5011, Museum of the City of New York. His will is dated Apr. 14, 1700.

[94]For biographical information, see L. Effingham De Forest, *The Van Cortlandt Family* (New York: Historical Publication Society, 1930).

[95]N.Y. Wills, 1st ser., no. 749.

widow owed her economic success to a seven-hundred-pound legacy
from her own mother as well as to her life-interest in her deceased
husband's properties.[96] Dutch family assets in the early colonial period
were usually the product of a married couple's joint efforts, not simply
the patriarch's fortune.

The people of New York recognized Gertrude Van Cortlandt as a
prominent member of the community. More than four hundred men
attended her funeral, including representatives of the Bayard, De Lancey, Livingston, Schuyler, and Van Rensselaer families. While the Van
Cortlandts had political and social ties to the elite, they were also leading
members of the Dutch community. Most of the guests at the funeral
were Dutch in origin, including burghers from such middle-class families as Boelen, Clock, Ten Eyck, and Van Wyck. Although honoring a
woman, the *begraaf lyst* (or funeral list) mentions only three women by
name: Catharine Philipse, Cornelia Schuyler, and Sophia Teller—all
sisters-in-law to the deceased.[97] The list therefore reflects the achieve-
ments of a particular woman, while indicating women's subordinate social status.

Dutch burghers from the 1660s through the 1720s seem to have expected their widows to manage the family business if they so desired.
One Klaas Janse Bogert, the owner of a substantial bakery, composed a
will in 1726 that offers particular insight into Dutch family values and
concerns. Declaring the testament at age fifty-eight, he conveyed the use
of his entire estate to his wife, Margaret, and allowed her the option of
being sole manager of his business for as long as she was widowed. This
grant of power is especially noteworthy for two reasons. First, Bogert
regarded his wife as the immediate successor to family property even
though he had four sons, three of whom were over twenty-one years old
at the time he dictated his testament. Second, he did not limit his
spouse's share of the estate because she was his second wife. Since he had
been married to Margaret for nearly twenty years and had five children
by her, he appointed her as an executor with provisional control of
property. She might use the income from the bakery for herself and the
support of underage children, but she could not sell the shop itself, any
tools of the trade, household goods, or slaves without the consent of five
other executors—the testator's two eldest sons, two brothers-in-law, and
one particular friend. Like other Dutch bakers and brewers, Klaas Janse
Bogert offered his sons the choice of purchasing the business from the

[96]Gertrude Van Cortlandt was the daughter of Philip Pieterse Schuyler and Margareta
Van Slechtenhorst. For Margaret Schuyler's will, see Pelletreau, *Abstracts of Wills*, 2:73–74,
will not dated, proved in Albany on June 27, 1711.
[97]Van Cortlandt Family Papers, V1959, Sleepy Hollow Restorations, Tarrytown, N.Y.

other heirs—but only after the widow's death or remarriage. Despite being mature men, they would have to work under Margaret Bogert's management until she herself decided to yield control of the estate. Since she survived her husband by more than fifteen years, the oldest sons were more than forty years old by the time they gained their inheritance.[98]

Some widows had little opportunity to pursue trade because they were preoccupied with survival. When a carter named Christian Heartman died in 1737, his wife, Sarah, was bound to sell the family house and lot according to his will. Since she could hardly follow his occupation, her goal was simply to gain sufficient income to pay his debts and to lease a small house for herself and her underage children. Unfortunately, there is no record of how the widow actually supported herself for the remainder of life.[99]

A small but growing number of New Yorkers during the mid-1700s offered specific instructions to their executors concerning their business affairs. These testators were generally wealthy men who did not expect a widow to assume the leading role in managing financial assets or family enterprises. Such a man instead appointed his spouse as one of the executors in order to protect her interest in the estate and to strengthen her influence over other family members. Andrew Barclay, a merchant who prepared a will in 1763, appointed no less than eight executors: his wife, three sons who were approaching their majority, brother, father-in-law, brother-in-law, and son-in law. Authorizing the executors to sell or rent his real estate, he also directed that they operate his sugar refinery in partnership with two brothers-in-law, Jacobus and Isaac Roosevelt, for the support of the widow and underage children. Andrew Barclay wished his wife to receive the income of most of his estate, but he did not allow her to control his business or to decide how much money his five sons and six daughters were to receive as they came of age. The appointment of his wife's kin as executors itself guaranteed that her interests would be respected in the management of business. Alloting six hundred pounds to each child as he or she came of age, Barclay ordered that his heirs divide the remainder of the estate among themselves after his wife's remarriage or death. The children in this case received their

[98]N.Y. Wills, 1st ser., no. 713, Sept. 17, 1726. Margaret Bogert was buried on Sept. 10, 1742. See "Record of Burials in the Dutch Church, New York," *Year Book of the Holland Society of New York* (New York: Knickerbocker Press, 1899), 147. Dutch women also assumed an active role in their husbands' business affairs in early eighteenth-century Albany. See Alice P. Kenney, *The Gansevoorts of Albany: Dutch Patricians in the Upper Hudson Valley* (Syracuse: Syracuse University Press, 1969), 166–67.
[99]Ibid., Liber 13:211–12, Dec. 23, 1728.

shares at a fairly young age since their mother died before their father's will was probated in 1776.[100]

Because men seldom expressed their motives in either bequeathing property or appointing executors, it is easier to document shifts in the use of the will than to explain those changes. New patterns of will writing in eighteenth-century New York City reflected hundreds of individual decisions rather than a coordinated response to a specific law or government directive. When city residents limited their wives' authority over their estates, they were surely unaware that their wills formed part of an historical trend extending beyond their town and province. Recent scholarship indicates that men in several regions imposed tighter restrictions on their widows' control of property during the late colonial era. This trend was especially pronounced among well-to-do colonists whether those men were New England landowners, New York City merchants, or southern planters.[101] Men's wills during the late colonial era generally placed widows in a dependent position but did not leave them without some property rights or some influence over family affairs in their common capacity as co-executors of the estate.

As historians learn more about the early American family, they are confronting the problem of relating data derived from legal documents or vital records to literary evidence. Personal letters and diaries, largely written by members of the privileged classes, indicate that family life became less rigidly patriarchal over time and more oriented toward satisfying the individual needs of children.[102] As the relations between parents and children grew more intimate, many New Yorkers began to restrict their wives' rights to their estates in favor of the younger generation. These trends were doubtless mutually reinforcing since both patterns of social change developed most fully among the "genteel" classes. The decline of Dutch customs of inheritance may therefore be related to a shift in the social values underlying family life in eighteenth-century America, particularly among well-to-do colonists.

[100]Ibid., Liber 30:184–88, Aug. 12, 1763.

[101]Carole Shammas, Marylynn Salmon, and Michel Dahlin, *Inheritance in America: From Colonial Times to the Present* (New Brunswick: Rutgers University Press, 1987), 59–61. Mary Beth Norton, "The Evolution of White Women's Experience in Early America," *American Historical Review* 89 (1984): 603.

[102]Daniel Scott Smith, "Inheritance and the Social History of Early American Women," in Hoffman and Albert, *Women in the Age of the American Revolution*, 52–53, 63–66. Daniel Blake Smith, "The Study of the Family in Early America: Trends, Problems, and Prospects," *William and Mary Quarterly*, 3d. ser., 39 (1982): 3–28.

## Chapter 4

# From Parents to
# Their Children

The act of declaring a will obligated parents to confront the prospect of death and to direct their concerns to the future well-being of their descendants. This dual aspect of inheritance—preparation for death and provision for the living—bound the passing of one generation to the rise of its successor. Because fathers were usually the heads of households, they most commonly had responsibility over the bequest of property. In New York City 823 fathers and 147 mothers prepared wills between 1664 and 1775. Since 125 of the women (or 85 percent) were widows, they had the task of completing a social and legal process already begun by their deceased husbands.

By declaring a last will and testament, colonial parents had the legal power to circumvent the laws of intestate succession and to bequeath property according to their own particular needs and desires. The great majority of New York City testators who had children purposefully evaded primogeniture—the English custom requiring all real estate to descend from parent to eldest son. Though primogeniture was the law of intestacy in the province, it was sometimes evaded or ignored even when the head of the household died without a will.

Testators usually offered their children unrestricted control of their inheritance unless heirs required some special degree of protection. Married daughters were most apt to receive such assistance since their property would otherwise be subject to their spouses' control. New Yorkers were generally reluctant to bequeath property in order to punish individual children or to elevate personal favorites above the rest. Rather than unconditionally disinherit children, parents were more inclined to deprive heirs of certain benefits if the latter challenged or opposed their wills. It is striking that the threat of disinheritance appears most frequently in wills written from 1680 to 1710—those years in which Dutch fear of primogeniture was most intense. Dutch anxieties about inheritance gradually lessened as burghers and their widows learned to write wills that circumvented the English law of descent.

The nature of governmental controls over family life changed significantly after the English conquest of New Netherland. The demise of the Dutch Orphan Masters court in the late 1660s, for example, left New York City without any effective public oversight of minor children's property rights. Dutch colonists initially responded to this deficiency by themselves appointing guardians in their wills. By 1730, however, this customary practice had all but disappeared. Though testators commonly asked their kin or neighbors to act as executors, they seldom directed them to serve as their children's legal guardians. The guardianship of children became a largely private concern rather than one effectively regulated by the state.

## THE GUARDIANSHIP OF CHILDREN

Colonial New Yorkers often used the term "nonage" (i.e., no age) to describe the status of children during their minority—the period prior to age twenty-one. Jurists commonly dubbed all minors "infants" since they were dependent persons subject to parental control. If concepts such as "nonage" and "infancy" succinctly express colonial attitudes toward parent-child relations, they offer only a partial view of minority status. Though children did not attain full age under English common law until their twenty-first year, they were judged legally competent for certain purposes before that point. Either male or female might lawfully select a guardian at age fourteen and serve as an executor at age seventeen. Though a person could not devise real estate by will until age twenty-one, he or she might bequeath personal property before then. A young woman could make a valid testament at age twelve, a young man at fourteen.[1] This power was largely theoretical since no colonial wills were executed by such youthful persons.

William Blackstone described the civil disabilities of minority status as privileges since they were extended for the protection of individuals not competent to manage their own affairs. Minors could not be sued alone,

[1] Sir William Blackstone, *Commentaries on the Laws of England,* ed. James DeWitt Andrews, 4th ed., 2 vols. (Chicago: Callaghan and Co., 1899, 1, bk. 1:464.

only jointly with their legal guardians. With certain exceptions, they could not alienate lands, perform any legal acts, make any deeds, or enter into contracts that would bind themselves. (Exceptions were contracts of guardianship and agreements to pay for necessaries toward their education or support.) In general, minority status precluded independent control over one's own inheritance.[2]

It is significant that young persons reached full legal age later in Roman-Dutch law then in English common law. Majority in New Netherland was not reached until age twenty-five—a custom that reinforced the authority of the old over the young.[3] By 1700, Dutch colonists throughout New York had adjusted to the English definition of majority status. Wills commonly provided that children receive some portion of their inheritance as they married or turned twenty-one, whichever came first. Daughters occasionally were awarded their legacies at age eighteen—an acknowledgment that some young women wed in their late teens.[4] A bride's dowry, of course, by no means signaled her independence since her property generally came under her husband's control.

Both Dutch and English common law distinguished between guardianship over the persons and over the property of minor children. Though parents were bound to care for and maintain their offspring, they had limited powers over their children's estates. According to Roman-Dutch law, neither father nor mother could administer a minor child's inheritance unless appointed by a court or nominated by last will and testament. English common law recognized the father's prior right of guardianship but required that he account to his children for the management of property once the heirs came of age. If the father was dead, the question of guardianship depended on the type of property to be inherited. Though a mother might administer her children's personal property under court supervision, her power did not extend to real estate. The common law provided that male kin serve as guardians to children who inherited land.[5]

The institution of guardianship differed significantly under Dutch and English colonial rule. The New Amsterdam Court of Orphan Masters insisted that guardians be appointed over minor heirs who lost either parent. New York statute law required that courts take such action only if both parents had died and the heirs had no surviving kin. County and local officials were then to assume responsibility for the orphans'

[2]Ibid., 465–66.
[3]See above, Chap. 2.
[4]See, for example, the will of Philip French, merchant. N.Y. Wills, 1st ser., no. 231, May 27, 1706.
[5]Blackstone, *Commentaries* 1, bk. 1:461–63.

care and administer their personal property until they came of age.[6] The appointment of guardians in other cases depended on petitions from the interested parties themselves rather than mandatory court intervention.

New York law offered a limited degree of protection for minor children whose fathers died intestate. No statutory provision was made for the mother's death since she was presumed to be propertyless within marriage. If a man died intestate, his widow received the sole right to administer his personal estate. Should there be no widow, that responsibility fell to his next of kin. Administrators were required to take an inventory of the estate and to give security that the lawful shares of minors would be paid when the latter came of age.[7] These procedures were only partially effective, however, because just a fraction of all intestacy cases were reported to public authorities.[8] New York statutes omitted any reference to the administration of heirs' real estate since that form of property was to descend according to English common law—a legal system foreign to many colonists.

Both Dutch and English colonial law sanctioned the appointment of guardians by last will and testament. Although New York City testators fairly commonly selected such overseers during the early colonial era, they seldom did so after 1725. Consider, for example, the case of married men who had at least one minor child at the time they prepared their wills. Between 1664 and 1725, 24 percent of these men chose guardians other than their wives. Only about 5 percent of fathers followed this procedure during the remainder of the colonial era (see Table 4.1).

Men's reliance on their wives helps to explain why many testators neglected to appoint legal guardians. More than 90 percent of all fathers with minor children were married at the time they prepared their wills (488 men among 534 testators fall into this group). Even widowers very seldom bothered to designate formal guardians; instead they implicitly entrusted their children's care to their executors. Only four among forty-six widowed men selected guardians throughout the English colonial era.

Dutch colonists were almost solely responsible for the appointment of guardians in wills written between the 1660s and 1720s. More than four-fifths of all fathers who chose such overseers during this period were of

[6]Charles Z. Lincoln, comp., *The Colonial Laws of the State of New York*, 5 vols. (Albany: J. B. Lyon, 1894), 1:56, 154, 300–302. The most significant laws concerning guardianship were enacted in 1665, 1684, and 1692.

[7]Ibid., 1:300–302.

[8]See below, Appendix.

**Table 4.1** Married men's appointment of guardians in wills

| Period | Married men having minor children N* | Married men appointing guardians (besides wife) N | % |
|---|---|---|---|
| 1664–95 | 54 | 13 | 24.1 |
| 1696–1725 | 130 | 31 | 23.8 |
| 1726–50 | 114 | 6 | 5.3 |
| 1751–75 | 190 | 9 | 4.7 |
| Entire period | 488 | 59 | 12.1 |

*A minimum of 488 testators (or 71.4 percent of 683 married men) had at least one minor child at the time they executed their wills.

Dutch origin.[9] These burghers continued to respect the traditional Dutch notion that widowed parents should not be entrusted with sole responsibility over minor heirs. The subsequent decline in the appointment of guardians can be traced to the waning influence of Dutch legal practices—a trend that was evident in rural settlements as well as Manhattan.

The appointment of guardians by last will and testament changed little in the immediate aftermath of the English conquest of New Netherland. Married couples who executed mutual wills in the 1670s and 1680s commonly empowered the surviving spouse to choose guardians for their minor children. In keeping with Dutch tradition, husband and wife granted each other broad discretionary powers over property during widowhood, while safeguarding their heirs' rights in case of a parent's death or remarriage.[10] With the demise of the Dutch mutual will by the mid-1690s, fathers selected their children's guardians in their own wills rather than leaving this decision to their widows. Though armed with paramount legal authority, men often respected their wives' interest in selecting guardians and bequeathing family property. Jacob Teller, a well-to-do merchant, conveyed his entire estate to his wife in 1696, exempting her from giving an inventory or accounting to any person as long as she was widowed. The couple's infant was to be protected by three guardians: the testator's brother and two brothers-in-law.[11] The appointment of the wife's kin as well as the testator's kinsman achieved a balance between the widow's and child's needs.

[9]Among forty-four married men who appointed guardians between 1664 and 1725, thirty-eight (or 86.3 percent) were of Dutch origin.

[10]See, for example, the will of Christopher Hoogland and Catharina Cregiers in N.Y. Wills, 1st ser., no. 79, Mar. 12, 1676.

[11]Ibid., Liber 5–6:157, Aug. 17, 1696.

No simple pattern governed the selection of guardians in wills written during the early colonial era. Men commonly asked their male friends and business associates as well as kinsmen to oversee their minor children's welfare. Johannes Hardenbrook, a Dutch colonist involved in the bolting or milling business, chose his two friends Nicholas Roosevelt, a bolter, and Garret Van Laer, a baker, as guardians. Giles Shelley, a merchant and immigrant from London, called upon two fellow traders, the Englishman Robert Lurting and the Scotsman Robert Watts.[12] As one might expect, ethnic and occupational ties strongly influenced the selection of guardians during the late seventeenth and early eighteenth centuries.

Widows occasionally appointed guardians over their children by utilizing legal powers under their husbands' wills. In February 1686, Frederick Hendrick de Boogh, a New York City boatman, bequeathed possession of his entire estate to his wife, Elizabeth Salomons, and ordered that all family property remaining after her death be divided equally among the couple's ten children, all of whom were still minors. In addition to appointing his wife as sole executor, de Boogh named her as *tutrix*, the Dutch legal term for a female guardian. The will specifically granted her "such ample Power & authority as . . . Tutors . . . ought to have," including the responsibility of selecting guardians to assist her or take her place.[13] Within three months of her husband's death, Elizabeth Salomons herself declared a will so as to prepare for the day "when the Lord God shall call me out of this sorrowful world." Ordering that the family estate be divided among the children according to her late husband's will, she appointed her brother-in-law, William Beekman, and cousin, Isaac Van Vleck, as tutors to her children and "Regents of their Goods."[14] Lacking the power to bequeath family property, she nevertheless felt bound to protect her children's interests through the appointment of guardians. Her two kinsmen were both prominent burghers who were likely to fulfill their family obligations.

Unlike Elizabeth Salomons, the overwhelming majority of New York women failed to leave behind any written, legally binding instructions concerning their children's upbringing and care. Once deprived of the opportunity to declare mutual wills, wives usually deferred to their husbands' choice concerning the guardianship of minor heirs. They very seldom selected any legal overseers to assume this responsibility after their own death.

If a father failed to appoint guardians in his will, it was quite unlikely

---

[12]Ibid., 1st ser., no. 423, Sept. 12, 1702; no. 350, Sept. 22, 1702.
[13]Ibid., Liber 19B:172, Feb. 22, 1686.
[14]Ibid., 175.

that the colony's legal institutions would select overseers after his death. The appointment of guardians in such cases depended on petitions presented to a court on behalf of minor heirs. By the early eighteenth century, the provincial Court of Chancery emerged as the primary judicial body concerned with minors' legal rights.[15] Located in New York City, this court received 168 requests for the appointment of guardians between 1691 and 1775. Seventy-five of these petitions (or 45 percent) concerned Manhattan residents.

The great majority of petitions concerning guardianship were presented during the late colonial era. The Chancery received 102 petitions, or 61 percent of all documented colonial cases, between 1756 and 1775. Eighty-eight requests (52 percent of the total) were dated between 1766 and 1775. Since the court's orders are extant for most of the eighteenth century, the increase in cases during the late colonial era cannot be attributed simply to more efficient record-keeping. The growing number of petitions indicates that the general populace was becoming increasingly knowledgeable about the use of provincial legal procedures and institutions. Parents began to seek judicial approval for powers that they had previously assumed entirely of their own accord. Rather than being limited to the colonial elite, petitions for guardianship served the needs of children from widely varying social backgrounds.

Because of omissions in court records, one cannot always determine whether Chancery cases involved children who had lost one or both parents. At least 53 petitions, or 31 percent of all 168 requests for guardianship, were made on behalf of minors whose father and mother had died. Though disinterested individuals occasionally served as guardians in these cases, it was more common for overseers to have some financial or personal relationship with the orphans' parents. Minors themselves looked for assistance from those persons who could be expected to protect their interests. William Heysham, an eighteen-year-old orphan, petitioned the Chancery in 1760 that George Duncan Ludlow, a city merchant, be appointed as his guardian. Ludlow's deceased father-in-law, Thomas Duncan, had previously served as an executor of the Heysham family estate. This case also indicates how the appointment of a legal guardian was often a last resort—a measure undertaken when other means of guidance were no longer possible. William Heysham himself only petitioned the Chancery after the death of his father's three executors—the boy's widowed mother and two family friends.[16]

---

[15] Kenneth Scott, ed., *Records of the Chancery Court, Province and State of New York* (New York: Holland Society of New York, 1971).

[16] Ibid., 12. William Heysham's father, Thomas, had appointed Thomas Duncan as an executor of his will. Duncan referred to his son-in-law, George Duncan Ludlow, in his will. N.Y. Wills, Liber 17:343–44, Jan. 11, 1750; Liber 22:197–98, Nov. 9, 1758.

Unlike Dutch legal practice, the Court of Chancery recognized the right of female kin and nonrelatives as well as males to serve as guardians. In practice, however, men accounted for the great majority of appointed overseers. Male kin were commonly chosen as guardians even when the orphans' closest surviving relations were women. After William and Mary Browne of Massachusetts died in 1766, the couple's two daughters came under the personal supervision of three aunts, all of whom lived in New York City. While these women were responsible for the girls' upbringing, their husbands petitioned to be appointed as guardians of their property. The court readily granted this request, thereby distinguishing between the orphans' financial and personal needs.[17]

Widowed mothers usually served as their children's guardians without being formally appointed by a court. They might, however, petition for official designation if they needed to represent the minors' interests in any legal proceedings. Elizabeth Clarkson, for example, acted as her children's guardian in successfully prosecuting a suit against a brother-in-law who had attempted to abscond with the orphans' inheritance.[18] The Chancery recognized a widowed mother's prior right of guardianship unless the deceased father had appointed other overseers by legal deed or will.

Though Dutch magistrates in New Amsterdam had required widowed parents to settle their children's inheritance before remarrying, New York law was much more permissive in this area. The Chancery court records from 1701 through 1775 include thirty-two petitions for guardianship when the children's mother had remarried. These petitions represent the total number for the entire province and obviously pertain to a small percentage of all instances of remarriage. The Chancery followed quite different rules in appointing guardians than did the New Amsterdam Orphan Masters. Dutch custom required the designation of either disinterested men or kinsmen who were blood relations to the minors. The Chancery often sanctioned the appointment of stepfathers—an unthinkable practice in Dutch law. Among all thirty-two cases concerning remarriage, the Chancery appointed the stepfather alone as guardian eleven times. The stepfather was chosen with the children's mother in three additional cases. Most of the remaining eighteen cases involved the appointment of disinterested men or kin.[19]

[17]Scott, *Records of the Chancery Court,* 16.
[18]See David Clarkson, Jr. and Matthew Clarkson by Elizabeth Clarkson, their Guardian and next Friend v. Levinus Clarkson, Chancery Decrees Before 1800, C 73, July 12, 1773, N.Y. State Archives, Albany (hereafter N.Y. Archives). See also Clarkson v. Clarkson, Chancery Records, BM 918-C, Mar. 24, 1775, County Clerk's Office, New York County.
[19]Scott, *Records of the Chancery Court.*

Minors who were fourteen years old and above sometimes themselves petitioned that their stepfathers be their legal guardians. They thereby strengthened their ties to a surrogate parent while protecting their own inheritance. Since guardians had to give security before the Chancery, they risked financial penalty if they violated their trust.[20] This requirement was obviously important considering the potential abuse of parental authority. Given the limited number of guardianship cases reviewed by the Chancery, however, one can assume that most adults preferred to administer minors' property with as little court supervision as possible. Public oversight of orphaned children usually yielded to private control after the English conquest of New Netherland.

## THE EDUCATION AND MAINTENANCE OF CHILDREN

Dutch colonists' wills during the late 1600s followed a distinctive pattern in several areas: the bequest of property, the appointment of guardians, and the education of children. Indeed, only the ethnic Dutch during this era tended to offer any instructions concerning their children's upbringing. Maintaining practices already established under Dutch rule, burghers and their wives commonly insisted on two points— that their minor heirs be taught how to read and write and that they be instructed in a trade. Nevertheless, parents seldom directed that boys or girls receive any formal schooling.[21] Wills allowed the surviving parent or guardian ample discretionary power in deciding how to serve the children's educational needs.

Dutch colonists assumed that boys and girls would receive vocational training appropriate to their sex and social class. Only a few parents required any specialized instruction for their children. Declaring a will in 1678, Grietie Wessels directed that her daughter Elbertje be taught to sew as well as to read and write.[22] Hendrick Boelen, a blacksmith, simply requested in his will that his son Abraham "learn A trade for which he Shall have A minde So by which he may live in the future."[23] This will suggests that parents and overseers may have often considered their ward's particular interests and inclinations in arranging his apprenticeship. The commonly used phrase "a trade by which he may live"

---

[20]Ibid., vii.

[21]Evert Wessels, a carpenter, and his wife, Jannetie Claes, asked that their children be taught how to read and write at school. See N.Y. Wills, 1st ser., no. 109, Nov. 1, 1683.

[22]N.Y. Wills, Liber 14A:151, Apr. 13, 1678. Wessels executed this will with her husband, Jan Janse Langedyck, the girl's stepfather.

[23]Ibid., 1st ser., no. 121, May 15, 1691.

reflects the fact that most residents of seventeenth-century New York had limited aspirations for their children. As Gary Nash has written, most burghers regarded "security from want, rather than the acquisition of riches," as their primary social aim.[24]

By the 1720s, Dutch New Yorkers no longer approached the issue of education in a distinctive manner in their wills. Irrespective of national origin, most colonists outlined the same general guidelines concerning their children's upbringing. Rather than specify instruction in basic literacy and a trade, testators simply required that their minor heirs be "educated and maintained" during their minority. The use of this general formula in will after will indicates that men were willing to allow their widows and executors considerable latitude in raising their children. Eighteenth-century wills—whether written by merchants, artisans, or mariners—differed very little in this respect.

A few wills went beyond the customary formula to reveal the testator's goals for his children. As in the seventeenth century, fathers did not necessarily assume that sons would follow their own trade. James Arden, a tallow chandler, ordered in 1764 that all the tools of his business— "Soap kettles, tallow pots, ladles, skimmers, soap frames, and gages"—be sold after his death. He meanwhile offered his only son, Samuel, another set of tools if he wished to learn carpentry, cabinetmaking, or the carver's trade. If the young man declined this opportunity, all woodworking tools were to be sold and the proceeds shared by Samuel and his two sisters.[25]

While some merchants expected their sons to enter trade, they also acknowledged that the young had some degree of choice regarding their vocation. Declaring a will in 1763, Andrew Barclay ordered that his sons be instructed in "the art and Mystery of Merchandizing or any other art or Mystery." He also requested that his widow "give to all my children a good and due education, and if any of my sons shall desire a liberal education at the College of the City of New York, they are to be permitted."[26] Barclay offered no specific instructions regarding his daughters' education—a subject that he apparently considered to be his wife's concern. Similarly, innkeeper Ezekiel Archer simply ordered that his two daughters "be brought up to Learning," while his only son was to be trained in navigation and accounting.[27]

As might be expected, some members of the colonial elite expended a significantly greater amount of money and attention on their sons' edu-

[24]Gary B. Nash, *The Urban Crucible: Social Change, Political Consciousness, and the Origins of the American Revolution* (Cambridge: Harvard University Press, 1979), 9.

[25]N.Y. Wills, Liber 25:38–39, Dec. 3, 1764.

[26]Ibid., Liber 30:184–88, Aug. 12, 1763.

[27]Ibid., Liber 29:34–35, July 25, 1773.

cation than their daughters'. Stephen De Lancey, the founder of one of
New York's leading mercantile families, bequeathed a thousand pounds
to each of his three younger sons and five hundred pounds to his youngest daughter as an equivalent to several sums spent on eldest son
James's "travelling and education" and second son Peter's inheritance.[28]
Educated at Cambridge University and the Inns of Court, James De
Lancey was well prepared for a career in New York politics and law.
Lewis Morris of Morrisania was yet another member of the colonial elite
who distinguished between his children's education according to their
birth order as well as sex. While transmitting his library along with his
manor to his eldest son, Lewis Jr., he marked certain books for his
younger son Richard. He also allowed Richard the joint use of all other
books as long as the young man continued to practice law, provided that
none of the library's holdings be removed from Morrisania or loaned out
to any person. Lewis Morris, Sr., made only passing reference to his
daughter's education while expressing a deep personal concern about
instruction for his youngest son, Gouverneur:

> It is my desire that my son, Gouverneur Morris, may have the best educa-
> tion that is to be had in Europe or America, but my express will and
> directions are that he never be sent for that purpose to the Colony of
> Connecticut, lest he should imbibe in his youth that low craft and cunning
> so incident to the People of that Colony, which is so interwoven in their
> Constitutions that all their art cannot disguise it from the World; though
> many of them, under the sanctified garb of Religion, have endeavored to
> impose themselves on the World for honest men.[29]

New York's gentry sought to instill in their sons the manner, talents, and
outlook of the English upper class. It would simply not do if the young
were to be tainted by Yankee acquisitiveness, parsimony, and moralism.

Before the 1720s, few testators offered any specific instructions on
how their children were to be maintained during their minority. Because
the great majority of men were married when they declared their wills,
they generally authorized their widows to arrange their minor heirs'
support. Stepmothers as well as natural parents were allowed discretionary power in meeting this goal as long as they remained widowed.
Though most fathers requested their spouses to maintain their offspring
until the age of majority, a few testators distinguished between the care
of young children and the care of adolescents. Hendricus Ten Broeck, a
carpenter who made a will in 1712, empowered his wife, Tryntie, to sell

28Ibid., Liber 14:91–95, Mar. 4, 1735.
29Ibid., Liber 23:426–30, Nov. 19, 1760.

or mortgage any part of his estate for the family's support after his death. Appointing his wife and brother-in-law as guardians, he asked Tryntie alone to "nurrish traine and bring up my sd children til Every one of them cometh to the age of fourteen or fifteen without the least or any Charge against them."[30] Ten Broeck evidently expected his children to be apprenticed at that point or no longer dependent on parental assistance.

By the 1720s, fathers became increasingly likely to restrict their widows' share of the estate for their children's benefit. Men did not wish their wives to bear the direct costs of child support nor did they want their heirs' property to be consumed for this purpose. A growing number of colonists therefore ordered that legacies be "put out to interest" in order to pay for children's maintenance and educational needs. More than 30 percent of all fathers with minor children followed this procedure during the late colonial era (see Table 4.2). Samuel Weaver, a well-to-do artisan, granted five hundred pounds to his wife in 1742 while bequeathing the remainder of the estate to his young son and daughter. Ordering the sale of some property, he directed that three male friends invest one thousand pounds for the children's support. Once each heir reached age twenty-one or married, he or she was to receive five hundred pounds of the principal sum. Like most testators, Weaver offered only general instructions concerning the investment of assets and left the details of management to his executors.[31]

Wealthy New Yorkers were the first social group to order that their children's inheritances be used to generate interest income. Before 1750, merchants and well-to-do mariners accounted for about 70 percent of all testators who placed their children's shares "out to interest." Over the next twenty-five years, it became quite common for persons of more modest wealth to emulate this practice. From 1751 to 1775, artisans, shopkeepers, and laborers together accounted for more than one-third of all testators who directed that their children's legacies be invested in some manner.[32] Rather than allow money to sit idle, these colonists were willing to take some risks in order to enhance their heirs' future prospects.

A few wealthy testators established special funds for the purpose of supporting their underage heirs. The merchant Gulian Verplanck directed his executors in 1750 to pay an annuity to his wife for his chil-

[30]Ibid., 1st ser., no. 399, July 30, 1712.
[31]Ibid., Liber 14:305–7, Aug. 31, 1742.
[32]Sixty-four testators utilized this practice in wills written during the late colonial era. They included twenty merchants, eleven artisans, eight shopkeepers, seven mariners, and four laborers.

Table 4.2 Fathers ordering that children's legacies
be "put out to interest"

| Period | Fathers having minor children N* | Fathers investing children's shares N | % |
|---|---|---|---|
| 1664–95 | 57 | 0 | 0 |
| 1696–1725 | 138 | 23 | 16.7 |
| 1726–50 | 130 | 33 | 25.4 |
| 1751–75 | 209 | 64 | 30.6 |
| Entire period | 534 | 120 | 22.5 |

*This table pertains to widowers as well as married men who had at
least one minor child at the time they prepared their wills.

dren's care and education: thirty-five pounds for each child under age
fourteen and sixty pounds for each one between fourteen and twenty-
one years old. Discriminating on the basis of age alone, Verplanck offered the same amount of support to his three daughters as his only son.
He undoubtedly recognized that older children required a more inten-
sive, specialized, and hence a more expensive education than their
younger siblings. His will was unique in protecting his heirs against the
possible depreciation of New York currency. If "a large quantity of paper currency" was issued and the value of money decreased, he requested his executors to transfer his credits "to some part of Europe and
to put the same into some good fund there" for the children's benefit.[33]
Verplanck's will included some unusual provisions, but it typified parental aspirations during the late colonial era. Well-to-do testators were as
interested in increasing their orphaned children's future wealth as in
protecting their security.

INTESTACY LAW AND PRIMOGENITURE

The most knowledgeable practitioners of law in colonial New York
were continually frustrated by the ambiguities of their province's legal
system. William Smith, Jr., the preeminent legal scholar of the late colonial era, issued this complaint in 1757:

The state of our laws opens a door to much controversy. The uncertainty
with respect to them renders property precarious, and greatly exposes us
to the arbitrary decisions of bad judges. The common law of England is
generally received, together with such statutes, as were enacted before we

[33]N.Y. Wills, Liber 18:68–75, July 5, 1750.

had a legislature of our own. But our courts exercise a sovereign authority, in determining what parts of the common and statute law ought to be extended; for it must be admitted, that the difference of circumstances necessarily requires us, in some cases, to reject the determinations of both. In many instances they have also extended, as I have elsewhere observed, even Acts of Parliament, passed since we have had a distinct legislation, which is adding greatly to our confusion. The practice of our courts is not less uncertain than the law. Some of the English rules are adopted and others rejected.[34]

Smith's proposed solution to this problem was twofold: first, an Act of Assembly specifying the extent to which English law applied in the province; second, judicial establishment of a general set of rules governing legal practice.

William Smith's complaint is certainly supported by an examination of New York intestacy law. The Duke's Laws of 1665 intentionally adopted New England practices concerning the succession to personal property, but not for the descent of land. If a man died intestate, his personal estate "shall be . . . divided between the Widow and Children, viz., one third . . . to the widow and the other two thirds amongst the Children, provided that the Eldest Sonne shall have a double portion, and where their are no Sonnes the daughters shall inherit as Copartners."[35] Though New York was hardly a Puritan commonwealth, its "double portion" law was derived from the Mosaic Code (Deuteronomy 21:17). The English Statute of Distributions of 1670 provided, by contrast, that each child should receive an equal portion of personal property. While New York courts acknowledged this statute by the 1750s, the provincial assembly did not officially adopt it until 1774.[36] The movement for legal reform finally achieved results, but only after years of uncertainty and confusion in colonial law.

The rules governing the descent of real estate were initially no more certain than those regulating the succession to personal property. The Duke's Laws offered no specific guidelines concerning the inheritance of land, thereby implying that the common law rule of primogeniture obtained in the province. The New York assembly clearly adopted this interpretation in the Charter of Liberties of 1683. Drafted by Englishmen who intended to establish their own legal institutions at the

---

[34]William Smith, Jr., *The History of the Province of New-York*, ed. Michael Kammen, 2 vols. (Cambridge, Mass.: Belknap Press, 1972), 1:259–60.

[35]Lincoln, *Colonial Laws*, 1:9.

[36]Herbert Alan Johnson, "English Statutes in Colonial New York," *New York History* 58 (1977): 285–86. See also Charles M. Andrews, "The Connecticut Intestacy Law," *Tercentenary Commission of the State of Connecticut* (New Haven: Yale University Press, 1933), no. 2.

expense of Dutch colonists, this document declared that "Noe lands Within this province shall be Esteemed or accounted a Chattle or personall estate but [instead] an Estate of Inheritance according to the Custome and practice of his Majesties Realme of England."[37] Though the charter was soon revoked, its conscious policy of Anglicization marked a turning point in the evolution of provincial law. The colony's highest legal institutions—the Supreme Court, Prerogative Court, and Chancery Court—all acknowledged primogeniture as the law of descent from the 1690s to the Revolution.

By the mid-eighteenth century, New York intestacy law conformed to southern colonial practice while diverging sharply from intestate succession in Pennsylvania and New England. Primogeniture was established by statute in Maryland, Virginia, and the Carolinas between 1705 and 1715. These colonies also adopted the English Statute of Distributions by requiring the equal division of personal property among all children. Pennsylvania and New England instead allowed the eldest son a double portion of both real and personal property, while granting his siblings only a single share. Regardless of variations in colonial law, the eldest son in all regions obtained certain advantages when his father died without leaving a will.[38]

## THE PROBLEM OF THE HEIR AT LAW

Primogeniture was only one possible outcome of intestacy in colonial New York. If no eldest son survived, common law determined who was entitled to be "heir at law," representative of the deceased and claimant to his real estate. Without outlining all the rules governing inheritance in such cases, I want to emphasize several points concerning children's property rights: first, real estate descended to the deceased person's legitimate issue in an infinite line of succession, thereby excluding ascendants (parents or other ancestors); second, male issue inherited before female; third, the eldest male alone inherited if there were two or more males related in the same degree to the deceased; and fourth, females inherited jointly in the absence of a male heir. While English common

[37]Lincoln, *Colonial Laws*, 1:114. For the political background to the Charter, see John M. Murrin, "English Rights as Ethnic Aggression: The English Conquest, the Charter of Liberties of 1683, and Leisler's Rebellion in New York," in William Pencak and Conrad Edick Wright, eds., *Authority and Resistance in Early New York* (New York: New-York Historical Society, 1988), 56–94.

[38]Carole Shammas, Marylynn Salmon, and Michel Dahlin, *Inheritance in America: From Colonial Times to the Present* (New Brunswick: Rutgers University Press, 1987), 32–35.

law advantaged both male issue and the firstborn among males, it did not exclude inheritance by females. A daughter would inherit before any collateral kin. If a male heir himself died without sons, his own daughters assumed precedence over his younger brothers. Two or more female heirs inherited as "coparceners," persons entitled to an equal share of real property.[39]

Since the Statute of Wills of 1540, Englishmen might devise land to persons of their choice and therefore defeat the claims of the heir at law. Testators first obtained this power over all their freehold land and two-thirds of knights' service realty. With the abolition of feudal tenures in the 1670s, men could freely devise nearly all their fee-simple lands (those held by an individual, his heirs, and assigns without limitation or condition). The conveyance of real estate by will was an increasingly common practice among the English middle class, including shop-keepers and yeomen, during the seventeenth and eighteenth centuries. In gentry families, by contrast, heirs often lacked the power to alter marriage settlements that fixed the succession to the estate from father to eldest son. Primogeniture remained a custom among the landed elite, but it was not necessarily the rule of descent followed in yeomen's or merchants' wills.[40]

Because the Statute of Wills was never formally incorporated into New York law, many colonists were uncertain whether they could legitimately devise real estate by last will and testament. Dutch colonists became especially fearful that they lacked this right after the provincial assembly adopted English common law rules governing inheritance in 1683. Cornelius Steenwyck, a wealthy city merchant and recent mayor, pre-pared a mutual will with his wife the following year that openly defied the legislature's action. Declaring his own lands to be chattels, he avowed his right to bequeath them as he pleased "any Law or Statute to the contrary . . . notwithstanding." His wife, Margareta Riemers, herself re-jected English law, stating with him that their property would descend "according to the Regulations Customs Laws & Statutes of the Nether Dutch nation."[41] Since Steenwyck and Riemers had no surviving chil-dren, they bequeathed nearly all their property to the widowed spouse, provided that their respective kin inherit equal shares of the estate after the survivor's death. Steenwyck and Riemers justified their action by citing the English guarantee of Dutch inheritance customs according to "the articles made upon the Surrendering of this place" in 1664. Given

[39]Blackstone, *Commentaries* 1, bk. 2:202–20.
[40]Shammas, Salmon, and Dahlin, *Inheritance in America*, 26–30.
[41]N.Y. Wills, Liber 19B:135–40, Nov. 20, 1684.

the strong Dutch influence in local affairs, the Steenwyck-Reimers will was probated without any challenge.[42]

While few testators took the extraordinary measure of declaring their real estate to be personal property, the great majority circumvented primogeniture by some means. By the early 1700s, most landowners in New York City and rural regions offered a small cash sum or other gift to the heir at law in lieu of any claim to all their real estate. While testators generally offered token bequests for this purpose, some parents granted valued heirlooms or personal items. John Ewets, a carpenter, left his eldest son a gold seal ring, a silver-headed cane, and a silver tobacco stopper; Garret Van Horne, a merchant, gave his firstborn the family portraits, his own apparel, several pistols, and the choice of his mus-kets.[43] Whether allowing the heir the family Bible or a shotgun, men almost never granted him any real estate based on birthright itself.

New Yorkers might employ similar legal stratagems against any poten-tial heir—whether or not the latter was eldest son. Samuel Bensing (Benson), a pot maker, bequeathed twenty shillings to his orphaned grandson, eldest son of the deceased heir, "wherewith I Cut him of[f] and Utterly Debarr him from any further Claim or Pretension as being my Heir at Law."[44] Testators of diverse ethnic origin carefully drafted their wills in order to evade English inheritance law. Joseph Bueno de Mesquita, a Jewish merchant who had no surviving children, chose to leave most of his estate to his wife, his sister, and his brother's children. Recognizing that his brother was his lawful heir, he granted him "my five bookes of [the] law of Moses in Parchment together with the two Orna-ments of plate thereto belonging in full of all his pretentions and de-mands of my Estate whatsoever."[45]

A few colonists were not content with simply offering an heir a token bequest in satisfaction of his lawful claims. They instead threatened him with disinheritance if he should seek to exploit his privileged status in any manner. Coenradt Ten Eyck, a tanner, posed this warning while offering his firstborn son one hundred guilders more than any of his other children in the final division of the estate. Declaring his preference for a nearly equal sharing of wealth, Ten Eyck counseled his children to "Unity peace and quietness As Ought to bee Amongst brothers and Sisters."[46] A small additional bequest might satisfy the eldest son's desire

[42]Ibid. Apart from bequests to male and female relatives, the will conveyed land in Westchester County to the Dutch Reformed Church.

[43]Ibid., Liber 18:161–62, July 6, 1751; Liber 25:80–82, Dec. 8, 1761.

[44]Ibid., 1st ser., no. 1068, July 20, 1726.

[45]Leo Hershkowitz, ed., *Wills of Early New York Jews (1704–1799)* (New York: American Jewish Historical Society, 1976), 15–17, Oct. 20, 1708.

[46]N.Y. Wills, Liber 3–4:58–59, Sept. 4, 1686.

for special recognition, while the threat of disinheritance would discourage him from undermining family harmony.

Dutch women as well as men throughout the province sought to prevent the eldest son from claiming his full legal privileges under common law. Margaret Schuyler, a wealthy Albany widow, executed a will about 1707 for the specific purpose of ensuring an equitable division of the family estate among all her children. Noting that she and her deceased husband had executed a mutual will some twenty-eight years previously, she now explained that her younger children feared that the original testament might be judged invalid under English common law, thereby depriving each heir of an equal share of real estate with the eldest son. While Margaret Schuyler expressed some confidence that her eldest son would not seek to overturn the mutual will, she nevertheless took no chances with his generosity. Her last will and testament confirmed a family agreement of 1707 that apportioned the bulk of real and personal property equally among all seven Schuyler children and the heirs of one deceased son. Typical of Dutch parents, Schuyler listed her children's names in her testament by birth order, not gender. She thereby implicitly reinforced the idea that each child was entitled to an equivalent share of property.[47]

Without including a prohibitory clause in their wills, testators had little defense against heirs who desired to press their legal claims to all real estate. In decisions made in 1707 and 1722, the New York Court of Chancery declined to uphold a last will and testament challenged by the heir at law.[48] The individual's right to devise real estate depended ultimately on family cooperation rather than the force of judicial opinion.

It is worth reviewing one of these cases in order to examine the potential sources of conflict between family members. Beginning in 1706, Helena Rombouts, a well-to-do widow and merchant, found her title to her deceased husband Francis's real estate in Manhattan challenged by her son-in-law and daughter. Sixteen years previously, Francis Rombouts had prepared a Dutch-language will that divided his property between Helena and the couple's only child, Katherine, then just three years old. The will first offered particular benefits to each party: four thousand guilders to the widow; three thousand guilders and some land at Wap-

[47]Pelletreau, *Abstracts of Wills on File in the Surrogate's Office, City of New York, 1665–1801*, 17 vols., Collections of the New-York Historical Society (New York, 1893–1909), 2:73–74, will not dated, proved June 27, 1711. For the mutual will, see Court of Probates wills, AS 2, N.Y. Archives. Margaret Schuyler had earlier used her maiden surname, Van Slechtenhorst.

[48]*Orders in Chancery, Mar. 29, 1705 to Sept. 16, 1708*, 85–95; *Orders, Dec. 22, 1720 to June 5, 1735*, 4–7, 23–32, N.Y. Archives.

pinger's Falls to the daughter. The remainder of the estate, including all Manhattan property, was to be divided equally between them, provided that young Katherine received her portion when she married or came of age. While Rombouts prepared his own will, he acknowledged that his estate had been held as community property since his wife, Helena, had been previously wed and had contributed significantly to his personal wealth. Though he had initially promised her just fifteen hundred guilders as a legacy in their marriage contract, he had more than doubled this sum in recognition of her value as a wife.[49]

Francis Rombouts died in 1692, leaving his wife to manage his estate as executor and to care for their child. The relationship between widowed mother and daughter changed in 1703 when sixteen-year-old Katherine married Roger Brett, an English colonist and navy officer. After living with the widow for seventeen months, the daughter and son-in-law moved into the second family house on Broadway. The facts of the case after this point are subject to dispute. Helena Rombouts claimed that her son-in-law had promised to lease the house from her, but he denied offering any rent. His alterations of the garden and erection of a beehive provoked his mother-in-law still more. As their personal relations deteriorated, Roger Brett and his wife decided to move from their house and to lease the property. Helena Rombouts proceeded to evict the new tenant and to pull down several fences built by her son-in-law.

Beginning with petty concerns, this dispute escalated into a conflict over all Rombouts family real estate. In June 1706, Roger and Katherine Brett entered a plea of trespass in Supreme Court against Helena Rombouts in order to recover the property from which their tenant had been evicted. Arguing that Katherine was her father's heir at law, their attorney in a related suit maintained that she had a right to all his real estate, including this particular house that the widow had built on his land since his death.[50] Since Helena Rombouts recognized that she had no remedy at common law, she petitioned the Court of Chancery for an injunction to stay all legal actions in Supreme Court against her. Stating that the Manhattan real estate was community property, she asked the

---

[49]For the antenuptial contract and will, see Francis Rombouts Estate, New York City Estates, New York Public Library. The contract was dated Sept. 20, 1683, while the will was written Jan. 9, 1691.

[50]Brett v. Rombouts, June 1706, Supreme Court Parchments, P-241-C-1, New York County Clerk's Office. The evicted tenant successfully sued Rombouts for damages. See Crabtree v. Rombouts, 1706–7, P-219-C-3. Roger Brett and his wife commenced an action against Helena Rombouts in Chancery to force her to account for her administration of her deceased husband's estate. See *Orders in Chancery, 1705 to 1708*, 39, 41–42, 46. Their attorney's argument is stated in Brett *et ux* v. Rombouts, Oct. 3, 1706, Chancery Decrees before 1800, R19, N.Y. Archives.

court to honor her deceased husband's will, which had allotted widow and daughter an equal share of this family wealth.[51] Since the court dismissed Helena Rombouts's complaint as having no standing in equity, her daughter and son-in-law were free to prosecute their case at common law against her. They were also encouraged to continue a related suit in Chancery in order to force the widow to deliver deeds to the real estate and to account for her management of her deceased husband's personal property—goods and assets in which they had a half-share.

Though heirs might legitimately challenge a will, such cases were exceedingly rare. There are apparently no more than three court cases during the colonial era in which heirs attempted to obtain all real estate after being granted a lesser share by their ancestor's will. It seems that eldest sons and other claimants were extremely reluctant to claim legal privileges at the risk of alienating other family members. They might also have to contend with juries that respected the testator's right to devise real estate as he pleased. Roger and Katherine Brett themselves secured title to one Manhattan property, but they never obtained judgment against Helena Rombouts for the house where she herself lived. The widow died in 1708 while still engaged in litigation with her daughter and son-in-law. Her own will left Katherine the insulting amount of nine pence while dividing the remainder of her wealth among her six children by a former husband, Hendrick Van Baal.[52] Rather than remain in contention with the Van Baals, the Bretts mortgaged their city house and then built a homestead and gristmill along the Fishkill in Dutchess County—on land inherited from Francis Rombouts. Katherine Brett herself outlived her husband by many years, became a successful businesswoman like her mother, and died in 1764 at age seventy-six. It is perhaps not surprising that, having herself been heir at law, she allowed her own eldest son the substantial bequest of one hundred pounds "as Primogeniture."[53] Like most New York testators, however, she did not grant all her real estate to a single heir but instead left five farms, all leased to tenants, to her eldest son, and five other leases to her younger son's children.

Some eldest sons regarded family harmony as so important that they relinquished all claims to their siblings' inheritance if acquired by last will and testament. When Hendrick Van Der Heul, a Manhattan shop-

[51]Rombouts v. Brett *et ux*, Feb. 13 and Mar. 6, 1707, *Orders in Chancery, 1705 to 1708*, 65–66, 85–95.

[52]N.Y. Wills, 1st ser., no. 226, Nov. 20, 1706. Rombouts was widowed three times.

[53]Ibid., Liber 24:336–40, Dec. 13, 1763. For the Rombouts and Brett family history, see Harold Donaldson Eberlein, *The Manors and Historic Homes of the Hudson Valley* (Philadelphia: J. B. Lippincott, 1924), 180–84.

keeper, died in 1718, he left behind three sons: seventeen-year-old Abraham and the younger Jan and Hendrick. Each son was guaranteed an equal share of property by their father's will, provided that the eldest received an additional five pounds in recognition of his birthright. Five years later, Abraham mortgaged his third part of the family house and lot on Dock Street. Just prior to executing this deed, he released all claim to the remaining two-thirds "for and in Consideration of the Love and Affection which he hath and beareth unto his Brothers."[54] Despite having been granted an equal share of real estate from their father's will, the younger sons apparently believed that their title was insecure until it was acknowledged by their eldest brother, the heir at law.

Eldest sons might themselves benefit by cooperating with other family members in the division of real estate. Abraham De Peyster, heir of Abraham Sr., declined to exploit his father's mental incapacity during old age at the expense of his younger siblings. Though the elder De Peyster lived twenty-six years after preparing his will in 1702, he failed to draft a codicil concerning two vital matters: the birth of two new children and the purchase of additional real estate during the intervening years. According to common law, these offspring might be deprived of any benefit and the eldest son himself might claim all real estate acquired since the will was written.[55] Neither possibility occurred. Abraham De Peyster, Jr., maintained his family's goodwill by reaching a legal settlement with his widowed mother and siblings shortly after the father's death. All parties recognized the youngest children's right to share equally in the greater part of the estate with the other heirs. Abraham himself agreed to relinquish all interest in any lands acquired by his father after the will was drafted. He also accepted an additional legacy of six hundred pounds rather than insisting on the one thousand previously bequeathed to him. In return for these concessions, his siblings pledged to assume an equal cost in defending any legal suits brought against him as heir. They were also to incur an equal share of any losses if judgment should go against him. This guarantee was important given the De Peyster family's history of litigiousness. Finally, it should be noted that the De Peysters did not settle their differences on good faith alone. All parties bound themselves in the sum of four thousand pounds for the contract's performance.[56]

[54]Conveyance Libers (Microfiche) 31:510–11, Aug. 19, 1723, City Register, New York City. For Hendrick Vanderhule's will, see Pelletreau, *Abstracts of Wills*, 11:26, Feb. 17, 1710. Eldest sons in rural areas of New York also frequently relinquished their rights as heir at law.

[55]Blackstone, *Commentaries* 1, bk. 2:379.

[56]Articles of Agreement, Dec. 9, 1728, Duane Papers, New-York Historical Society (hereafter NYHS). For Abraham De Peyster's will, see N.Y. Wills, 1st ser., no. 910, Sept. 18, 1702.

One eldest son who initially refused to acknowledge a younger sibling's inheritance had to recognize her rights after she sued him in Supreme Court. In 1739, forty-seven-year-old Gerardus Stuyvesant defended his title to the family farm at the Bowery against his widowed sister, Anna Pritchard, then fifty years old. Both had claims to the estate, long ago their grandfather Pieter Stuyvesant's property, based on their deceased father Nicholas's will. In 1698 the testator had left nearly all his wealth, including the farm, to his wife on condition that it eventually would be divided equally among the couple's three children, Petrus, Anna, and Gerardus. Unfortunately, the will defined Anna's inheritance in ambiguous terms. While she was granted an equal third with her brothers, her right to the estate might be satisfied as a dowry if "her . . . mother sees Cause."[57] Anna married in 1706, undoubtedly received some property then, but still demanded an inheritance equal to her sole surviving brother's after her mother died in 1738. She sought thereby to prevent Gerardus Stuyvesant from claiming all family real estate based on his status as heir at law to their father, Nicholas, and deceased brother, Petrus.

Since Anna Pritchard's petition before the Supreme Court is not extant, her attorney's precise argument is unknown. It is clear, however, that the plaintiff persisted in her demands. After three years' delay, Chief Justice James De Lancey ordered a jury in 1742 to partition the Stuyvesant estate so that Anna Pritchard received one-third of the property's value, while her brother obtained two-thirds. Without stating its rationale, the court presented this award as complying with law and custom in both England and New York.[58] The decision favored the male heir, but it did not recognize him as sole claimant. It also implicitly affirmed the individual testator's right to devise real estate by last will and testament to heirs of his own choice. Moreover, a daughter's claim to inherit land through a will was upheld despite her having previously received a dowry. The jury awarded Anna Pritchard three separate parcels comprising 192 acres, including a farm of 131 acres along the East River and bordering the King's Highway from Bloomendal to Harlem. (Gerardus Stuyvesant was awarded roughly 275 acres, including the central portion of the estate with its homestead and nearby church.) Finally, it should be noted that Anna Pritchard sold the 131-acre parcel in 1746 but still held the remainder at her death thirteen years later. Having no children, she bequeathed most of her estate to her nephew Nicholas William Stuyvesant, brother Gerardus's eldest son.[59] Her pre-

[57]Stuyvesant v. Pritchard, July 1739, Legal Documents, no. 3014, Museum of the City of New York.
[58]Ann Pritchard-Writ, y-1742-April 17, NYHS.
[59]I. N. Phelps Stokes, *The Iconography of Manhattan Island, 1498–1909*, 6 vols. (New York:

vious challenge of her brother's legal claims was based on self-interest rather than any consistent stance against the right of heirship.

There was considerable resistance to primogeniture as the law of intestacy in rural areas, particularly during the early eighteenth century. Considering the importance of land as an economic resource, a yeoman's younger children, particularly sons, could not readily accept the eldest son's right as heir without sacrificing their own future well-being. Two Dutch families in Kingston in 1709 and 1710 even concluded formal contracts compelling the eldest son to relinquish his birthright when the head of the household died without leaving a will. Andries De Witt was killed suddenly in July 1710 when two wooden beams crashed down on him as he slept in his house. Since he had no time to prepare a will before dying, his eldest son, Tjerck, was entitled to inherit all of his father's real estate. Despite his privileged status as heir at law, Tjerck could press his advantage only at the risk of alienating other family members. He therefore reached a formal agreement with his mother, four brothers, and three sisters that specified a more equitable division of the deceased man's property among all concerned.[60]

The De Witt family contract is particularly significant because it followed legal procedures commonly used by yeomen in drafting their wills. In keeping with Dutch custom, the deceased man's spouse was to remain in possession of nearly the entire estate during widowhood. The couple's four sons and four daughters, ranging in age from seven to twenty-seven years, had to await their mother's death before acquiring their inheritance. Though the males alone were eventually to inherit land, they had to compensate all their siblings for their real estate's appraised value. All children therefore received economic benefit from their father's land. The eldest son himself received special treatment within certain strictly defined limits. Although Tjerck alone gained the right to choose one of his father's slaves and also inherited the family Bible, he had to divide the remainder of the deceased man's personal property in a nearly equal manner with his siblings. His share of the estate was similar to what he might have received if his father had written a will.[61]

New England settlers in eastern Long Island followed inheritance customs different from those of Dutch colonists, but they also opposed primogeniture. When John Cooper of Southampton died intestate in

---

R. H. Dodd, 1915–28), 6:141, 169. For Anna Pritchard's will, see N.Y. Wills, Liber 21:358–60, June 7, 1759.

[60]The agreement, written in Dutch, is found in Ulster County Deeds, Liber BB, pp. 89–92, Sept. 8, 1710, County Clerk's Office, Kingston, New York. A translation is published in *Olde Ulster* 8 (1912): 71–75.

[61]Ibid.

1677, he left behind a wife, a daughter, and three sons. Acting as administrator of the estate, the widow bought out the daughter's interest five years later with a cash payment and a small parcel of land.[62] Unlike females in Dutch colonial families, New England daughters were not considered to have any necessary claim to either their deceased father's real estate or its monetary value. Having reached maturity, the Cooper sons agreed in 1689 to divide all family houses and lands among themselves. The two eldest heirs, who shared the homestead, assumed the responsibility of caring for their widowed mother during the remainder of her life. She relinquished her claim to the estate in return for maintenance—sixteen pounds each year paid in oil and beef, the use of the east room in the main house, and all things necessary for her support.[63]

One sign that eastern Long Islanders rejected primogeniture is apparent in the division of town lands—a continuous source of prosperity to long-established families. After a man's death, his right to the still-undivided commons generally descended to all his sons. As in New England, this system of partible inheritance customarily excluded daughters from any share in family real estate.[64]

## THE ADVANCEMENT OF CHILDREN

Whether father or widowed mother was the head of the family, parents in colonial New York City generally offered their children some form of material support as the latter married or came of age. The most common form of parental assistance was a gift of personal property or cash known as the "outset," a term derived from the Dutch *uitzet.* Daughters received their outset with the understanding that they were now expected to be dependent on their husbands; sons henceforth had to be self-sufficient in business or trade. The outset was not simple largesse but counted toward a child's inheritance when both parents eventually died. According to the Dutch custom called *inbreng,* children might participate in the final division of the family estate only if they accounted for all previously received parental gifts. They would forfeit their inheritance should they fail to bring such property back into the household.[65]

---

[62]See William J. Post and William S. Pelletreau, eds., *Records of the Town of Southampton,* 6 vols. (Sag Harbor, N.Y.: John H. Hunt, 1910), 5:204. For the widow's appointment as administrator, see Pelletreau, *Abstracts of Wills,* Liber 1:156, July 8, 1677.

[63]Post and Pelletreau, *Records of Southampton,* 5:239, 258–60.

[64]Ibid., 3:149–54.

[65]R. W. Lee, *An Introduction to Roman-Dutch Law,* 5th ed. (1953: rpt. Oxford: Oxford University Press, 1961), 355.

Coenradt Ten Eyck, a shoemaker who prepared a will in 1698, was typical of seventeenth-century Dutch colonists in allowing his widow to control the children's outsets, though not their final inheritance. She was to retain possession of the family estate, grant the children an amount she could "conveniently" spare as they respectively came of age, "charging their account debtor for ye same . . . to be deducted . . . from ye Inheritance after her decease, when my sd children shall by equal partage and division inheritt my estate."[66] Widowed mothers were ordinarily expected to give each newly adult child the same value of property that older sons or daughters had already received.[67]

Testators usually directed that sons and daughters receive their outsets at age twenty-one or marriage. In practice, however, a young woman's advancement was linked to marriage regardless of her age. Since her outset consisted largely of household goods and clothing (or money to purchase these items), her parents had little reason to offer her such goods until she was ready to marry and to establish her own home. Thus Jacobus Goelet, a shopkeeper of mixed Dutch and French ancestry, directed in 1722 that his eighteen-year-old daughter Aefje, if still unmarried at his death, "shall be furnished with wedding and mourning robes, and Reasonable Linning [i.e., linen] and housing stuff as becomes a young woman of our degree."[68] Similarly, Samuel Bayard, a wealthy merchant, allowed his youngest daughter, twenty-five-year-old Anne, an additional legacy of £150 to buy household goods if she had not yet wed at his death.[69] David Provoost's will of 1723 offered special assistance to his thirty-one-year-old daughter Belia precisely because she seemed unlikely to marry. Since Provoost himself was widowed, he chose to foster his daughter's independence rather than rely on other family members to provide for her. In addition to granting her an equal share of his residual estate with her brother and married sister, he allowed her one hundred pounds, three city lots, a black slave girl, and all remaining household goods: wrought silver plate; pewter, brass, copper, and ironware; mirrors, paintings, bedding, chairs, a clock and Dutch cupboard. All this property, he explained, "I give to her . . . Because she . . . [is] a Maiden Girl and otherwise not able to Maintain her self." If she were to wed before his death, however, her inheritance was to be only an equal portion of the estate, "excepting that she shall have [an] out set at her marriage of £100 [which] I promised to her while I am alive." As chance

66N.Y. Wills, 1st ser., no. 546, Nov. 5, 1698.

67See the wills of Andries Brestede, cooper, and Gerardus Beekman, gentleman. N.Y. Wills, 1st ser., no. 430, July 27, 1709; no. 698, Nov. 10, 1722.

68N.Y. Wills, 1st ser., no. 1156, Sept. 15, 1722.

69Ibid., Liber 15:486–90, Apr. 1745.

**Table 4.3** Average age at first marriage among testators and their wives*

| Period when married | No. of men | Average age | No. of women | Average age |
|---|---|---|---|---|
| 1670–99** | 56 | 24.2 | 50 | 22.1 |
| 1700–1729 | 92 | 24.4 | 74 | 20.7 |
| 1730–59 | 64 | 26.2 | 56 | 22.6 |
| Entire period | 212 | 24.9 | 180 | 21.7 |

*Because the vital registers of the Dutch Reformed church are more comprehensive than those of other congregations, the ethnic Dutch account for 85 percent of the grooms and 87 percent of the brides considered here.
**Using a somewhat different sample, Joyce Goodfriend has obtained very similar figures concerning the age at marriage of men and women in late seventeenth-century New York City. See "'Too Great a Mixture of Nations': The Development of New York City Society in the Seventeenth Century" (Ph.D. diss., UCLA, 1975), 78.

would have it, Belia was able to gain the best of both worlds—the additional bequest followed by marriage. She was still unmarried at her father's death in 1725 but wed just one year later at age thirty-four.[70] It is therefore quite likely that her substantial inheritance enabled her to attract a husband.

Belia Provoost's case was unusual because most women in colonial New York wed during their late teens or early twenties. Consider, for example, the average age at first marriage for testators' wives who wed during three periods: 1670–99, 1700–1729, and 1730–59. The average bride was 22.1 years old during the first period, 20.7 years during the next, and 22.6 years during the last (see Table 4.3). These statistics reflect the social experience of a limited group of white women, mainly those of Dutch descent from the middle or upper ranks of the social scale. It is striking nonetheless that a growing number of females wed at age twenty-five or above during the mid-eighteenth century. Only 8 percent of brides were of this age between 1700 and 1729, but 28 percent were within that group between 1730 and 1759 (see Table 4.4). While a growing percentage of women married relatively late, a significant portion still wed before age twenty-one. (This fact helps to explain why the average age of first marriage for women remained quite low.)

New York City men who left wills tended to marry during their mid-twenties. The average age at first marriage was 24.2 years between 1670 and 1699, 24.4 years during the next thirty-year period, and 26.2 years from 1730 through 1759 (see Table 4.3). It seems, therefore, that both

[70]Ibid., 1st ser., no. 660, Oct. 2, 1723. See also Edwin R. Purple, "Biographical and Genealogical Sketch of David Provoost, of New Amsterdam, and Some of His Descendants," *New York Genealogical and Biographical Record* 6 (1875): 10–11.

**Table 4.4** Age at first marriage among testators' wives, by date of marriage

| Age | 1670–99 | | 1700–1729 | | 1730–59 | | Entire period | |
|---|---|---|---|---|---|---|---|---|
| | N | % | N | % | N | % | N | % |
| Under 21 | 14 | 28.0 | 39 | 52.7 | 22 | 39.3 | 75 | 41.7 |
| 21–24 | 27 | 54.0 | 29 | 39.2 | 18 | 32.1 | 74 | 41.1 |
| 25–29 | 8 | 16.0 | 6 | 8.1 | 11 | 19.6 | 25 | 13.9 |
| 30 and above | 1 | 2.0 | 0 | 0 | 5 | 8.9 | 6 | 3.3 |
| Totals | 50 | 100.0 | 74 | 100.0 | 56 | 99.9 | 180 | 100.0 |

men and women were likely to wed at a somewhat later age during the mid-1700s than had been typical among the previous generation. During the period 1730–59, 18.7 percent of bridegrooms in the sample were thirty years old or above—nearly twice the percentage in that age group between 1700 and 1729 (see Table 4.5). There was little change over time in the percentage of men who first wed below twenty-one years of age. Only 8 percent of bridegrooms in the entire sample had not yet reached their majority.

The average age at marriage differed significantly between merchants and artisans during the mid-1700s. During the period 1730–59, twenty-five merchants who eventually left wills first wed at an average age of 27.6 years. The average age at first marriage for nineteen artisans was 23.6 years. This discrepancy is especially striking because there had been little difference between merchants' and artisans' ages at marriage during the late seventeenth century. From 1670 through 1699, both groups wed at an average age of about twenty-four years. The average age at first marriage increased steadily among New York City merchants while changing little among artisans (see Table 4.6).

In general, young men within the mercantile community probably postponed marriage because of their own individual preferences rather than family constraints. Since they commonly received their outset at age twenty-one, the delay of marriage until their late twenties and early

**Table 4.5** Age at first marriage among male testators, by date of marriage

| Age | 1670–99 | | 1700–1729 | | 1730–59 | | Entire period | |
|---|---|---|---|---|---|---|---|---|
| | N | % | N | % | N | % | N | % |
| Under 21 | 5 | 8.9 | 5 | 5.4 | 7 | 10.9 | 17 | 8.0 |
| 21–24 | 29 | 51.8 | 53 | 57.6 | 20 | 31.2 | 102 | 48.1 |
| 25–29 | 19 | 33.9 | 25 | 27.2 | 25 | 39.1 | 69 | 32.5 |
| 30 and above | 3 | 5.4 | 9 | 9.8 | 12 | 18.7 | 24 | 11.3 |
| Totals | 56 | 100.0 | 92 | 100.0 | 64 | 99.9 | 212 | 99.9 |

**Table 4.6** Average age of first marriage among testators (merchants and artisans)

| Period when married | No. merchants | Average age | No. artisans | Average age |
|---|---|---|---|---|
| 1670–99 | 16 | 24.2 | 22 | 23.4 |
| 1700–1729 | 21 | 25.6 | 36 | 24.4 |
| 1730–59 | 25 | 27.6 | 19 | 23.6 |

thirties cannot be attributed to a lack of parental support. It is also worth noting that there was no lack of brides who might satisfy their needs. Beginning in the early 1700s, women outnumbered men in the city's population.[71] Young merchants probably tended to delay marriage because they did not wish family responsibilities to absorb their energies and resources during their initial years in business. There would be time enough for a wife and children once a man had established himself in trade.

The Byvanck family papers offer an unusually detailed view of the economic bonds between fathers and sons in New York City Dutch households. John Byvanck's accounts with his father's estate over some forty years also disclose how personal tensions might shape this basic family relationship. Born in Manhattan in 1731, John (christened Johannes) was the eldest among four Byvanck sons and one daughter who survived to maturity. His father's business partner from an early age, he became convinced that he was exploited in the management of family concerns. Looking back from the 1780s, he recounted how his father had introduced him to trade during boyhood but had seemed only to hinder his advancement upon reaching adulthood. The father, Evert Byvanck, a bakery owner as well as a merchant, began to invest in business ventures for his son when the latter was just twelve years old. Selling goods to the West Indies at a profit of 100 to 300 percent, he amassed five hundred pounds for John by the time the youth reached his majority. The son's sense of grievance stemmed from the fact that his father maintained control of this capital sum and nearly all profits from subsequent voyages financed by both men. While John's younger siblings married and received outsets of five hundred pounds each, he remained a bachelor who felt unrewarded for his investment of time and money in the family's business. He was especially embittered at not being paid for risks incurred in smuggling for seventeen and a half years: "I earned by

[71]Bureau of the Census, *A Century of Population Growth* (Washington, D.C., 1909), 170–83. For corrections in the 1731 census, see Robert V. Wells, "The New York Census of 1731," *New-York Historical Society Quarterly* 57 (1973): 255–59.

[the] Running of prohibited goods at Least £100 a year thou[gh] that was Performed in the night When If a Servent works he Ought to [be] Intiteld to the Wages of a Servent clear to him self, I never had any Reward for braking my Rest."[72]

John and Evert Byvanck viewed their partnership from distinct and conflicting perspectives. The eldest son could not easily accept his father's words that a bachelor had little need of an outset. Was it not customary for a son to receive this gift as soon as he reached adulthood? While harboring a sense of grievance, John did not directly challenge his father's authority while he was still single. His own economic fortunes were too tightly bound with the family business for him to risk a break with his father. He also clearly hoped that his periodic demands would eventually bring satisfaction. Evert Byvanck himself attempted to assure John that he would eventually receive treatment equal to his siblings' even if his outset was delayed. He fulfilled this promise in 1766 by granting thirty-four-year-old Johannes £1,283 at marriage—the original principal sum of five hundred pounds together with interest accrued since the son was twenty-one. This payment did not, however, satisfy John's demand for £100 a year in wages earned since entering his father's business.[73]

After marriage John Byvanck continued his efforts to gain some control over the management of family resources. In 1770 he leased his father's bakery, storehouse, and six slaves for one year at two hundred pounds—his rent to be paid in quarterly installments.[74] Though subsequently caring for his father in old age, he never attained his wish for the division of the family partnership prior to Evert's death in 1782. An account from 1778 indicates that John charged seventy-eight pounds for thirty-five weeks in which he provided "board, washing, mending, and lodging" to his father, youngest brother Abraham who was mentally incompetent, and family servant Sam. Rather than demanding immediate payment, he followed typical practice in debiting these expenses to his father's estate. He neglected no cost however small, even the £1, 16s. necessary to purchase cloth and then to make four pair of drawers for his father and brother.[75] The Byvanck family papers offer just one example of how accounting practices worked at various stages of the

---

[72]"The State of my Father Evert Byvanck's Affairs," undated manuscript in Byvanck-Bleecker Papers, NYHS. See also John's "sketch of my concourse with my father" in the same papers.

[73]Ibid.

[74]"Proposall of John Byvanck to his Honored Father," Feb. 15, 1770, Byvanck-Bleecker Papers, NYHS.

[75]"Evert Byvanck Sr. [Debtor] to John Byvanck," Byvanck-Bleecker Papers, NYHS.

parent-child relationship. Parents charged sons and daughters for any sums of money or other forms of material assistance received upon marriage or during adulthood. These costs were eventually deducted from the children's inheritance in order to ensure a fair division of family property among all concerned. Children were at the same time credited for offering any services to their aged parents. Their inheritance often reflected both their initial dependence on their elders and their subsequent role as family providers.

John Byvanck was himself extremely dissatisfied with his father's will because it awarded him an equal share of the family estate with his siblings. Citing years of unpaid wages and profits from joint trading ventures, he claimed property far in excess of the other heirs' legacies.[76] After several years of family conflict, the Byvanck heirs finally all recognized that John Byvanck had special rights to the partnership while forcing him to yield certain claims from the past. Apart from minor issues, all parties agreed that any money due to the Byvanck family business was to be divided into two equal shares—one-half to John Byvanck alone and one-half to be divided equally by the five surviving heirs, including John himself. Liability for debts still owed by the partnership was to be apportioned in the same manner. All five children acquired an equal share of their deceased father's residual estate.[77] This agreement accorded well with Dutch traditions of distributing family assets to benefit all children, not the eldest son alone.

John Byvanck's long apprenticeship to his father did not lead him to promote his own son's advancement at an early age. When John prepared his will in 1788 at age fifty-seven, he bequeathed an outset of five hundred pounds each to his only son, Evert, and his daughters, Mary and Jane. While the daughters were to receive their portions as soon as they married or reached age twenty-one, Evert was to obtain his gift only when he wed or reached his twenty-fifth year—the age of majority in Roman-Dutch law. Though John Byvanck lived during the revolutionary era, he shaped his own will with respect to ancient Dutch customs.[78]

## THE TRANSMISSION OF REAL ESTATE

Charles Wooley, an English visitor to New York in 1678, was surprised to learn of the differences between his own country's inheritance laws

[76]N.Y. Wills, Liber 36:494–96, June 11, 1776. Evert and John Byvanck accounts, Byvanck-Bleecker Papers, NYHS.
[77]"Indenture," Byvanck-Bleecker Papers, NYHS, Box 2-1786.
[78]N.Y. Wills, Liber 41:41–44, Aug. 31, 1789.

and Dutch social customs. Speaking to a Dutch burgher, he remarked that Frederick Philipse, "the richest mijn heer" in Manhattan, was said to have one son and daughter: "I was admiring what a heap of Wealth the Son would enjoy, to which a Dutch Man replied, that the Daughter must go halves, for so was the manner amongst them, they standing more upon Nature than Names; that as the root communicates itself to all its branches, so should the Parent to all his off-spring which are the Olive branches round about his Table."[79]

This statement succinctly expresses the Dutch notion that all children had an equal claim—at least in principle—to the family estate. Wooley himself commented favorably on Dutch inheritance customs while misinterpreting the burgher's pronouncement in several ways. First, he confused the Dutch preference for equality of division among all children with the Kentish custom of gavelkind—the equal partition of lands among sons alone. An advocate of English colonization, Wooley was so interested in promoting younger sons' economic prospects that he ignored the issue of women's legal rights.[80] Moreover, he failed to recognize basic differences between colonial social practice and law. Most Dutch colonists adhered to their own traditions in bequeathing property despite the institution of primogeniture as the law of descent. Finally, Wooley understandably failed to anticipate the assimilation of English law among the upper ranks of the colonial elite, including men such as Frederick Philipse himself.

Dutch colonists were by no means alone among New York City testators in favoring an equal division of wealth among their children. Between 1664 and 1775, 389 fathers who had at least one son and one daughter conveyed real estate by last will and testament (see Table 4.7). Nearly two-thirds of the entire group ordered their realty to be divided equally among all their children. An additional 9 percent apportioned their housing and land in a nearly equal manner among their offspring. While most men instituted equality of division, a significant minority in eighteenth-century New York left all or most of their real estate to sons. Whereas less than 10 percent of fathers had favored sons between 1664 and 1695, 18 percent chose this course between 1696 and 1725. During the remainder of the colonial era (1726–75), more than one-fourth of testators substantially favored sons over daughters in devising real estate.

---

[79]Charles Wooley, "A Two Years Journal in New York," in Cornell Jarray, ed., *Historical Chronicles of New Amsterdam, Colonial New York and Early Long Island,* 1st ser., 2 vols. (Port Washington, N.Y.: Ira J. Friedman, Inc., 1968), 58. Wooley's account was first published in London in 1701.

[80]Ibid., 57–58.

**Table 4.7** Testators' distribution of real estate among their sons and daughters

| Period | Equal | | Near equal | | All or bulk to sons | | Other | | Total | |
|---|---|---|---|---|---|---|---|---|---|---|
| | N | % | N | % | N | % | N | % | N | % |
| 1664–95 | 42 | 82.3 | 3 | 5.9 | 5 | 9.8 | 1 | 2.0 | 51 | 100 |
| 1696–1725 | 68 | 73.1 | 7 | 7.5 | 17 | 18.3 | 1 | 1.1 | 93 | 100 |
| 1726–50 | 58 | 56.9 | 9 | 8.8 | 31 | 30.4 | 4 | 3.9 | 102 | 100 |
| 1751–75 | 90 | 62.9 | 18 | 12.6 | 32 | 22.4 | 3 | 2.1 | 143 | 100 |
| Entire period | 258 | 66.3 | 37 | 9.5 | 85 | 21.8 | 9 | 2.3 | 389 | 99.9 |

The movement toward favoring sons was linked to the process of economic development—the establishment of businesses such as warehouses, tanneries, flour mills, breweries, and sugar refineries that entrepreneurs wished to preserve for particular sons. Most proprietors allowed their heirs some choice in deciding whether they wished to purchase the family home and business. Few sons acquired this privilege free of cost. Johannes Kip followed a common procedure in a will of 1702 by offering his eldest son, Jacobus, the right of first refusal to his house and brewery after both the testator and his wife had died. Rather than establish a fixed price, Kip left that responsibility to arbitrators who might be acceptable to all his surviving children. After an appraisal was made, the privileged heir was asked to pay the brewery's value to his deceased father's estate. The purchase price, together with the remainder of family property, was then to be divided equally among all daughters and sons, including the eldest son himself. This procedure reflected the Dutch custom known as *uitboedeling*—a process by which privileged heirs bought out their siblings' share in the family *boedel* or estate.[81]

Dutch yeomen in Long Island and the Hudson River Valley were especially likely to require their male heirs to compensate other family members, usually daughters, for real estate. By the early 1700s, this practice became an economic and social necessity as fathers attempted to preserve farmland for particular sons while arranging an equitable division of wealth among all their children. While daughters did not necessarily receive the full market value of sons' real estate, their cash legacies were usually quite substantial. By contrast, Yankee farmers in eastern

[81]N.Y. Wills, 1st ser., no. 351, Sept. 16, 1702. For the meaning of *uitboedeling*, see A. S. de Blécourt, *Kort Begrip van het Oud-Vaderlands Burgelijk Recht*, ed. H. F. W. D. Fischer (Groningen: J. B. Wolters, 1950), 373. For additional evidence of this practice, see H. Blink, *Geschiedenis van den Boerenstand en den Landbouw in Nederland*, 2 vols. (Groningen: J. B. Wolters, 1902–4), 2:268.

Long Island seldom required sons to compensate daughters in like fashion for their inheritance in land. There is little doubt that daughters generally received a larger share of family wealth in Dutch rural settlements than in Yankee communities.[82]

As in New York's rural areas, fathers in eighteenth-century Manhattan increasingly specified the precise amount of money their sons had to pay for family property. By deciding this issue in their wills, men lessened the possibility of sibling conflict over the inheritance. John Groesbeck, a merchant who left a will in 1750, directed that his only son, John, pay seven hundred pounds to his seven sisters for the right to inherit the family house, storehouse, and other buildings. (Each daughter was to receive two payments of fifty pounds within two years after their brother came of age.) John Groesbeck, Sr., recognized that his son might decline the responsibility of ownership with its attendant financial obligations. If his son refused payment, the testator ordered that the real estate be sold and that the proceeds be divided equally among his widow and all eight children.[83] He was obviously unwilling to promote an only son's economic advancement at the expense of his spouse's welfare or his daughters' property rights.

Though sons generally had to await their father's death before inheriting real estate, some heirs purchased the family home and business before that point. On December 22, 1730, Garret Van Horne, a fifty-nine-year-old widower and leading merchant, sold his house, storehouse, and lot fronting Queen Street and bordering the East River to his eldest son, thirty-six-year-old Cornelius, for £1350.[84] Six days later the elder Van Horne, though then in good health, prepared for death by making his last will and testament. Stating that he wished to treat his children as similarly as possible, he directed that the remainder of his estate be divided into five equal parts—one each for his son and three daughters, and one to be shared by his three orphaned grandchildren. (The latter were heirs of the testator's deceased daughter, Anna Maria.)[85] Garret Van Horne obviously wished to distinguish between the conveyance of his principal residence and the succession to other prop-

[82]David E. Narrett, "Men's Wills and Women's Property Rights in Colonial New York," in Ronald Hoffman and Peter J. Albert, eds., *Women in the Age of the American Revolution* (Charlottesville: University Press of Virginia, 1989), 120–30. Firth Fabend maintains that cash payments to daughters in the Haring family were by the 1770s only a fraction of the value of sons' farms. These sums were not, however, token amounts. See Firth Fabend, *A Dutch Family in the Middle Colonies, 1660–1800* (New Brunswick: Rutgers University Press, 1991), 119–27.

[83] N.Y. Wills, Liber 18:109–11, May 14, 1750.

[84]Conveyance Libers (Microfiche), Liber 31:521–23, Dec. 22, 1730, City Register, New York City.

[85]N.Y. Wills, Liber 13:124–26, Dec. 28, 1730.

erty, including real estate. While his only son had to pay a substantial sum for his father's home and business, he regained one-fifth of his cost at the final division of the estate. It is also apparent that Cornelius purchased this property partly through parental assistance, undoubtedly his outset received when attaining his majority. The elder Van Horne's will required that all previous gifts advanced to his children be counted toward their inheritance.

Cornelius Van Horne followed a somewhat different strategy than his father when he came to prepare his own will in 1747. Then fifty-three years old, he ensured his wife's security by allowing her the choice of any of his houses in Manhattan and the income of one-third of all remaining real estate during widowhood. Rather than convey his principal residence and business to any particular heir, he simply ordered that most of his estate be divided equally among his four sons: the eldest, Garret, by his first wife, Joanna Livingston, and the others—Augustus, Cornelius, and David—by his current spouse, Judith Jay. The testator was so concerned with equity that he compensated his youngest sons for their elder brother's inheritance from his deceased mother.[86] Like most city landowners, Van Horne encouraged the partition and sale of real estate rather than its preservation within the family.

While Cornelius Van Horne's sons received most of their father's personal property upon his death in 1752, they waited until his widow died more than six years later before disposing of family real estate. In February 1759 alone, the heirs sold four separate houses and city lots, including their father's former dwelling and storehouse on Queen Street. This last property was sold for £3,700, nearly three times the amount that Cornelius Van Horne had paid for it in 1730. Since Cornelius himself failed to designate any privileged heirs, his three surviving sons—the youngest had died—themselves had to decide the selling price of houses and land. Only Cornelius Jr., the third son, decided to purchase any family property, buying a house and lot on Dock Street for £1,760. This sum in typical fashion was paid to the deceased man's residual estate and then divided equally among all heirs.[87]

Finally, it should be noted that the Van Horne heirs had not resolved all issues concerning inheritance after selling their deceased father's real estate. Since his widow, Judith Jay Van Horne, had owned land in her own right, her two surviving sons, Augustus and Cornelius, had to dispose of her property as well. Augustus might have claimed all his deceased mother's real estate as heir at law since she had died intestate. But

---

[86]Ibid., Liber 18:124–27, Sept. 3, 1747.
[87]Augustus Van Horne Account Book, NYHS.

he instead decided to divide the sale price of £683 equally with Cornelius.[88] His generosity offers yet another example of an eldest son who relinquished his right of primogeniture in the interest of family unity.

Excluding some wealthy entrepreneurs, most city dwellers were content to divide their real estate among all their children, occasionally including their wives as co-equal heirs with their offspring. By granting fractional shares of houses and city lots, testators encouraged family members to sell their property and to use the proceeds for their own purposes. Men seldom expected that a particular residence would serve as the center of family life over the course of generations. Consider, for example, the sale and resale of one particular property in eighteenth-century Manhattan. In 1702, one Samuel Burt ordered that his entire estate, including his brick house on King Street, be divided equally among his wife and children after his death. Anticipating that the heirs would need a source of income more than any particular place of residence, he authorized his executors to sell his home at their discretion. In 1712, the testator's only surviving child and heir, Mary, decided to sell the house for £350. John Latham, the buyer, wrote a will just one year later that directed his widow to dispose of all his real estate for his family's support. The house on King Street was sold to one John David, who soon conveyed it to his son-in-law, John Dupuy. Dupuy, a physician, lived in the house for nearly thirty years and attempted to preserve it for his family after death. Preparing a will in 1741, he granted the use of the house to his widow, provided that the property descend to his three sons and two daughters in equal shares after her death. By 1752, the testator's widow was dead, two of the original heirs had also died, and one married daughter had sold her interest in the house to another individual. Rather than maintain their fractional shares for rent income, the owners eventually chose to sell the residence to an outsider for one thousand pounds—nearly three times the purchase price forty years previously.[89]

Whereas most property holders might leave a single residence to several heirs, Manhattan's wealthiest merchants owned various forms of real estate, including city houses, vacant lots, and vast tracts of land in rural areas of the province. When fifty-six-year-old Stephanus Van Cortlandt prepared a will in 1700, he was among the very richest men in the province. His holdings included the Manor of Cortlandt, itself comprising about eighty-six thousand acres in the lower Hudson River Valley, as well as substantial real estate in Manhattan, several New York counties,

---

[88]Ibid. (See account of the "Real Estate of Judith Van Horne, deceased," Feb. 21, 1759.)

[89]N.Y. Wills, 1st ser., no. 296, Aug. 21, 1702; Liber 15:265–67, May 27, 1741. Indentures dated Nov. 10, 1712, and July 5, 1764. Byvanck-Bleecker Papers, NYHS, Box 2.

and New Jersey. He and his wife, Gertrude, were prolific parents, having fourteen children between 1672 and 1698. Four sons and seven daughters lived to adulthood. Unlike most burghers, who pledged only cash or personal property for their children's outsets, Stephanus Van Cortlandt provided in his will that all his underage heirs should receive a city lot for the construction of a house when they married or came of age. Postponing the transmission of any other real estate until his wife's death, he was far more concerned with treating all his children equitably than with preserving any particular estate for a single heir. After granting his eldest son, Johannes, a 915-acre tract of land within his manor, he ordered that the remainder of his real estate be divided equally among his eleven children.[90]

Sung Bok Kim attributes Van Cortlandt's decision to divide his lands among many heirs to the difficulties of maintaining manorial lordship against encroachment by local governments and the provincial assembly. According to this theory, political frustrations induced Van Cortlandt to oversee the fragmentation of his vast holdings within three years after he had founded the manor itself.[91] It seems just as likely, however, that Van Cortlandt's will was shaped by Dutch cultural and social traditions. Like most burghers in the early 1700s, he postponed the major portion of his children's inheritance until his wife's death or remarriage. He also offered preferential treatment to male heirs while dividing most of his real estate equally among all his children. His will allowed his sons the right to choose by birth order those particular houses and lands they would inherit. It should be stressed, however, that Van Cortlandt accepted privilege based on gender and age only on condition that each child's portion be of equal monetary value.

Stephanus Van Cortlandt's heirs finally agreed on a division of his Manhattan and New Jersey real estate in 1730—twenty-nine years after his will was probated and seven years after his widow's death. Remarkably, ten of the original eleven heirs were still alive at that point. Although the precise reasons for the delay of partition are not apparent, it was obviously difficult to divide numerous and substantial properties among many heirs. According to New York law, the consent of all interested parties (the devisees) was necessary to arrange the division of land among co-owners or tenants-in-common. A schedule of the partition agreement indicates that the Van Cortlandt heirs were scrupulous in executing their deceased father's will. The city and New Jersey real

[90]Wills, no. 5011, Apr. 1700, Museum of the City of New York.
[91]Sung Bok Kim, *Landlord and Tenant in Colonial New York: Manorial Society, 1664–1775* (Chapel Hill: University of North Carolina Press, 1978), 88–89.

estate was appraised and then divided into ten nearly equal parts, each valued at between £412 and £440. Those heirs who drew the most valuable properties by lot had to compensate the others with small cash payments. After agreeing to the partition of the Manhattan real estate in 1730, they waited two more years before beginning to divide their father's manor lands. Other substantial Van Cortlandt properties in New York and Pennsylvania were held in common until the mid-1750s.[92] There was little reason for the surviving heirs to divide certain undeveloped lands until they were prepared to lease or sell them. Inheritance in major landholding families was therefore linked to the development of the colonial population and economy.

A few members of the Anglo-Dutch elite sought to perpetuate their vast estates in the Hudson River Valley for future generations of male heirs. Frederick Philipse, the founder of Philipsburgh manor, was himself a onetime Frisian immigrant who had arrived in New Amsterdam in the 1650s as a carpenter and contractor to the Dutch West India Company. After marrying a widow who was a successful merchant, he proceeded to accumulate a fortune through overseas trade and land acquisitions—activities that depended on close political relations with a series of English colonial governors. By the time he declared his will in 1700, Philipse was the owner of ninety-three thousand acres in Westchester County as well as valuable New York City real estate.[93] Rather than follow the English custom of primogeniture, he divided his manor between two heirs: two-year-old grandson Frederick, heir to his deceased son, Philip; and his only surviving son, Adolph. Each beneficiary was to receive the use of property for life on condition that it descend to "ye heires male of his Body lawfully to be begotten."[94] By entailing the manor lands, Frederick Philipse allowed his immediate successors to enjoy the income of the estate but not to alienate the inheritance itself.

---

[92]"A Division made by the heirs of Col. Stephen Van Cortlandt, Deceased," Nov. 12, 1730, Van Cortlandt–Van Wyck Papers, Box 2, New York Public Library. See also Indenture, Dec. 14, 1753, Van Cortlandt–Van Wyck Papers, Box 5. Kim, *Landlord and Tenant,* 180–83. The problem of dividing large land grants is analyzed in Armand La Potin, "The Minisink Grant: Partnerships, Patents, and Processing Fees in Eighteenth-Century New York," *New York History* 56 (1975): 29–50.

[93]Kim, *Landlord and Tenant,* 41, 67–69, 73–74; Robert C. Ritchie, *The Duke's Province: A Study of New York Politics and Society, 1664–1691* (Chapel Hill: University of North Carolina Press, 1977), 118–21, 150–52; Linda Briggs Biemer, *Women and Property in Colonial New York: The Transition from Dutch to English Law* (Ann Arbor: UMI Research Press, 1983), 36–43.

[94]Frederick Philipse's will, Oct. 26, 1700, Philipse Papers, PA815, Sleepy Hollow Restorations Library, Tarrytown, N.Y. Sung Bok Kim's superb study of the New York manors is incorrect in stating that Philipse devised his manor in fee simple to his heirs. See Kim, *Landlord and Tenant,* 95.

Frederick Philipse's will reflects the customs of the Dutch gentry as well as the use of English legal procedures such as entail. Like major landholders in Holland, he favored male heirs in apportioning real estate without necessarily resorting to primogeniture. Grandson Frederick and son Adolph each received Manhattan properties in the same restricted way that they inherited manor lands. Daughter Annatje and stepdaughter Eva acquired a life-interest in the city houses where they lived with their husbands. The will provided that these properties were to descend to each woman's second son, thereby insuring the heirs' welfare against their elder brothers' right of primogeniture. Finally, it should be noted that Frederick Philipse favored male descendants in conveying real estate but ordered that most of his personal property be divided equally among his grandson, son, daughter, and stepdaughter.[95]

Frederick Philipse II came to write his own will in 1751 at age fifty-three, completing this task just four days before his death. Having recently succeeded his uncle Adolph, who had died without issue, he commanded both the "upper" and "lower" parts of the manor that had previously been divided by his grandfather's will.[96] As a man who shunned commerce for the life of a country gentleman, Frederick II may have been especially attracted to the English custom of primogeniture. He entailed his manor and certain Manhattan real estate to three successive generations: his eldest son, Frederick, the latter's eldest surviving son, and finally the next generation of males. If Frederick III were to die without any appropriate heirs, his inheritance was guaranteed to another line of males: his younger brother Philip, Philip's son Adolph, Adolph's eldest son, and that heir's male issue. The testator's three daughters were to inherit the manor only if both their brothers died and left no surviving sons, grandsons, or great-grandsons.[97]

While keeping his manor intact for his eldest son, Frederick Philipse II apportioned other real estate in the Hudson Valley and New York City among several children. His younger son, Philip, and three daughters were to share equally in the substantial Highland Patent lands located to the east of the Hudson River. Though not entailing these lands to a succession of male heirs, Philipse still wished to keep them among his descendants, at least for two generations. He therefore required that each child's share descend to his or her respective "heirs of the body."[98]

[95] Ibid. For inheritance practices among aristocratic Dutch families, see Sherrin Marshall, *The Dutch Gentry, 1500–1650: Family, Faith, and Fortune* (New York: Greenwood, 1987), 106–7.
[96] Kim, *Landlord and Tenant*, 193.
[97] N.Y. Wills, Liber 18:1–9, June 6, 1751, codicil July 22, 1751.
[98] Ibid.

According to this provision, an original heir might convey or devise his portion of real estate only to lineal descendants, whether male or female. Having limited the succession to the Highland Patent, Philipse granted at least one city house and lot in fee simple to each of his children, thereby allowing the heirs to dispose freely of their respective Manhattan properties. Ironically, neither the city real estate nor manor lands would remain long under the Philipses' control. Because of Tory loyalties, the family had its vast estates confiscated by New York State during the revolutionary war.[99]

## THE BEQUEST OF PERSONAL PROPERTY

Unlike the devise of real estate, the bequest of personal property changed little during the colonial era. Fathers generally offered some small advantage to the eldest son, while dividing the greatest portion of their movable goods equally among all their children. It is especially striking that few men offered particular articles of clothing, household goods, or cash sums to individual heirs. Burghers instead usually apportioned personal property into fractional shares, thereby inviting their executors to sell their possessions for the payment of legacies.

The small number of specific bequests is somewhat surprising considering the nature of Dutch inheritance customs. According to Roman-Dutch law, testators might offer any child an additional bequest above his or her *legitim* or legitimate share (the minimal portion of the estate guaranteed to each heir except in cases of disinheritance). This special gift, known as a prelegacy, allowed parents to single out certain children—and not just the eldest son—for special treatment.[100]

Thus Hendrick Kip, a seventy-one-year-old burgher, made a Dutch-language will in 1671 that promised the following items to his children "by title of prelegacy" (*bij titule van prelegaet*): his everyday clothes, shirts, and linens to his eldest son, Isaac; his best black coat and a particular Dutch landscape painting to his younger son, Jacob; a wardrobe, dresser, and his bed with all its furnishings to his daughter, Tryntie; a silver spoon to several orphaned granddaughters and a gold bodkin to another granddaughter, undoubtedly a personal favorite. After his eldest son's death, Hendrick Kip added a codicil to his will that benefited his only surviving son, probably because the latter provided shelter for his father in his own home. Jacob Kip's new prelegacy included not only

[99]Eberlein, *Manors and Historic Homes*, 95–98.
[100]Blécourt, *Oud-Vaderlands Burgelijk Recht*, 329.

Hendrick's clothing but also some goods that had previously been earmarked for all the testator's heirs: books, chairs, pillows, paintings, a big and a small leaf-table, a jug-rack, lantern, mirror, spectacles, and certain pewterware. Having singled out his son for special treatment, Hendrick Kip reserved his real estate as well as his plate, silver, and money in wampum for all his heirs.[101] Favoritism to a single child—no matter how justified—had its limits within the Dutch colonial family.

Some parents transferred possession of personal property to their children just before death rather than leaving their heirs to decide this matter among themselves. Christopher Bancker, a wealthy merchant of Dutch ancestry, used his last will and testament as only one instrument in the distribution of wealth. Preparing this document in 1756, the fifty-seven-year-old widower ordered that nearly his entire estate be divided equally among his five sons. The eldest son, Evert, was to receive just ten pounds more than his brothers in satisfaction of his claim as heir at law.[102] Six years after declaring his will, Christopher Bancker decided to give some of his household goods, including valuable silverplate, to his children. Although his precise motives are not known, it is likely that ill health prompted him to anticipate death by overseeing his sons' inheritance. Bancker family financial accounts indicate that Evert spent one hundred pounds in 1762 for his father's board and lodging during his final illness and for the maintenance of four slaves. Evert made certain to charge Christopher Bancker's estate for these expenses, including his cost "for keeping Extraordinary fires in the Parlor from the beginning [of] August & in the Winter" until his father died on April 13, 1763.[103]

The Bancker heirs received their portions of personal property in two stages. The first division occurred one year before their father's death; the second took place just one week after he died (and five weeks before the deceased man's will was probated). In the first stage, each of the four surviving sons (one had died since Christopher Bancker's will was drafted) was allocated $44\frac{5}{16}$ ounces of silverplate. The precise weight of each article was noted in the family account book in order to verify the equal sharing of property.[104]

After Christopher Bancker's death, each of his sons acquired an additional $64\frac{10}{16}$ ounces of plate. The division of property reflected each heir's individual preferences as well as Dutch social customs. After an initial selection of plate was made, Evert Bancker decided to give a punch bowl

[101]Simon Hart, "How Hendrick Kip Bequeathed His Estate," *de Halve Maen* 37 (1962): 9–10, 12.
[102]N.Y. Wills, Liber 24:44–45, Feb. 22, 1756.
[103]Account Book (Christopher Bancker Estate), Bancker Papers, NYHS.
[104]Ibid.

and strainer to his brother Adrian in return for a tankard and pepper box. Since Evert received a somewhat greater value of plate in this exchange, he agreed to pay the difference to Adrian.[105] A fair division of property depended on cooperation among siblings and a commitment to common family values and traditions. Since the Bancker children (all adults at the time of Christopher Bancker's death) were their father's sole executors, they were able to arrange the settlement of the estate without intermediaries.

Household goods were distributed within the Bancker family in much the same way as the plate. In the initial division of 1762 each son received a small portion of goods that were listed but not appraised. After Christopher Bancker's death the next year, however, a strict valuation of all household furnishings was made. Each son was allowed £23, 6s., 3d. worth of movables—a sum that purchased a considerable amount of goods. Evert Bancker's legacy, for example, included a mahogany cupboard, an oval walnut table, seven leather chairs, an oval tea table with two tea boards, as well as a leather couch. Evert also obtained a large painting of the Magi and portraits of his father and mother. While he may have initially been granted these family portraits because of his status as eldest son, he chose to exchange all three paintings for three others and a walnut desk from his youngest brother, William. Evert obviously had a liking for biblical scenes since his new pictures were listed by inventory as "Queen Sheba," "Moses Rescuing the Woman," and the "Birth of our Savior."[106]

Finally, the Bancker papers again underscore the position of the eldest son in the Dutch colonial family. Though Evert received certain minor privileges, he had to divide the bulk of the family estate equally with his siblings. Just before dying, his father offered Evert a special gift: the choice of a clock, twenty-five pounds in cash, or a six-year-old black girl. Evert chose the slave, but was not awarded his prize until he relinquished all claim as heir at law to a deceased brother's estate. His release, acknowledged before an attorney, ensured that the younger son's inheritance would be shared equally by all four surviving Bancker children.[107]

## WILLS OF FATHERS AND WIDOWED MOTHERS

Fathers were generally more concerned with ensuring an equal division of personal property among their offspring than with bequeathing

[105]Ibid.
[106]Ibid.
[107]Ibid.

certain goods to particular children. Though widowed mothers usually granted similar portions of personalty to their descendants, a minority of women favored daughters over sons in their wills. From 1664 to 1775, seventy-six widows in New York City bequeathed personal property to at least one son and one daughter. Seventeen women (or 22 percent of the entire group) offered preferential treatment to a daughter, while forty-eight (or 63 percent) granted equal or nearly equivalent portions to each child. Three widows (or 4 percent) favored sons, while eight others (11 percent) chose an idiosyncratic manner of distribution.

Some degree of favoritism to daughters might be expected given the importance that colonial women attached to clothing, jewelry, and household furnishings. Indeed, widows tended to bequeath certain items to their female descendants even when offering all children a substantial portion of their overall wealth. Phebe Outman, a merchant who ran a store for sixteen years after her husband's death, declared a will on March 27, 1732, just one day before her death and burial. While her son and two married daughters received equal portions of their mother's merchandise and financial assets, the women alone shared her household furniture, plate, jewels, and clothes. An inventory of the widow's estate, taken ten days after her death, appraised these items at £217, nearly one-fifth of her total wealth. Each daughter garnered slightly more than 35 percent of her deceased mother's net worth while their brother gained just under 30 percent.[108]

Phebe Outman's testament was nearly a mirror image of her husband Johannes's will, probated in 1716. She favored her daughters in the division of personal property; he granted the principal family house to his son while conveying less valuable real estate to one daughter and to another daughter's children.[109] Like many widows, Phebe Outman was herself unable to control the succession to real estate since she held only a life-interest in her deceased husband's houses and lands.

Whether married or widowed, women expressed their affection for family members through the bequest of personal effects and household goods. Christina Cappoens, who executed her last will in 1687, devoted great care to the bequest of valued possessions to her daughter and granddaughters. Daughter Maria received a silver beaker, gold vase, diamond ring, pepper box, two silver cups, and three silver spoons. Granddaughter Sara, perhaps the widow's personal favorite, acquired a saltcellar and other silverware engraved "J.H.," the initials of Christina

---

[108]N.Y. Wills, 1st ser., no. 1049, Mar. 27, 1732. N.Y. inventories, Part III, no. 325, 1732, NYHS.

[109]N.Y. Wills, 1st ser., no. 358, Jan. 8, 1714.

Cappoens's first husband. She also gained her grandmother's church book with silver clasps and chain, one great ear spangle with ear jewels, her largest hoop ring, and a gold finger ring with a diamond in it. The other granddaughter's special gifts were a silver beaker and six spoons.[110]

Margaret Van Varick, a minister's widow and merchant, carried the Dutch preoccupation with material possessions to an extreme by placing all her silverplate, jewelry, and personal effects into several bundles to be distributed after her death among her four children, Johanna, Marinus, Rudolphus and Cornelia—heirs listed in her will by birth order. After Van Varick's death in late 1695 or early 1696, her executors—three leading New York merchants—opened each bundle, listed its numerous contents item by item, and then locked the great chest holding the entire *boedel* until the payment of legacies was made. The division of goods was by no means simple. Margaret Van Varick gave each child a bundle marked with the recipient's name, but she also included other bundles or baskets to be shared either by her sons, her daughters, or all children jointly. While each beneficiary received his own napkin containing silverware and jewelry, the daughters gained larger portions of these goods. The widow left it up to her children to distribute particular items of men's and women's clothing among themselves. The daughters alone were to share equally a vast quantity of children's and babies' clothing and linens.[111]

While certain small objects were grouped in bundles, other possessions were placed loosely in the great chest or left in the house for distribution to particular heirs. The eldest child, Johanna, acquired the biggest and finest "turkey carpet" while her sister obtained the second best. The eldest son made do with a less valuable oriental rug and a satin-flowered carpet while the youngest gained a flowered carpet stitched with gold and also a calico rug. The eldest daughter received a portrait of Johanna Van Varick, undoubtedly her grandmother; the youngest son obtained his father's portrait. Son Marinus's pictures included a landscape while daughter Cornelia inherited a still life of a flower pot. Only the Bible was considered sufficiently important among books to justify a bequest to a particular child. After giving her Dutch Testament with gold clasps to her eldest daughter, Margaret Van Varick divided her remaining Dutch books among her four children. These volumes, not listed by title, included thir-

[110]Ibid., Liber 5–6:7–11, June 17, 1687, codicil Sept. 2, 1693. For an inventory of her estate, see Inventories and Accounts, Series J0301, Jan. 15, 1694, N.Y. Archives.

[111]For Van Varick's will see N.Y. Wills, 1st ser., no. 139, Oct. 29, 1695, codicil Nov. 16, 1695. The contents and value of her estate are recorded in Inventories, May 29, 1696, Museum of the City of New York.

ty-seven in quarto, forty-six in octavo, and four in folio. The widow's executors mentioned another "parcel of printed books most [of] them High German and foreign languages, so of little value here; wherefore they are packed up to be kept for the use of the children when at age."[112]

Though female landowners accounted for only a small minority of all widows, their wills are revealing about attitudes toward property and family relations. Like fathers, most widowed mothers who left wills divided their realty in an equal or nearly equal manner among their children. Between 1664 and 1775, forty-six female landowners having at least one son and one daughter declared their testaments. Twenty-two (or 48 percent) ordered that their houses and lands be shared equally among all their offspring. Eight mothers (or 17 percent) showed some favoritism to a certain child while dividing the greatest portion of the real estate in an equal manner. Only seven widows (or 15 percent) strongly favored sons; the remaining women showed no clear pattern of preference in their wills.

Widowed mothers were somewhat more likely than fathers to give special consideration to daughters in the conveyance of real estate, particularly if their female heirs had some special need. Cornelia Norwood, a woman of Dutch descent who had married an English colonist, had three surviving sons and two daughters when she made her will in 1722. Although she ordered that her own house be sold immediately at death, she allowed her daughters to live in her rented house as long as they were unmarried. Once both had wed, that property was also to be sold and the proceeds shared equally among all five children. The widow typically set aside certain household goods for her daughters alone: two dozen cane and leather chairs, her two best and largest mirrors, a small dressing mirror, her best chest of drawers, cooking utensils, and sufficient money to purchase "a decent suit of silk apparel."[113]

Some daughters who received special benefits also incurred extraordinary obligations. Helena De Key, an elderly widow who left a will in 1735, ordered that most of her estate be divided into three equal parts: one part each for her children, Helena and Hillegonde, and a third for her deceased daughter Catherine's children. While directing that most

[112]Ibid. After reading the wills of Christina Cappoens and Margaret Van Varick, one can readily visualize a New England woman's description of New York fashion in 1708: "The English go very fasheonable in their dress. But the Dutch, especially the middling sort, differ from our women, in their habitt go loose, wear French muches wch are like a Capp and a head band in one, leaving their ears bare, which are sett out wth Jewells of a large size and many in number. And their fingers hoop't with Rings, some with large stones in them of many Coullers as were their pendants in their ears, which You should see very old women wear as well as Young." Quoted in Michael Kammen, *Colonial New York: A History* (New York: Charles Scribner's Sons, 1975), 154.

[113]N.Y. Wills, 1st ser., no. 661, May 20, 1722.

of her real estate be sold immediately at death, De Key allowed her widowed daughter, Helena Sheffield, to live in her own house provided that she maintain her incompetent brother, Johannes, "with good & Sufficient Diet Washing Lodging and apparrell." If the daughter remarried and still chose to live there, De Key recognized that Johannes himself might prefer to live elsewhere. In that case, daughter Helena was to pay twenty-four pounds each year for his upkeep. Finally, all De Key heirs were required to offer security for this expense if Helena Sheffield predeceased her brother or if the house stood empty for any time and failed to produce the annual sum. Helena De Key was typical among colonial parents in assuming that her adult children would wish to live separately from each other—except if forced to care for each other by necessity. After Johannes's death, the house was to be sold "to the best advantage" and the proceeds divided among the surviving heirs.[114] A widowed daughter's use of the family home lasted only as long as a more pressing family need existed—the care of an incompetent son.

Women generally had the most latitude over the bequest of property when they had accumulated or inherited an estate in their own right. Consider, for example, the case of Mary Alexander, one of the wealthiest merchants in eighteenth-century New York. Born in 1694 to a Scots immigrant merchant and a Dutch colonial woman, she was undoubtedly familiar with commerce from an early age. Her maternal grandmother, Cornelia De Peyster, was herself a leading female trader of the early colonial era. Mary Alexander's first husband, the merchant Samuel Provoost, died in 1719, granting her a £750 cash legacy as well as real estate previously secured for her sole use by several deeds. There is little question that Provoost regarded his wife (who happened to be his elder brother's stepdaughter) as the principal beneficiary of his estate. Ten days after drafting his will, he executed a codicil that allowed her the unusual privilege of purchasing all his household goods and personal effects for fifty pounds—this sum itself to be part of the general estate divided equally between the widow and the couple's three children.[115] Provoost undoubtedly recognized that his own wealth had depended on his wife's bounty since she had brought a substantial inheritance to their marriage.

Two years after Provoost's death, his widow married James Alexander, a leading attorney as well as New York Council member. Like other prominent female merchants, Mary Alexander remained committed to

[114]Ibid., Liber 13:19–22, Jan. 31, 1735.
[115]Ibid., no. 576, July 21, 1719, codicils July 24 and July 31, 1719. For biographical information, see Alice Morse Earle, *Colonial Days in Old New York* (1896: rev. ed. New York: Charles Scribner's Sons, 1915), 162–64.

business despite her new family obligations. According to James Alexander, she personally sold more than thirty pounds worth of goods in her store the day after giving birth to a daughter. In all, she had two sons (one of whom died young) and five daughters by her second spouse. James Alexander himself was at least as devoted to Mary as her first husband had been. His will, written in 1745, granted particular bequests to the couple's children while allowing his widow absolute freedom in disposing of the estate as a whole. William, their only son, inherited one thousand pounds, and the daughters each received five hundred pounds in addition to an outset in household goods and other personal property. The son's inheritance included the family mansion while the female heirs acquired less valuable tracts of undeveloped real estate. Finally, Alexander stated that William should receive twice the value that each daughter was given of any properties that Mary Alexander did not dispose of by last will and testament.[116]

Mary Alexander utilized her authority under her husband's guidelines while using her will to meet her special concerns. She first bequeathed five thousand pounds to her son, John Provoost, thereby satisfying her obligations to the only surviving child by her first husband. She divided the bulk of her estate equally among her five surviving children by James Alexander rather than favoring her only son as her husband had done. After conveying the mansion on Broad Street to William as her husband had wished, she also bequeathed him two carpets and both his parents' portraits. Dividing most of her silver equally among all children, she left her daughters nearly all other household goods. Since the youngest daughter, Susannah, was still unmarried, she received the most valuable legacy and outset: fifteen hundred pounds to make her equal to her older sisters and a large quantity of particular items including mirrors, marble and mahogany tables, numerous chairs, the green Russell bed with bedding as well as the chintz bed, window curtains, a large Holland cupboard, the square tea table with the china upon it, linens, and additional china, pewter, and silver. While ensuring that her youngest daughter had a suitable outset for a gentlewoman, Mary Alexander favored her eldest daughter, Mary (the wife of Peter Van Brugh Livingston), with all her clothing and jewelry. The eldest also received a chaise all to herself while her younger sisters shared another. The widow Alexander was most concerned that Mary's legacy should not be used by Livingston to pay off large debts that he had accumulated as a war contractor. She therefore executed a codicil to her will in 1758 requiring that her younger daughters hold their sister's jewelry and apparel in

116N.Y. Wills, Liber 19:437–44, Mar. 13, 1745, codicil Jan. 28, 1751.

trust until the British government paid her son-in-law for his expenses.[117]

After Mary Alexander's death in 1760, her son William, by then the self-proclaimed Earl of Stirling, calculated her net worth at just over £100,000—a sum equaled by only a handful of New Yorkers during the late colonial era. Her assets included an estimated £52,600 in bonds and debts due to her estate as well as £13,500 in account with the English trading firm Barclay and Sons.[118] The widow's concern with her children's inheritance is indicated by a letter from David Barclay, a Quaker, addressed to her just two years before her death. He assured her of the safety and liquidity of several £1,200 annuities purchased for her account. This investment, he explained, would not be jeopardized by her death since the annuities were "absolutely thine & thy Heirs' Property, equally the same as any other Part of thy Fortune, wch thou mayst dispose off at any time, or bequeath to any Person thou pleases, who will by Virtue thereof, become intitled to both Principal & Interest due thereon at such time."[119] The purchase of Bank of England funds, yielding just 3 percent annually, may have served as a counterweight to more speculative colonial bonds that usually paid from 5 to 7 percent.[120] Mary Alexander, being an immensely wealthy merchant with transatlantic trading connections, could exploit investment opportunities available to the privileged few.

### DISCIPLINARY PROVISIONS AND DISINHERITANCE

Parents were most likely to restrict the succession to property in order to protect their most vulnerable heirs, especially married daughters and their daughters' children. Given their dependent status in common law, married women possessed little control over their own inheritance. Their husbands could claim ownership of any cash legacy or gift of personal property; husbands also had the right to administer their wives' real estate for their own profit. Though most testators trusted their sons-in-law not to abuse these powers, a significant minority did not. Twenty-four fathers and thirteen widowed mothers in colonial New York City included provisions in their wills that granted daughters the separate use of property during marriage. Testators usually achieved this goal

---

[117]Ibid., Liber 22:55–66, July 27, 1756, codicil Feb. 29, 1758.
[118]Alexander Papers, Box 8, NYHS. This account was not dated.
[119]David Barclay to Mary Alexander, May 13, 1758, Alexander Papers, Box 8, NYHS.
[120]For typical yields, see Virginia D. Harrington, *The New York Merchant on the Eve of the Revolution* (Gloucester, Mass.: Peter Smith, 1964), 131–32.

through the establishment of a life estate—an arrangement entitling the beneficiary to use property, but not to sell or alienate the inheritance itself. Johanna De Bruyn, an elderly widow who declared a will in 1709, allowed her married daughter Petronella the annual rent from several houses and the interest income from a £150 legacy throughout life. Petronella's children were to administer the inheritance for her sole benefit and to share it among themselves at her death. Johanna De Bruyn then explained why she had granted a life estate to one married daughter while allowing two others to receive unrestricted control of property. She had not limited Petronella's rights out of any disrespect to her "but because her husband who does deserve so little at her hands should reap no further benefit by any part of my estate."[121] The widow evidently loved her daughter but feared that she might eventually yield to her husband's demands. She therefore threatened to disinherit any heirs, including Petronella, who opposed her last will and testament.

Other parents restricted their married daughters' inheritance not because they disliked their sons-in-law but simply in order to guarantee the descent of property to their grandchildren. Mary Sinclair accumulated a substantial estate after her husband's death in 1704 and subsequently assisted her son-in-law, Charles Crommelin, in establishing a major transatlantic trading firm. Her will of 1721 absolved him from repaying the principal and interest on a loan of eight hundred pounds that she had previously given him. Though favoring her son-in-law to some degree, Sinclair reserved nearly her entire estate for her only child, Hanna, Charles Crommelin's wife, and the couple's four children. She directed her executors to lease all her city real estate and to pay the rents and profits, deducing the costs of taxes and repairs, to her daughter throughout life. After Hanna Crommelin's death, all property was to descend to her children, including those lawfully "Begotten & to be begotten Either by the Said Charles Crommelin or by any other Husband." The widow took great care in specifying the succession to household goods and personal effects from her daughter to grandchildren. While Hanna's children were to share most of these goods after their mother's death, certain heirs gained title to particular items. For example, Sinclair's will granted Robert Crommelin a gold ring and a silver tankard engraved with his maternal grandfather's coat of arms. Granddaughter Mallie received a large pearl necklace, a pair of gold rings with large pearls set in them, a silver powder box, a pepper box, and a Dutch Bible with gold clasps and a gold cross inlaid with precious stones.[122]

[121]N.Y. Wills, 1st ser., no. 490, Nov. 30, 1709.
[122]Ibid., Liber 13:50–57, July 20, 1721, codicil Aug. 23, 1730. For Crommelin's business activities, see Harrington, *New York Merchant*, 119.

Mary Sinclair, born Mary Duyckinck in New Amsterdam, prized her household goods and personal possessions as much as any Dutch colonial matron. Though she trusted her son-in-law to care for her grandchildren if her own daughter died, she did not allow him to interfere with their inheritance.

The New York Court of Chancery recognized a married woman's right to sole benefit from property bequeathed for her separate use. Unless assisted by relatives or friends, however, she might have little opportunity to protect her inheritance from an abusive husband. Jane Barnet of Jamaica in Queens County relied on her brother, Eldert Eldert, and uncle, Hendrick Eldert, in bringing suit against her husband, Joseph. Her father, Luke Eldert, had written a will in 1752 that directed his executors (the two kinsmen mentioned above) to pay Jane Barnet the annual interest from one-half of his personal estate during life. Luke Eldert evidently despised his son-in-law because he included the extraordinary condition that his daughter receive this income only "for so long a time as she shall remain Childless." If she had any children, the executors were to hold the principal and interest for their benefit after Jane's death. Joseph Barnet himself did little to hide his contempt for his wife and father-in-law. Writing to Luke Eldert in 1754, he openly expressed his hatred:

> your Jayne as I call her for She is not worthy of Being called my wife is Crasy and I have put her under Confinement and do in a Short time Design to put her in the work house to Beat the Block[,] for no other place is fit for her and with me She Shall not Live[.] you may think of this as you Please for I shall do as I Please for I neither Love you nor fear you for it is not my Duty to Love you and it is not in your power to make me fear you and I hate and Despise your name . . . my name is too good for you to Read so I only put these two Letters J.B.[123]

Given Joseph Barnet's hatred for the Elderts, it is not surprising that he opposed his father-in-law's will. Suing in Chancery, he claimed that Luke Eldert's executors should pay the annual income of his wife's legacy directly to him. Jane's uncle and brother countered that Joseph had continually abused his wife without reasonable cause—beating her, turning her out of doors, and forcing her to pawn her clothes for basic necessities. They also testified that Luke Eldert had openly expressed his desire to support his daughter out of his estate without giving any benefit to his son-in-law. Because Eldert had intended the inheritance for his daughter's separate use, Chancellor Cadwallader Colden ordered that

---

[123]Eldert v. Barnet, Nov. 24, 1763, Chancery Decrees, B 66, N.Y. Archives. For Eldert's will, see N.Y. Wills, Liber 20:112–14, Aug. 28, 1752.

the deceased man's executors pay the interest income to her alone.[124]

Very few parents attempted to influence their children's choice of a spouse from beyond the grave. Wills almost always assigned outsets or dowries without requiring that the beneficiaries obtain either a widowed mother's or guardian's consent before marrying. Testators seem to have assumed that children would seek their elders' approval in marriage; they seldom threatened disinheritance if their offspring wed contrary to their wishes.

Because Jews were especially concerned about maintaining communal integrity, they were more likely than other colonists to influence their children's marriages through the bequest of property. Isaac Rodriguez Marques, a Sephardic merchant, bequeathed one-third of his estate to his daughter Esther, allowing her an additional fifty pounds to buy jewelry when she either reached age eighteen or married with her mother's consent. A few parents relied on the threat of punishment rather than positive incentives to induce their children to avoid an early and possibly unwise marriage. Isaac Levy, writing a will in 1776, directed that his son Asher and daughter Esther be disinherited if either wed before age twenty-one. Judah Hayes dismissed his daughter Rachel with a mere five shillings for marrying against his will.[125]

The resiliency of the Jewish community was tested by its small numbers, transient nature, and ethnic divisions. In a community of some twenty households, it was by no means easy for young persons to find a suitable marriage partner. Some residences represented little more than a home base for merchants engaged in international commerce. The difficulty of marrying within the faith was compounded by tensions between New York's Ashkenazic and Sephardic Jews. Abigail Franks, a prominent matron of Ashkenazic heritage, scoffed at the possibility of marriage between her daughter, Richa, and David Gomez, a member of Manhattan's wealthiest Sephardic family: "david Gomez for this Some Years has had an Inclination to Richa but he is such a Stupid wretch that if his fortune was much more and I a begar no child of Mine . . . Should . . . have my Consent And I am Sure, he will never git hers."[126] While

---

[124]Barnet v. Eldert, Feb. 7, 1765, *Orders in Chancery, May 13, 1740 to Mar. 30, 1770*, 217–18. Jane Barnet subsequently had to sue her own kinsmen to ensure that she received the interest from her inheritance. See Executors of Lucas Eldert v. Jane Barnet, Chancery Decrees, E 13, Aug. 28, 1765. Barnet by Eldert v. Eldert, Sept. 1, 1765, *Orders in Chancery, 1740 to 1770*, 240. Barnet and Another v. Executors of Lucas Eldert, Chancery Records, BM-417-B, May 15, 1770, New York County Clerk's Office.

[125]Hershkowitz, *Wills of New York Jews*, Oct. 17, 1706, 8–9; Oct. 22, 1776, 158–59; July 2, 1763, 118–20.

[126]Abigail Franks to Napthali Franks, Dec. 5, 1742, in Leo Hershkowitz, ed., *Letters of the Franks Family (1733–1748)* (Waltham, Mass.: American Jewish Historical Society, 1968), 110. See the editor's introduction for biographical information and an overview of New York City's Jewish population.

Richa apparently never married, her two brothers, Napthali and Moses, wed their first cousins.

Given her strong sense of Jewish identity, Abigail Franks was greatly disappointed that two of her children wed outside the faith. Writing to her son Napthali, she expressed shock upon learning of the secret marriage of her daughter Phila to Oliver De Lancey. Undoubtedly fearing her parents' disapproval, Phila had lived at home for six months after the marriage without informing the family of her change in status. She finally left in March 1743 in order to live with her husband—probably at his country estate in Bloomingdale just north of the city. Abigail's letter written soon after these events recounts her "Severe Affliction": "I can hardly hold my Pen whilst I am writing. . . . Itts wath I Never could have Imagined Especially affter wath I heard her Soe often Say that noe Consideration in Life should Ever Induce her to Disoblige Such good parents." Abigail would not accept the consolation of Christian friends "whoe allow She has DisObliged Us but in noe way bin Dishonorable being married to a man of worth and Character."[127] Refusing her son-in-law's repeated requests to see her, she vowed not to set eyes upon her daughter again or even to allow other family members to see her. After her son David married a Christian, she expressed a similar attitude in another letter to Napthali: "As to wath you Say of david doe Just As you think proper[.] for my part if I cant throw him from My heart I Will by my Conduct have the Appearance of it."[128]

Though Abigail Franks would have nothing to do with Phila, her husband, Jacob, decided not to harm his daughter by alienating the powerful De Lancey family. He therefore asked his son residing in London to remit Phila's inheritance of one thousand pounds bequeathed to her by her late uncle Isaac who had lived in England. The will specified that the legacy be paid when Phila came of age or married, provided that she wed with her father's and uncle Aaron's consent. Jacob Franks felt bound to explain to his son why he favored paying the legacy even though he disapproved of his daughter's actions:

> It may seem strange to you t[ha]t I should Desire ye same but if you concedor wee live in a Small place & he [i.e., Oliver De Lancey] is Related to ye best family in ye place & though yr sister has Accted so very UnDutyfull yet it would Give Me & family a great Deall of Trouble was she to be Ill Used by her husband or Relations which at present is other ways, but should he be kep[t] from Said mony . . . it might be other ways[.] he Seems

127Ibid., June 7, 1743, 116–17.
128Ibid., Nov. 25, 1745, 131.

to be a Carefull Young Man & will Not spend his Estate all which I would have you Mention to yr Uncle Aaron.[129]

Phila De Lancey had seven children by her husband, who later served as a British officer during the revolutionary war. After the conflict the family fled to England, where Phila died in 1811.

A mere five parents in colonial Manhattan disinherited any of their children by last will and testament. Those testators who took this extreme measure felt bound to give a token bequest in order to satisfy an heir's potential claims against the estate. Hendrick Bosch, a sword cutler, gave just one shilling to each of two married daughters, Hillegonda and Dorothy, because of their "Stubborn & disobedient carriage towards me these many yeares." He further castigated Hillegonda for her "Scandalous & unclean way of living."[130] Widow Marite Aertsen was one of those few parents who used their wills to both punish and reward particular children. Her youngest son, Johannes, accused of being an "undutiful child," received just one shilling "and no more in full of all pretences that he shall or may claim to all or any part of my estate." She then awarded all her personal estate to her daughter Wyntie "for her dutiful care and attendance and trouble which she hath and may have with me." It is striking that the widow disinherited Johannes while awarding his children a major portion of her real estate.[131] Though expressing her disapproval of her son, she still felt committed to assist his heirs, her own lineal descendants.

Though very few parents categorically disinherited children, a greater number threatened recalcitrant heirs with the loss of property if they acted disobediently. Dutch New Yorkers were especially apt to adopt this tactic in wills written during the early colonial era. Between 1664 and 1775, twenty-eight wills deprived children or grandchildren of certain benefits if they failed to follow the testator's wishes. Ten of these documents were executed by Dutch burghers or their wives from 1679 to 1710, a period of political and social turmoil. Because provincial law was so uncertain during this era, some colonists felt bound to secure their final wishes against any potential legal challenge—even from their own children. The threat of disinheritance—though virtually unknown in New Netherland wills—became fairly common as a means to guard against foreign customs, especially primogeniture. As Dutch New Yorkers adjusted to English law, they gradually learned how they might

---

[129]Jacob Franks to Napthali Franks, Nov. 22, 1743, in Hershkowitz, *Letters of the Franks Family*, 124–25.
[130]N.Y. Wills, 1st ser., no. 299, Apr. 27, 1701.
[131]Ibid., no. 1009, Apr. 8, 1730.

achieve their own personal goals through properly executed testaments. Though parents in eighteenth-century New York continued to counsel individual children against disobedient behavior, they seldom issued a direct warning against heirs who challenged their wills' legitimacy.

Before 1710 several colonists linked their children's compliance with parental wishes to their obedience to God. Steeped in Calvinist culture, the Dutch were particularly likely to couple moral advice to their children with the threat of punishment for disobedience. Johanna De Bruyn, a wealthy widow, requested that her heirs "rest contented with my disposition of my estate . . . without difference of its being unequally shared or otherwise[,] as they will expect God to bless them." She then demanded that her daughter Katalina relinquish all claim to her deceased uncle's and father's estates since her share had already been "considerably overpaid." If Katalina and her husband failed to comply, they were to be denied all benefits, including forgiveness for debts that they still owed the widow.[132] Johanna De Bruyn's testament reminds us that the term "patriarchy" is inadequate to describe the Dutch colonial family. Widowed mothers were as likely as fathers to institute disciplinary measures against children.

William Beekman is a good example of a Dutch patriarch of the early colonial era. Arriving as a young man in New Amsterdam in 1646, he accumulated a substantial estate and became a perennial municipal leader under both Dutch and English rule. Declaring his will in 1701, the seventy-eight-year-old widower divided most of his estate equally among his four sons and granddaughter Magdalena, heir of a deceased child. Though offering his eldest son, Henry, the right of first refusal to the family house and brewery, he threatened to deny him one-third of his inheritance if Henry himself claimed any birthright. The testator also warned all heirs that they would forfeit their shares if they violated or opposed any provision of his will. Beekman followed a typical procedure by ordering that any disobedient heir's property be equally divided among the other claimants. He then admonished his sons and granddaughter to avoid any discord in dividing the estate "which the Lord in his Mercy hath lent me":

> So that my desire after my decease [is] that you receive it [the inheritance] from God with a Thankfull and Contented mind and pray to God to bless it to you all and Every one of your own posterity: The Same Advice that Joseph gave to his Brethren I leave among you all and that is Se[e] you fall not out by the way: Whilst you live in this world Se[e] that ye be kindly,

---

[132]Ibid., no. 409, Nov. 30, 1709.

Affectionate one towards another: that what by Gods Blessing I Advanced
I have Endeavored and Laboured to Gaine it honestly so would I have you
to do, and so keep faith and Good Conscience always.[133]

Colonial fathers implicitly recognized that having a disinherited son
was worse than having a recalcitrant one still subject to parental discipline. They occasionally maintained their power after death by appointing executors as overseers of their children's behavior. Lewis Bongrand,
a Huguenot merchant, ordered his executors to invest the proceeds of
his estate for the benefit of his eighteen-year-old son, Lewis Jr., and he
also requested that they pay Lewis the annual income in quarterly installments after he came of age. If the boy should "Waste" or "Dissipate" the
interest, however, they were to withhold successive payments and finally
to deny him any money if he continued for several years "to lead not a
life agreeable to God and Man." Bongrand hoped that God would "In-
spire" his son to abandon seafaring and dreams of privateering for a
trade by which he could earn a "Decent Livelyhood." (It is quite remarkable that there was but one will of this type written in colonial Manhattan, a major port.) The testator hesitated to disinherit Lewis, an only
child, as much out of concern for future descendants as for the young
man's welfare. If young Lewis returned from the sea, he was to receive
only a life-interest in the estate. The inheritance would descend automatically to his lawful issue at death. Lewis Bongrand the elder even
granted this bequest in a conditional form. He allowed his son a mere
ten pounds if he wed an Indian or Negro woman—perhaps the ultimate
horror to a colonist concerned with his lineage. Failing legitimate issue,
the Huguenot church of New York was to receive the bulk of the estate.
The will also disinherited Lewis if it was discovered that he had married
without his father's knowledge or consent.[134]
Lewis Bongrand the younger apparently never returned to New York.
His name is absent from colonial probate records, tax rolls, and the
register of city freemen. His father's will was not typical because it openly
expressed anxieties that were usually left unstated, at least in written
form. The great majority of parents sought to influence their offspring
without threatening them with disinheritance.

[133]Ibid., no. 233, Dec. 13, 1701. See also Philip L. White, *The Beekmans of New York in
Politics and Commerce, 1647–1877* (New York: New-York Historical Society, 1956).
[134]N.Y. Wills, 1st ser., no. 193, Oct. 24, 1709.

# Chapter 5

# Kinship and Communal Ties

M ost heads of households naturally focused on the future security and well-being of their wives and children. Although nearly all parents could agree where their principal duties lay, not all persons placed the same importance on less intimate bonds of kinship or friendship. The provision of wills reveal several important ways in which individuals expressed their ties to the wider society around them: by conveying property to their relatives, friends, or acquaintances; by appointing them as executors; by leaving behind a charitable bequest; or by choosing to bequeath slaves to family members or instead to manumit them. Although each of these acts depended partly on individual preference, each was also directly influenced by the testator's family circumstances, economic position, or ethnic origin.

## BEQUESTS TO KIN, FRIENDS, AND ACQUAINTANCES

Apart from a testator's spouse and children, all other beneficiaries fall into three general categories: kin, friends, and acquaintances. Since most men and women specified how they were related to their heirs, one can usually distinguish among various types of kin, both persons related by blood and those related through marriage. The term "friend," used in many wills to designate an heir, poses greater problems of definition. During the eighteenth century, a small number of New York testators directly referred to their kin as "friends." Regnier Tongrelou, a merchant who had no children, left his entire estate to his wife and directed that it be distributed after her death "between my friends and her friends being the next in blood."[1] Thomas Valentine bequeathed all of his property to his wife, Mary, but also requested "that as soon after the settlement of my estate is finished, she return to her friends in Ireland."[2] Much more commonly, however, the term "friend" referred to a close personal acquaintance who was not related through ties of kinship. Thus one Paul Richard, a merchant, ordered his executors to give "a complete suit of mourning to my worthy friend Elizabeth Sharpas," a single woman, "for her to remember me by and as a token of the good will I have always born [sic] to her, as my spouse's intimate friend and acquaintance." James Jarvis, a hatter, similarly appointed his wife, brother, "and my friend and partner" Isaac Stoutenburgh as the executors of his estate.[3]

A final category of heirs consisted of persons who were identified neither by a term of kinship nor by the designation "friend." George Norton, a butcher, appointed his wife and nephew as beneficiaries but also left fifty pounds to one Mr. Samuel Pennant and ten pounds to a Mrs. Stales.[4] Since terms of kinship were used so commonly in wills, even to describe distant relatives, one can assume that other heirs were not related to the testator. For lack of a more precise term, such persons can be considered acquaintances, as opposed to kin or friends of the deceased.

The inheritance of kin, friends, and acquaintances depended largely on the nature of a testator's own familial responsibilities. Although most fathers left property to their wives and children alone, a considerable number of men left substantial bequests to their grandchildren—typically as heirs of a deceased child. Leonard De Grauw divided nearly all his property into five equal parts: one share to each of his three children and two sets of grandchildren, the heirs of his deceased son Isaac and daughter Aryantie. According to this common method of distribution, each grandchild acquired an equal portion of his deceased parent's inheritance. Like nearly all Dutch colonists, De Grauw bequeathed the same amount of property to each set of grandchildren, whether the heirs of a son or daughter.[5]

By leaving property to their grandchildren, parents expressed a

[1]N.Y. Wills, 1st ser., no. 403, Nov. 1, 1708.
[2]Ibid., Liber 29:46–47, Dec. 2, 1773.
[3]Ibid., Liber 20:151–57, Mar. 9, 1749, codicil Sept. 19, 1756; Liber 29:242, Aug. 1772.
[4]Ibid., 1st ser., no. 364, May 1, 1715.
[5]Ibid., Liber 15:584–87, Apr. 5, 1739. This manner of division was common among virtually all ethnic groups. See the wills of Obadiah Hunt and Ronald MacDougal. N.Y. Wills, Liber 22:236–38, Jan. 26, 1760; Liber 24:346–48, Mar. 1, 1763.

strong sense of obligation to their lineal descendants, even to heirs who had not yet been born. Jacobus Goelet, a shopkeeper, granted his widow the use of his estate and directed that his properties be apportioned equally among his children upon her death. Should any of his sons or daughters die before the division, however, their shares would pass to any children they might have "in Lawful Marriage."[6] This rule of inheritance was formally adopted by an Act of Assembly of 1774 that governed the succession to personal property. Should a man die intestate, his widow would receive one-third of his personal estate and the remainder would be equally divided among his children "and such Persons as legally represent [any deceased] . . . children."[7]

Although about 15 percent of all fathers bequeathed property to their grandchildren, more than half of all widowed mothers did so. This marked disparity is largely attributable to the advanced age of many widows. Since the average female testator was considerably older than her male counterpart, she was naturally far more likely to name grandchildren in her testament.[8] The distinctive family responsibilities of elderly widows also encouraged this pattern of bequests. Mary Ricketts had survived her husband, William, for almost five years when she executed a will in May 1740. Since her eldest son had already inherited a plantation in the West Indies, she reserved most of her estate for her unwed daughter, Elizabeth, and the children of her two married daughters. Other widows also advanced the fortunes of adult children while promoting their grandchildren's future prosperity.[9]

New York City testators seldom left any property to persons other than their wives, children, or grandchildren. Among 823 fathers, only 111 made such bequests throughout the English colonial era. Just 29 (or 3.5 percent of the entire group) offered a major portion of the estate to either kin or other persons beyond this narrow family circle. City residents were, however, considerably more likely to make such bequests

[6]N.Y. Wills, 1st ser., no. 1156, Sept. 15, 1722. Through another fairly common procedure, parents allowed their children a life-interest in certain properties but stipulated that the inheritance descend to any "lawful issue" that their offspring might have.

[7]Charles Z. Lincoln, comp., *The Colonial Laws of the State of New York*, 5 vols. (Albany: J. B. Lyon, 1894), 5:616–17. This law followed the same procedures as the English Statute of Distribution of 1670. See Herbert Alan Johnson, "English Statutes in Colonial New York," *New York History* 58 (1977): 285–86; Alison Reppy and Leslie J. Tompkins, *Historical and Statutory Background of the Law of Wills: Descent and Distribution, Probate and Administration* (Chicago: Callaghan and Co., 1923), 91–92.

[8]From 1664 through 1775, 823 fathers and 147 mothers executed wills in New York City. While 125 fathers (or 15.2 percent) designated grandchildren as beneficiaries, 78 mothers (53.1 percent) did so.

[9]N.Y. Wills, Liber 14:344–46, May 16, 1740. See also the wills of Mary Teller, Allette Douw, and Niesie Vinge. N.Y. Wills, 1st ser., no. 278, Nov. 1701; no. 608, Mar. 29, 1709; no. 611, June 24, 1716.

than Hudson Valley or Long Island farmers, whose loyalties centered almost exclusively on the homestead. In general, New York City men followed typical colonial practice in sharing wealth with members of the nuclear family or their lineal descendants alone.[10]

Even when testators expressed an obligation to their collateral kin, they seldom bestowed such generous legacies upon these heirs as they left to their children or grandchildren. Geertie Jans Van Langedyck bequeathed fifty pounds to her "cousins" Jan and Tryntie, the children of her deceased brother Peter; she set aside the remainder of her estate, including two highly treasured Dutch Bibles, for her orphaned grand-children, the heirs of her daughter Janneke and her son-in-law Frans Cornelissen, both deceased.[11] One Luis Gomez, a Jewish merchant, left most of his property to his five sons but directed that they pay an annuity of twenty-five pounds to his unmarried sister Ellenor. Should she prefer to live with the testator's "family," however, the will offered her "a Suffi-cient Maintenance" instead of a yearly sum. Luis Gomez clearly dis-tinguished between his obligation to support an unwed sister and his duty to transmit his wealth to his "family," his surviving children alone. Although he permitted his sister to use the services of a Negro woman, he directed that the slave descend to his sons upon her death.[12]

The commitment to children before kin did not necessarily extend to offspring born outside of wedlock. Although only a handful of fathers mentioned illegitimate children in their wills, nearly all these men chose to leave substantial bequests to other relatives. Thomas Walton, a wealthy merchant, granted a tract of land and £2,000 to his "natural son" James, but he also set aside several large sums for his kin: £500 for his mother, a total of £2,000 for three sisters, and £250 for each of his godchildren (his brothers' and sisters' children). He granted the re-mainder of his estate to his four brothers and appointed them as his executors. James Wright, a mariner, followed a similar course by be-queathing a substantial portion to his "natural son" James, but leaving most of his property to his two sisters' children.[13] These few wills suggest that fathers recognized their obligations to their illegitimate children but

[10]For evidence from specific colonies see Toby L. Ditz, *Property and Kinship: Inheritance in Early Connecticut, 1750–1820* (Princeton: Princeton University Press, 1986), 52–56; Carole Shammas, Marylynn Salmon, and Michel Dahlin, *Inheritance in America: From Colonial Times to the Present* (New Brunswick: Rutgers University Press, 1987), 48; John E. Crowley, "The Importance of Kinship: Testamentary Evidence from South Carolina," *Journal of Inter-disciplinary History* 16 (1986): 559–77.

[11]N.Y. Wills, 1st ser., no. 987, Sept. 5, 1702.

[12]Leo Hershkowitz, ed., *Wills of Early New York Jews (1704–1799)* (New York: American Jewish Historical Society, 1976), 62–63.

[13]N.Y. Wills, Liber 28:477–78, May 9, 1771, codicil May 18, 1772; Liber 36:468–70, May 31, 1770.

declined to support them to the same extent as their "lawful issue."
There is little direct evidence, however, of parents who willfully applied
the harsh rule of the common law that a "bastard can *inherit* nothing,
being looked upon as the son of nobody."[14]

Should a man leave behind a wife but no children, his relatives or
closest friends would sometimes inherit a major share of his estate. In
these cases, however, the testator's beneficiaries would not generally receive their full legacies until the widow's death or remarriage. This manner of division was fairly common because it allowed a man to fulfill his
primary obligations to his wife while also securing his estate for eventual
transfer to his nearest relations. Many married men dispensed, however,
with even this guarded commitment to their kin. Among all testators
who named a wife but no children, nearly two-thirds appointed the
widow as their sole heir.[15]

Some husbands were compelled by circumstances to arrange an immediate division of property among all their heirs. Lewis Rivard left the
greatest portion of his estate to his wife but ordered "that my dear
mother, Mary Rivard, shall take to herself all that she brought into the
house, viz., her bed and bedstead, two pewter dishes, a [pair of] bellows,
a pot hook and her clothes and linnen. And she shall have one third of
the price of two boats by me built when sold." Although Rivard did not
expressly state why he included such specific instructions in his will, he
may have feared that his wife and mother would no longer be able to live
peaceably together after his death. Should his mother choose (or be
forced) to leave her daughter-in-law's house, she would at least be able to
claim all her own household articles and an additional legacy. Since her
son regarded his marital obligations as his primary concern, however, his
wife would acquire the greater portion of the estate.[16]

The decision to bequeath property to one's immediate family inevita-
bly meant that more distant kin would receive little or no benefit.
Throughout the colonial period, only twenty-seven men made provision
in their wills for their wives' children by previous marriages. Although it
is impossible to determine how many testators could have left property
to stepchildren, it is almost certain that a considerable majority of these
men reserved all their possessions for their own offspring.

---

[14]Sir William Blackstone, *Commentaries on the Laws of England*, ed. James DeWitt Andrews, 4th ed., 2 vols. (Chicago: Callaghan and Co., 1899), 1, bk. 2:248. The stigma of
bastardy did not generally apply to children who had been "begotten" out of wedlock but
whose parents had married several months later. None of the New York testators who
mentioned "natural" or illegitimate children had married the mothers of these offspring.

[15]Throughout the colonial era, 240 men wrote wills that mentioned a wife but no
children. Eighty bequeathed property to individuals besides their spouses. Only 52 among
all 240 (or 21.7 percent) left a major share of the estate to someone other than a wife.

[16]N.Y. Wills, 1st ser., no. 273, Aug. 31, 1703.

Only the city's early Dutch settlers showed any inclination to bestow similar amounts of property on their wives' kin as on their own relations. Otto Van Tuyl directed that all his possessions descend to his three children after his widow's death, but he also arranged the succession to the estate should all his heirs die before attaining their majority. In that case, he ordered a partition of all property into two equal shares: one-half to be divided equally among his own brothers and sisters, the other half to be distributed among his wife's siblings in the same manner.[17] Like several other Dutch colonists, Van Tuyl acted on the principle that husband and wife possessed an equal claim to a common estate and that each spouse's heirs merited the same portion of property if the couple died without any children. Although this type of bequest was quite common before 1725, it very seldom appears in wills executed during the mid-eighteenth century. With the passing of the traditional Dutch custom of community property, husbands no longer felt an obligation to give any part of their estate to the wife's kin. (Under the English common law, a wife's heirs could only succeed to lands that she held in her own right, not to any personal property that she brought to her husband upon marriage.)[18]

Less than 4 percent of either men or women bequeathed any of their possessions to their mothers or fathers, probably because few testators failed to survive their parents. Rather than acquire full ownership over their children's property, several elderly parents were granted the use of their inheritance during the remainder of life. Thomas Marston, a merchant, set aside the annual interest on five hundred pounds for his "honored mother" and directed that the principal be distributed among his relations after her death.[19] Children were somewhat more likely to grant this type of legacy to their mothers than to their fathers, probably because mothers tended to have a greater need for some assured means of support during their old age.

Apart from a man's wife, children, and grandchildren, his most likely heirs were kin who were most closely related by blood, particularly brothers, sisters, or their children. Testators adopted various strategies in dividing property among these relations. Some men chose to grant substantial legacies solely to their nephews and nieces, whether or not the heirs' parents were still alive. One Raphael Goelet left most of his

---

[17]Ibid., no. 186, Nov. 12, 1707. See also the wills of Cornelius Steenwyck and Tymen Van Borsum. N.Y. Wills, Liber 19B:135–40, Nov. 20, 1684; 1st ser., no. 280, July 10, 1702. For a somewhat different procedure, see the will of Brandt Schuyler, no. 688, Jan. 11, 1701.

[18]W. S. Holdsworth, *A History of English Law*, 3d ed. rewritten, 13 vols. (Boston: Little, Brown, 1922–52), 3:525–27.

[19]N.Y. Wills, Liber 14:137–39, Sept. 9, 1740. See also the wills of Thomas Noble and Lydia Thorne. Liber 15:508–11, July 27, 1745; Liber 38:386–87, Feb. 6, 1761.

estate to his wife and directed that it descend upon her death to the children of his three brothers and deceased sister.[20] Other men preferred to transfer their possessions directly to their brothers and sisters, granting additional shares to the children of deceased siblings only. Henry Beekman, a bachelor, ordered the division of his estate into seven equal parts: one share each for his two brothers, three sisters, and two sets of orphaned heirs, the children of his deceased brothers Christopher and Jacobus.[21] This last method of distribution corresponded to the laws of intestate succession to personal property. Should a single person die without leaving a will, his movable goods would be apportioned equally among his brothers, sisters, and the children of any deceased siblings. Nephews and nieces would each receive an equal part of their deceased parent's full share.[22]

As in dividing property among their children or grandchildren, most testators arranged a fairly equitable division of property among their siblings. Of some thirty-five men who left real estate to their brothers and sisters, only four strongly favored their male over their female relations. Although the testator's brothers or nephews sometimes received an additional bequest, his sisters or nieces were seldom neglected.[23]

Several testators, particularly men without children of their own, demonstrated a clear preference for those male heirs who bore their name. Frederick De Peyster left one hundred pounds to each of three nephews but conveyed most of his estate to his namesake, one of his brother James's younger sons. Samuel Boyd, a tailor, divided his possessions among both his brothers and sisters, but left an additional ten pounds to "every brother's son that is named after me." One William Cox made a legacy to Samuel Bradley (his wife's brother) conditional upon a certain promise: "If God send my brother in law an heir, he shall call his name Cox Bradley and his children after him the same name."[24]

Although single women often gave property to their male kin, several "spinsters" placed a particular importance on the inheritance of their nearest female relations. Margaret Gouverneur named her brother Nicholas as an executor, gave relatively small legacies to her brother

---

[20]Ibid., Liber 16:227–29, Dec. 23, 1747.

[21]Ibid., Liber 15:91–92, June 19, 1727.

[22]Lincoln, *Colonial Laws*, 5:616–17, Mar. 1774.

[23]See the will of William Johnston in N.Y. Wills, Liber 29:7, Jan. 17, 1772. In addition to 31 men who left a major portion of realty to both brother(s) and sister(s), 55 men selected either group of siblings alone as their principal heirs: 34 testators chose their brother(s) exclusively, 21 testators chose their sister(s) alone. Unfortunately, one can seldom determine if these 55 men singled out either group of siblings for special treatment; some men may have simply had no surviving brothers or sisters.

[24]Ibid., Liber 29:5–6, Aug. 10, 1773; Liber 20:219–21, Feb. 7, 1757; 1st ser., no. 64, July 15, 1689.

Samuel and nephew Isaac, and reserved the greatest portion of her estate for five of her sister's daughters. Although she did not expressly state her reasons for making these bequests, one can safely assume that Gouverneur felt a special bond of kinship to and empathy for these nieces.[25] In some cases, female relations or friends may have also received preferential treatment because they could best utilize the household articles, apparel, and other personal effects that single women left behind at death. Catharine Bratt divided her estate among her brothers' and sisters' children but left a favorite niece all of her household goods and kitchenware.[26]

Some evidence indicates that elderly widows and single women became especially dependent on the care and assistance of their closest female kin and friends. Jane Crowley, the widow of a blacksmith and eighty-four years old when she made her will, left her house and lot to "my Dear and Well beloved Daughter Cornelia" in "consideration of the Great Trouble and Fatigue . . . she has had with me for these many Years in attending me, with many distinguished marks of her love and Affection." Elinor Bayne, a single woman, gave "all my Rings Buchels Buttons and all my other Silver and Gold Plate . . . to my loving Sister Mary Fox for her kind and tender Treatment of me During my Sickness." Mary Brockholst, a widow with no surviving children, divided most of her estate among her nephews and nieces but also set aside all of her clothing and household furniture for her "friend" Mrs. Mary Stuyvesant, "as a mark of my esteem and for the kindness and attention she has shown to me during my illness."[27] These wills suggest that female companionship was a highly prized asset to widows and single women, even to well-to-do women who could undoubtedly afford to pay for medical assistance. It should be emphasized that women were generally more likely than men to bequeath property to their kin or acquaintances. Among 125 widowed mothers who wrote wills from 1664 through 1775, 29 (or 23 percent) offered legacies to beneficiaries other than their children or grandchildren.

---

[25]Ibid., Liber 23:415–17, Nov. 4, 1758. For a brief genealogy of the Gouverneur family, see Edwin R. Purple, *Contributions to the History of Ancient Families of New Amsterdam and New York* (New York: privately printed, 1881), 19–20. Seven single women named their brothers or their brothers' children among their principal heirs. Ten single women left most of their property to their sisters or sisters' daughters. Of all twenty-eight single women who left wills, only five bequeathed substantial legacies to nonrelatives.

[26]Ibid., Liber 26:132–33, June 15, 1765. See also the will of Sarah Saunders, Liber 15:304–5, Apr. 29, 1743.

[27]Ibid., 1st ser., no. 1146, Apr. 30, 1728; Liber 28:378, Oct. 28, 1772; Liber 37:318–19, Mar. 9, 1775. In all six cases in which women left this kind of bequest, they appointed females as their beneficiaries.

The appointment of heirs followed a generally consistent pattern: lineal descendants before collateral kin, collateral kin before any persons related through marriage. Despite the prevalence of these customary patterns, the bequest of property was also a highly personal matter that reflected individual needs and concerns. John Moore, a wealthy merchant, conveyed his estate to his wife and nine children but decided to add a codicil after learning of his eldest son's unexpected death:

> I have been informed by Letters from my . . . son John's partner at Jamaica and others that in his late sickness not long before his death he declared he would make his Will and give the chiefest part of what he had unto his three maiden sisters Rebecca Susanna and Anne who he said were not so well able to provide for themselves as his Brothers were and that his eldest sister Frances being married was already well provided for.

In order to grant the dying man's "design and intention" as far "as in my power lies," John Moore bequeathed his eldest son's entire portion of personal property to these three young women.[28] Some men clearly believed that female kin, particularly if widowed or unwed, merited an additional share of their estate.

Though some testators acted out of sympathy for needy female relatives, other men did not hesitate to entrust major executory duties to women. After his eldest son and namesake died, Harmanus Rutgers hoped to leave his brewery to his grandson Robert, the deceased heir's eldest son. Since all of the testator's grandchildren were still minors, however, he authorized his son's widow, Elizabeth, to operate the business "so long as she shall Remain . . . unmarried." His will of 1750 directed that she possess

> All that my now Dwelling House Store House Malt house Brew house and Negro Kitchen . . . Together with all and Singular my Brewing Kettle Fatts [i.e., vats] Bags drays Wagons Casks Barrells Horses and all other Implements . . . belonging to or used with my aforesaid Brewhouse . . . for her Support and maintenance and to Support maintain bring up and educate the said children now Living of my said Son Harmanus by her begotten.[29]

Rutgers's will furnishes yet another example of women's economic responsibility within Manhattan's Dutch community during the mid-1700s.

It is especially important to note that Elizabeth Rutgers's privileges extended until her death or remarriage rather than merely to the point when her eldest son reached adulthood. Having asked his daughter-in-

---

[28]Ibid., Liber 17:44–51, Sept. 4, 1748, codicil Feb. 23, 1750.
[29]Ibid., Liber 18:347–55, June 26, 1750.

law to assume the responsibility of operating the brewery, Harmanus Rutgers may have felt obliged to prolong her authority, even at the price of delaying his grandson's inheritance. Elizabeth Rutgers gained possession of the brewery in 1753 and evidently operated the business for some time before deciding to lease it to her eldest son, Robert, the designated heir.[30] In this manner she continued to reap some of the profits of the enterprise while relinquishing the burden of management. Since her eldest son was still a tenant when he drafted his own will in 1770, he had to postpone any transfer of the brewery to his own heirs until after his mother's death. Elizabeth Rutgers finally died at the age of eighty-four in 1795, several years after bequeathing her estate to her two surviving daughters.[31]

Although relatives usually inherited property according to their degree of kinship to the testator, some heirs received preferential treatment because of special ties of affection or interest. Paul Richard conveyed much of his estate to his brothers' and sisters' children but gave an additional portion to one niece, "as she has been brought up in my family, and behaved herself dutiful."[32] In another case, one Samuel Bradley explained why he limited bequests to his own father and brother in favor of his brother-in-law, William Kidd, an influential Manhattan resident and a privateer who would soon become a notorious pirate:

> Whereas my loving brother in Law Capt'n William Kid, hath been very Carefull of me and hath Likewise for my Encouradgement now in my minority at my desire and request advanced and paid unto me the Summ of one hundred and fourty pounds ... which I now imploy in trade and merchandize, for and in Consideration of his So greate Love unto me as well as in recompense & in full satisfaction of the Said Summ of money ... I doe give and bequeath to my said Loving brother in Law [my share of a house on Wall Street and several city lots].[33]

[30]Although the date of the lease is not known, there is evidence that the widow still operated the brewery in 1757, four years after her father-in-law's death. On April 21, 1757, Colonel James Montressor recorded a payment of five pounds to "widow Rutgers's clerk for Beer." See G. D. Scull, "The Montressor Journals," in *Collections of the New-York Historical Society for the Year 1881* 14 (1882): 12.

[31]Robert Rutgers's will is found in N.Y. Wills, Liber 42:571–73, July 11, 1770, probate issued Jan. 18, 1798. Elizabeth Rutgers's will is in Liber 41:610, June 16, 1789. The Rutgers brewery itself was occupied by a British merchant during the Revolutionary war and subsequently destroyed by fire. Elizabeth Rutgers's suit for damages under the state Trespass Act occasioned Alexander Hamilton's famous legal argument against state laws in violation of federal treaties. For a brief analysis of the trial, see Forrest McDonald, *Alexander Hamilton: A Biography* (New York: Norton, 1979), 64–69.

[32]N.Y. Wills, Liber 20:151–57, Mar 9, 1749, codicil Sept. 19, 1756.

[33]Ibid., 1st ser., no. 268, July 5, 1693. For an excellent account of Kidd's activities, see Robert C. Ritchie, *Captain Kidd and the War against the Pirates* (Cambridge: Harvard University Press, 1986).

Although we should not doubt that Samuel Bradley felt a deep sense of affection for William Kidd, it is interesting to note how he equated his brother-in-law's love with the granting of a much-needed loan. Parents might be expected to manifest their love with gifts to their children, but an in-law's generosity surely could not be taken for granted. Bradley evidently did not accept this favor as an outright gift but instead viewed it as a sum he was obligated to repay.

The tendency to bequeath property beyond one's immediate family varied considerably according to a person's economic status, occupational background, and ethnic origin. Among all occupational groups, merchants and well-to-do professional men were the most likely to name heirs in addition to their own wives, children, and grandchildren. Even in these groups, however, most men confined their bequests to their spouses and lineal descendants (see Table 5.1). In some cases, the bestowal of gifts served as both a symbol of mourning and a token of friendship. Peter De Riemer named his wife and son as his principal heirs, gave a Negro girl and a suit of mourning to his sister, and left "my well beloved Brother . . . a gunn, and Pare of Pistoles the gunn being writ on . . . with my Name." Robert Watts reserved his most treasured personal belongings for his children alone but also gave a gold ring to five of his male and female friends.[34] Since mourning rings and apparel were often given to guests at funerals, the inclusion of these items in a will indicates that the testator wished to express a special bond of closeness to the recipients.

Some persons clearly intended that such gifts serve a commemorative purpose in the most literal sense—to remind the recipients of their obligations to the deceased man's family. William Bickley, a Quaker and wealthy shopkeeper, appointed his only child, Abraham, as his principal heir and sole executor, but he also requested the assistance of "my much respected friends," the merchants Richard Willett and Walter Thong,

> Desiring them whom I have found to bear Cordiall & Loving Kindness towards me, yt they Continue ye same favourable Kindness towards my son Abraham & afford him their best Advice & Councill in his Administration of this my Last Will & Testament, & that they accept from him One of ye best beaver hatt yt can be gott for money to Each of [them] to weare in remembrance of this my last request unto them.[35]

Hoping to achieve a similar end, Abraham De Peyster left substantial

---

[34]Ibid., no. 706, Dec. 17, 1725; Liber 28:308–9, Aug. 21, 1771. Although merchants and very wealthy men were the most likely to bequeath gifts of mourning, less well-to-do persons also followed this custom. See the wills of Richard Elliot (Ellett), cooper, and Edward Marshall, tailor. N.Y. Wills, 1st ser., no. 105, May 13, 1693; no. 261, Apr. 18, 1704.
[35]Ibid., no. 232, July 3, 1707.

**Table 5.1** Heirs named by testators within seven occupational groups

| Profession | N* | Testators naming additional heirs | |
|---|---|---|---|
| | | N | % |
| Professionals** | 95 | 25 | 26.3 |
| Merchants | 247 | 52 | 21.0 |
| Shopkeepers | 69 | 13 | 18.8 |
| Processors*** | 57 | 10 | 17.5 |
| Mariners | 137 | 20 | 14.6 |
| Artisans | 289 | 36 | 12.4 |
| Laborers | 46 | 5 | 10.9 |

*All testators considered here named a wife and either a child or grandchild.

**Includes attorneys, government officials, ministers, physicians, and persons who identified themselves by the titles of "gentleman" or "esquire."

***Includes men who were primarily concerned with the processing of food and drink: brewers, bakers, butchers, millers (bolters).

legacies to his three brothers and two friends—men who would be directly responsible for overseeing the welfare of his widow and children. He also set aside fifty pounds for his servant Hannah Krugers "for her true and faithfull Service," and promised her an additional thirty pounds "if she shall live with my Wife till ye Time of my . . . Wives [sic] decease."[36] The wills of some affluent men indicate that there were close connections between wealth, personal influence, and the scope of a network of kin and dependents. Because most merchants and professional men bequeathed property to their wives and children alone, only a few members of the colonial elite truly lived up to an old Irish saying: "The higher the man, the more people he has."[37]

Only one small group of testators, members of New York's Jewish community, tended to distribute their property among their relatives and friends as well as their wives and children.[38] Although Samuel Myers Cohen left behind a wife and four young daughters, he still set aside substantial bequests for his siblings and their children: the interest

[36]Ibid., no. 910, Sept. 20, 1702.

[37]See Conrad M. Arensberg and Solon T. Kimball, *Family and Community in Ireland* (Cambridge: Harvard University Press, 1940), 93. This tendency was also apparent in colonial South Carolina. See Crowley, "The Importance of Kinship," 571.

[38]Of twelve Jews who were married or had children, nine named additional heirs in their wills. Seven of the nine men were merchants, one was a shopkeeper, and another was a chandler.

on two hundred pounds for the "support of my brother Emmanuel," twenty-five pounds to each of his three sisters, and one hundred pounds to "my Niece Rose Bunn to be paid her at the day of her marriage provided always that she marries with the consent and approbation of my Wife otherwise not."[39] The need to promote group solidarity and to discourage intermarriage undoubtedly influenced some Jews to cultivate especially close relations with their kindred.

Several Jews possessed a deeply felt sense of obligation to relatives who lived in widely separate areas of the globe. Uriah Hyam, a chandler, left most of his property to his son Andrew "of the Island of Jamaica" but also bequeathed twenty pounds to his brother Enoch, "living in Bohemia."[40] Samuel Levy, a well-to-do merchant who left behind a wife and daughter, ordered his executors "to Remitt and pay out of my Estate to my brother Joseph . . . and his son Isaac Levy of London Merchants . . . the sum of Two Hundred pounds . . . to be Disposed of and Distributed . . . unto and amongst Such of my own poor relations Liveing in Germany as they in their Discretion shall thinke fitt." While Levy's business depended on the services of his kin in England, he also maintained a sense of brotherhood with his poorer relations of the diaspora. Nor did he neglect his familial obligations closer to home. He left an annuity of ten pounds to his mother-in-law and gave another ten pounds to Meriam Hart, "my Brother's Daughter . . . now wife of Moses Hart of the City of New York . . . to Buy a piece of plate in remembrance of me."[41]

One other group of colonists, immigrants from Scotland and Northern Ireland during the mid-eighteenth century, also retained particularly close ties with relatives in their native country. Duncan Brown, a well-to-do mariner, left most of his personal estate to his wife but also set aside "for my well Beloved Nephew Duncan Stone son of Robert Stone begotten on the Body of my sister Ann Brown living at Bellomony, in the County Antrim in Ireland my silver Watch, a silver hilted Sword, shoe and Knee Buckles gold sleeve Buttons and my Coat of Arms and gun." Since Brown had no children of his own, he also named his nephew as heir to all his real estate and "my Picture and Family Bible" after his wife's death.[42] David Young, an innkeeper who died single, authorized bequests that encouraged his kin to emigrate from Ireland to New York. He ordered the sale of most of his estate, granted two-ninths of the proceeds to his brother Samuel, of County Tyrone, and left the re-

[39]Hershkowitz, *Wills of Jews*, 65–68, Aug. 4, 1741.
[40]Ibid., 55–56, Nov. 1, 1740.
[41]Ibid., 27–29, Apr. 28, 1719.
[42]N.Y. Wills, Liber 28:182–83, Dec. 31, 1768.

mainder to "the sons of my brother John and the sons of my sisters, Jane and Mary, such as choose to come to this city . . . if they come within three years."[43]

Bachelors often demonstrated the importance of ties of kinship by appointing relatives as their principal heirs. Common sailors were the only group of single men who tended to bequeath their property to friends or acquaintances rather than their next of kin (see Table 5.2). As one of the most transient and youthful of the city's occupational groups, seamen often had neither wives nor children, nor any nearby relatives to whom they could leave their property after death. These men often prepared wills just before embarking on voyages and thereby granted all future wages and "prize money" to their closest friends or acquaintances. For example, William Flin, who boarded the privateer *Tartar* in 1758, bequeathed all his worldly goods and earnings to one Catherine Metcalf, "spinster."[44] Like nearly all common sailors, Flin executed a will in the simplest terms and did not openly state his motives for granting a legacy. One may wonder whether his "friend" Catherine Metcalf was a mistress on shore, or perhaps even a prostitute who might grant additional favors in return for the promise of a bequest.

Common sailors generally bequeathed their property to either fellow seamen, unmarried female friends or acquaintances, or innkeepers. Vintners and victuallers were likely beneficiaries in their roles as creditors. Since sailors lacked a steady income, they often had to pledge future earnings for their current shelter and fare. When William Topping, a ship surgeon, died intestate, an innkeeper requested that the Prerogative Court allow him to administer the deceased man's estate. The court readily granted this petition since the innkeeper had expended more than nine pounds on Topping's behalf "for sundry quantities of liquor, meat, drink, washing, and lodging . . . and the expenses of his funeral."[45]

## THE APPOINTMENT OF EXECUTORS

Although most men generally distributed their property among their closest relatives, they selected their executors from a much wider social circle. Rather than rely on their blood relatives alone, a considerable

---

[43]Ibid., Liber 27:137–39, Sept. 3, 1769.

[44]Ibid., Liber 21:317, Dec. 1758.

[45]See the petition of William May, Nov. 20, 1717, in Administration of Estates, Albany Court of Appeals, microfilm AAD 4, Paul Klapper Library, Queens College, New York City.

**Table 5.2** Heirs named by single men within four occupational groups

| Occupation* | Friends or acquaintances only | | Kin only | | Kin and friends or acquaintances | | Totals | |
|---|---|---|---|---|---|---|---|---|
| | N | % | N | % | N | % | N | % |
| Mariners | 77 | 68.7 | 29 | 25.9 | 6 | 5.4 | 112 | 100 |
| Professionals | 3 | 23.1 | 4 | 30.8 | 6 | 46.1 | 13 | 100 |
| Artisans | 6 | 22.2 | 19 | 70.4 | 2 | 7.4 | 27 | 100 |
| Merchants | 3 | 7.0 | 24 | 55.8 | 16 | 37.2 | 43 | 100 |

*I have excluded laborers, processors, and shopkeepers from this table because there are less than five cases for each of those professions.

number of testators entrusted this responsibility to their kin through marriage: sons-in-law and brothers-in-law (see Table 5.3). Because of an inconsistent use of terms of kinship, it is sometimes difficult to determine the exact degree of relationship between "in-laws." This suffix might sometimes refer to a stepson or stepbrother rather than a daughter's or a sister's husband. Several persons even dropped the designation "in-law" and identified their kin through marriage as though they were full blood relatives.[46] Despite these ambiguities, terms of kinship were frequently used in our modern sense. A "son-in-law" was usually one's daughter's husband; a brother-in-law was often any one of three relations: one's spouse's brother, one's sister's husband, or the husband of one's spouse's sister.[47]

Unlike most men, women were nearly as likely to appoint daughters as sons to be their executors (see Table 5.4). Since widowed mothers often bequeathed a major share of their household goods and personal effects to their daughters, they may have considered it especially important to allow their female heirs to play a direct role in the settlement of the

[46]See the wills of Ahasuerus Fromanteel and Alexander McBain. N.Y. Wills, 1st ser., no. 150, Apr. 2, 1694; Liber 25:98–100, Apr. 15, 1765. For a reference to affinal kin as blood relations, see the will of Nicholas Garretse. N.Y. Wills, 1st ser., no. 1028, Apr. 10, 1695. In their conversation or correspondence, the Puritans of seventeenth-century New England would often address their affinal kin as though they were full blood relations. New York testators seldom followed this practice, perhaps because the nature of the will required a more precise use of terms of kinship. See Edmund S. Morgan, *The Puritan Family: Religion and Domestic Relations in Seventeenth-Century New England* (1944; rpt. New York: Harper & Row, 1966), 150–60.

[47]Sons-in-law were appointed as executors in some 104 wills left by men and women. In at least 70 of these cases, testators used the term "son-in-law" to refer to their daughters' husbands. I have determined the precise meaning of the term "brother-in-law" in some 68 cases. Twenty-eight were brothers of the testator's spouse; 35 were husbands of the testator's sisters; another 5 were married to the sisters of the testator's spouse.

**Table 5.3** Appointment of relatives and friends as executors by male testators*

| Relation | No. cases appointed | Percent of 1,287 cases appointed | Relation | No. cases appointed | Percent of 1,287 cases appointed |
|---|---|---|---|---|---|
| Wives | 705 | 54.8 | Nephews | 26 | 2.0 |
| Male friends, acquaintances | 505 | 39.2 | Other female kin | 24 | 1.9 |
|  |  |  | Fathers-in-law | 21 | 1.6 |
| Sons | 221 | 17.2 | Mothers | 20 | 1.5 |
| Brothers | 136 | 10.6 | Female friends, | 19 | 1.5 |
| Daughters | 108 | 8.4 | acquaintances |  |  |
| Brothers-in-law | 108 | 8.4 | Fathers | 17 | 1.3 |
| Sons-in-law | 69 | 5.4 | Sisters | 16 | 1.2 |
| Other male kin | 45 | 3.5 | Grandsons | 4 | 0.3 |

*These figures are based on data from 1,287 wills written between 1664 and 1775.

estate. In most cases, however, widows requested that their sons-in-law assume these duties instead of their married daughters.[48] Some mothers thereby acknowledged the superior legal and social status of men within the family. Other women may have simply believed that their sons-in-law possessed necessary managerial skills that especially qualified them to serve as executors.

Both men and women frequently asked their principal female heirs to be executors of the estate. When choosing executors other than their chief beneficiaries, however, nearly all persons preferred their male relatives, friends, or acquaintances. Male friends or acquaintances were named as executors in some 601 wills, a figure surpassed only by the number of widows selected to that position. It is striking that the appointment of executors was shaped by neighborhood and business ties even more than by kinship.

Far from being a random process, the choice of an executor was often influenced by the testator's occupational and economic status. Merchants were, for example, extremely likely to place their trust in fellow traders who were best acquainted with their business affairs. Several men, such as William Butler, even designated one or more persons to undertake these responsibilities for a specific fee: "As it will be necessary to employ Jacob Rhinelander, one of my executors, in the settlement of my estate, he being best acquainted with the condition of my affairs, he shall have a

[48]Sixteen women appointed their married daughters as executors, five women called on the services of their sons-in-law and married daughters, and thirty women requested their sons-in-law to serve rather than their married daughters. For a detailed statistical analysis concerning executors' appointment, see David E. Narrett, "Patterns of Inheritance in Colonial New York City, 1664–1775: A Study in the History of the Family," (Ph.D. diss., Cornell University, 1981), 282–93.

**Table 5.4** Appointment of relatives and friends as executors by female testators*

| Relation | No. cases appointed | Percent of 228 cases appointed | Relation | No. cases appointed | Percent of 228 cases appointed |
|---|---|---|---|---|---|
| Male friends, acquaintances | 96 | 42.1 | Sisters | 12 | 5.3 |
| | | | Female friends, acquaintances | 9 | 3.9 |
| Sons | 50 | 21.9 | Other female kin | 9 | 3.9 |
| Daughters | 40 | 17.5 | | | |
| Sons-in-law | 35 | 15.3 | Grandsons | 8 | 3.5 |
| Other male kin | 29 | 12.7 | Fathers | 3 | 1.3 |
| Brothers-in-law | 20 | 8.8 | Mothers | 3 | 1.3 |
| Brothers | 14 | 6.1 | Fathers-in-law | 3 | 1.3 |

*These figures are based on data from 228 wills written between 1664 and 1775.

reasonable allowance, and the other executors [the testator's wife and son-in-law] are to allow him as they think reasonable."[49]

Because of the complexity of managing a great estate, merchants tended to name several people as executors. The appointment of four or five friends or relatives also served as a form of insurance should any of these men decline to carry out their obligations. Nathaniel Hazard appointed no fewer than seven executors: his wife, his two eldest daughters, a brother-in-law, two fellow merchants, and an attorney. He authorized these individuals, "or the major part of them," to continue his trade "if practicable" and to choose "some proper person" to serve "if necessary . . . as a Clerk or Bookkeeper to assist them." Although Hazard chose his two eldest children to act as executors, he appointed a sufficient number of other persons to counterbalance any possible bias. Should any of his children "endeavor to hinder or embarrass" the family business, those heirs would "be permitted to have no manner of Concern in the Management and direction" of trade. The authority of impartial executors would ensure, in Hazard's words, the continuation of "my present Trade and business in the Interest of my Family" and the "equal advantage Maintenance and Education" of all children.[50]

Seamen often selected executors who were of similar social background to themselves. Thomas Heysham, a prosperous mariner who owned a house and lot, appointed his two "friends," the wealthy merchants Thomas Duncan and James Tucker, as his executors.[51] William

[49]N.Y. Wills, Liber 29:448–49, May 11, 1775. Merchants were virtually the sole occupational group that was at all likely to leave gifts to their executors. A few merchants even set aside as much as 5 percent of the net proceeds of their personal property for this purpose. See the wills of Joshua Delaplaine and Samuel Bowne. Liber 28:87–90, Oct. 1, 1771; Liber 36:272–76, Nov. 5, 1771, codicil Jan. 4, 1784.

[50]Ibid., Liber 25:15–19, July 28, 1759, codicil July 13, 1761.

[51]Ibid., Liber 17:313–14, Jan. 11, 1750.

Murray, who left legacies totaling £1,318 to his wife and son, also called upon the services of reputable merchants, his "friends" Malcolm Campbell and Peter Van Zandt.[52] The needs of common sailors, who often had neither a wife nor children, were much simpler. These men frequently named a fellow mate, a female acquaintance, or an innkeeper as their principal heir *and* executor.

Not all groups showed a marked tendency to appoint executors from a similar occupational or economic status. While some artisans entrusted their affairs to men who worked at the same trade or a closely related skill, many others reached out to "friends" of a higher economic status: merchants or attorneys. This practice probably reflects the desire of middle-class men to appoint those who possessed a considerable degree of legal knowledge or managerial skills. It is also possible that craftsmen may have appointed professionals as executors when the latter were their creditors or were in a position to perform some special service for their families.

Because the selection of an executor was a highly personal process, it is often not possible to identify one determinative influence among several factors: ethnic and religious ties, associations at work or through neighborhood, and not least, a high degree of trust between friends or close acquaintances. It is clear, however, that New York City men overwhelmingly chose executors of the same national origin during the early colonial era. This practice diminished considerably after 1720 as colonists grew more accustomed to a pluralistic society and as the frequency of intermarriage increased. The importance of ethnic ties declined most markedly among the city's merchants, a group described by Virginia Harrington as "an aristocracy of wealth rather than lineage. Differences in nationality no longer counted for much," she writes, "because the original Dutch, French and English elements had by 1750 been so completely fused by intermarriage that few of their descendants could claim to be more one than the other."[53]

Although ethnic divisions had lost much of their intensity in mid-eighteenth-century New York, national ties still remained highly important to some recent immigrants. John Frans Walter, a carpenter, and recent colonist from Germany, named his two "good friends," the bakers Wilhemus Poppelsdorff and John Riple (also spelled Johannes Rypele) as his executors.[54] Ann Grant, a widow, was among the few immigrants

[52]Ibid., Liber 24:27–29, May 14, 1763.

[53]Virginia D. Harrington, *The New York Merchant on the Eve of the Revolution* (New York: Columbia University Press, 1935), 17–19.

[54]N.Y. Wills, Liber 27:83–84, July 13, 1742. See also the will of Alexander Wallace, a tallow chandler and native of Ireland, who appointed Daniel McCormick and John McDowell, two merchant "friends," as his executors. Liber 28:333, Sept. 8, 1772.

who openly expressed their fears that they would leave behind several "under Age" children in a "strange Country." She therefore appointed one John Small as an executor and the guardian of her children, "which trust I repose in him purely from the humane and charitable disposition he has on all Occasions shewn to me & my . . . children and also on Account of his personal Knowledge of my Relations & Connections in Scotland."[55]

## THE BEQUEST OF SLAVES AND CHARITABLE DONATIONS

Although relatives, friends, and acquaintances often served as executors, they seldom shared in the division of property between a man's wife and children. One would, of course, expect that heads of households would place their wives' and children's interests above all other concerns. What is particularly important, however, is the degree to which individuals felt called upon to part with any of their possessions for communal, religious, or humanitarian purposes. In colonial New York City, the decision to manumit one's slaves or even to leave behind a charitable bequest often hinged upon the extent of a person's familial obligations.

Throughout the English colonial era, 182 persons (or 11 percent of all New York City testators) transferred slaves in their wills. This number only partly indicates the extent of ownership since some masters undoubtedly wrote wills without specifying the possession of blacks. The omission of any reference to slaves may have been most common in seventeenth-century wills since early Dutch colonists often transferred the family estate as a whole rather than making specific bequests. The proportion of slaveowners among testators rose sharply during the early 1700s, an era in which New Yorkers came increasingly to rely on slave labor. While 8 percent of men referred to slaves in wills written from 1696 through 1725, nearly 14 percent did so from 1726 through 1775 (see Table 5.5). Colonial censuses reveal that blacks numbered between 14 and 19 percent of the city's entire population during this last period.[56] Among all northern seaports, New York was by far the most dependent on slave labor and the most fearful of slave rebellion. Public authorities brutally suppressed an uprising in 1712, and they responded

[55]Ibid., Liber 27:429–30, Feb. 2, 1769.
[56]Bureau of the Census, *A Century of Population Growth* (Washington, D.C., 1909), 170–83.

**Table 5.5** Ownership and manumission of slaves

| | No. leaving wills | No. specifying slaves | Percent specifying slaves | No. freeing slaves | Percent owners freeing slaves |
|---|---|---|---|---|---|
| **Men** | | | | | |
| 1664–95 | 120 | 3 | 2.5 | 0 | 0 |
| 1696–1725 | 285 | 22 | 7.7 | 5 | 22.7 |
| 1726–50 | 300 | 41 | 13.7 | 2 | 4.9 |
| 1751–75 | 634 | 87 | 13.7 | 9 | 10.3 |
| Entire period | 1,339 | 153 | 11.4 | 16 | 10.4 |
| **Women** | | | | | |
| 1664–95 | 38 | 4 | 10.5 | 1 | 25.0 |
| 1696–1725 | 51 | 3 | 5.9 | 0 | 0 |
| 1726–50 | 58 | 11 | 19.0 | 2 | 18.2 |
| 1751–75 | 107 | 11 | 10.3 | 4 | 36.4 |
| Entire period | 254 | 29 | 11.4 | 7 | 24.1 |

hysterically to an alleged conspiracy in 1741 by executing thirty-one blacks and transporting another seventy to the West Indies.[57]

Although the ownership of blacks was concentrated among merchants and well-to-do professionals, slaveholding was by no means limited to the elite. Merchants accounted for 31 percent of all city residents who referred to slaves in their wills. An additional 22 percent of slaveowning testators were shopkeepers, artisans, or other skilled tradesmen such as brewers and bakers. Women comprised 16 percent of all persons who owned slaves at the time that they prepared their wills.[58] While the overwhelming majority of masters owned blacks alone, seven persons mentioned Indian slaves in their wills. Six of the latter cases date between 1693 and 1710—a period in which the northern colonies imported a fair number of Indian slaves from Carolina.[59]

The ownership of slaves in early Manhattan was widely distributed among the urban populace rather than concentrated within a few households. Among all 182 testators who were proven slaveholders, seventy-two (or 40 percent) owned one slave, while thirty-one (or 17 percent)

[57]Edward McManus, *A History of Negro Slavery in New York* (Syracuse: Syracuse University Press, 1966). Gary B. Nash, *The Urban Crucible: Social Change, Political Consciousness, and the Origins of the American Revolution* (Cambridge: Harvard University Press, 1979), 106–9. Nash estimates that at least one-half of all New York City households owned at least one slave in 1746. Forty-one percent of families did so according to a census of 1703.

[58]The 182 owners included 57 merchants; 41 artisans, tradesmen, and shopkeepers; 14 mariners; 14 professional men, 3 laborers, 4 yeomen, 29 women, and 20 men whose status is not known. The female slaveowners included 28 widows and 1 single woman. In all, 14 percent of widows who left wills (28 among 196 women) mentioned slaves. These data are based on analysis of all New York City wills written from 1664 through 1775.

[59]Nash, *Urban Crucible*, 106.

possessed just two. Only thirteen New Yorkers (7 percent) definitely owned more than ten blacks at the time they prepared their wills.[60] By far the largest owner was Frederick Philipse, the second Lord of Philipsburgh manor, who bequeathed forty-six slaves in 1751: thirty-two to his eldest son and principal heir, two to his younger son, five among his three daughters, one to a granddaughter, and six to his wife. Though Philipse entailed Westchester lands to his children, he evinced no interest in keeping certain slaves within the family for two or more generations. He instead bequeathed individual blacks to each beneficiary as his or her absolute personal property. His eldest son acquired the bulk of slaves because he was the heir to farms where most of the Negroes labored. The remainder of Philipse family slaves were to serve primarily as household servants in Manhattan.[61]

Throughout the colonial era, only eight New York City testators offered their slaves the right to choose a master or mistress from among several white heirs or other persons. Samson Bensing, an illiterate potmaker who dictated a will in 1726, ordered that his Negro man Arcles be sold to the highest bidder among his six children, provided that the slave have his choice of owners outside the family if the heirs could not agree on a fair price among themselves. Isabella Morris was an uncommon mistress in directing her children to be kind to her "faithful servants, Harry and Old Hannah," who were both given their choice of owners from among five children. John Thurman was also an exceptional master in providing two types of protection for his slave Fooe: the latter was allowed his choice of master and was not to be sold outside the family without his consent.[62] Apart from these few cases, testators generally assigned slaves to particular heirs without any express regard for the blacks' wishes. Only a handful of masters, however, ordered that slaves be sold at public auction at their death. Wills generally regulated the transfer of blacks from owners to their spouses, children, or kin.

New York City men regarded their wives' comfort and security as their foremost goal when bequeathing slaves. While eighty-three burghers granted at least one slave for their spouse's use, sixty-five conveyed slaves to their children or grandchildren. It is also significant that widows tended to receive absolute ownership of blacks rather than a life-interest in such "chattels."[63] Many white women therefore had discretionary power to employ blacks in household labor, sell them for monetary gain,

[60]Twenty-six testators (14 percent among the 182 owners) owned three to five slaves, while forty testators (22 percent) held an indefinite number of slaves.
[61]N.Y. Wills, Liber 18:1–9, June 6, 1751, codicil July 22, 1751.
[62]Ibid., 1st ser., no. 1068, July 20, 1726; Liber 18:94–96, Aug. 9, 1746, codicil Feb. 16, 1747; Liber 37:262–64, Jan. 4, 1775.
[63]Among all eighty-three widows who obtained blacks from their husbands' wills, forty-nine (or 59 percent) acquired outright ownership of at least one slave.

or convey them eventually to children or kin. Parents tended to bequeath blacks to their children without undue favoritism to male or female heirs.[64]

While the bequest of slaves varied considerably with the individual owner's preference, it was also influenced by social custom and cultural attitudes. Sons and grandsons, for example, were most likely to gain possession of black men or boys as household servants. Though daughters might inherit women or children, they seldom obtained men—perhaps because of unspoken white fears about black male sexuality.[65] The bequest of slaves to white widows varied considerably in nature. Unlike daughters, their mothers tended to inherit control over black men as well as women or children. Some masters regarded their spouses' comfort as so important that they offered the widow her choice of slaves or authorized her to dispose of all blacks as she wished.[66]

Given the highly fragmented nature of slaveownership, blacks tended to be bequeathed as individuals rather than as members of family groups. Only thirteen colonial New York City wills explicitly referred to the presence of a black woman and her offspring within the same white household. Some masters owned a mother and children but took no measures to preserve these ties beyond their own death. During his last illness in 1762, Christopher Bancker offered his eldest son, Evert, his choice of twenty-five pounds, a clock, or his six-year-old black girl Mary as his birthright. Bancker's will, probated the following year, failed to mention either Mary's mother or his slave Tony, but instead included them within property to be divided equally among his five sons. The slave girl and her mother remained together only because Evert Bancker chose the girl as his birthright and then purchased her mother from his brother. There is no record of whether Tony (possibly the girl's father) was acquired by any Bancker heirs or sold by them at auction.[67] William Beekman was another New Yorker who left it to his children to deter-

[64]Twenty-four fathers bequeathed at least one slave to a son, while nineteen did so to a daughter. Ten widows offered at least one slave to a daughter, and seven did so to a son. An additional seven fathers and two mothers offered slaves for sale to all their children or gave blacks the right to choose their new owner from among male and female heirs.

[65]I have analyzed data from all thirty-six wills in which sons or grandsons inherited slaves. Thirty-one of these cases involved the transfer of at least one man or boy. Only twelve of the wills conveyed a woman or girl. New York City wills include thirty-three testaments by which parents bequeathed slaves to a daughter or granddaughter. Thirty of these wills conveyed a woman or girl, seven transferred a boy, and six granted a black man. (The total number of bequests exceeds the number of wills since some owners bequeathed several slaves.)

[66]See, for example, the wills of Peter and Adonijah Schuyler in N.Y. Wills, Liber 23:341–46, Mar. 21 and May 20, 1761.

[67]Account Book (Christopher Bancker Estate), Bancker Papers, New-York Historical Society (hereafter NYHS). For Bancker's will, see N.Y. Wills, Liber 24:44–45, Feb. 22, 1756.

mine his slaves' fate. He named his three daughters as equal owners of three black women, their children, and a man. He also bequeathed to his two sons a black couple and their two children living on his Manhattan farm.[68] The practice of dividing property equally among white heirs further undermined the maintenance of black family ties under slavery. Slaves were especially at the mercy of colonists in cases of intestacy. When Stephen De Lancey died intestate in 1747, his seven slaves were purchased by his two brothers, a sister, and a brother-in-law.[69] Inheritance led to the dispersal of blacks among the extended white family, lessening the slaves' chances to form stable social ties among themselves.

The number of owners who freed their slaves was quite small during the colonial era—only sixteen men and seven women among 182 slaveholders took this action in their wills. Though the level of manumission increased between 1726 and 1775, only nine among forty-nine slaveowning testators freed a black during the final decade before independence, 1766–75. It was only after the onset of revolution that New Yorkers began to free their slaves to a significant degree.[70] There was little change during the colonial period in the type of testators most likely to emancipate their slaves. Among all sixteen men who adopted this course, only nine were married and just four left behind any children. Five of the seven female emancipators were widows who had no surviving children. The decision to free one's slaves, of course, depended on personal concerns as well as family considerations. Some owners hoped to reward a slave for faithful service, to encourage the obedience of other bondsmen, or to express their own philanthropic instincts.[71] Clearly, however, few testators acted on these feelings if they had the opportunity to bequeath slaves to their own children.

Several testators demonstrated the primacy of their familial responsibilities by postponing the freeing of their slaves until after the deaths of their principal heirs. Elizabeth Vielle bequeathed her four "Negro Slaves" to her only child, Sarah, and ordered their manumission if they were still living at her daughter's death. Since Sara Vielle was only forty-eight years old when her mother died, her slaves might still have to wait many years before receiving their liberty.[72] Martin Clock's slave Frank

---

[68]For Beekman's will, see Nicholas Bayard Papers—Documents, Jan. 4, 1770, NYHS. An inventory of the estate is in the Beekman Family Papers, NYHS.

[69]See the list of slaves dated Feb. 27, 1747, in the De Lancey Papers, Document 40.190.108, Museum of the City of New York.

[70]McManus, *History of Negro Slavery*, 153. New York law entitled owners to manumit their slaves by deed as well as by will. My statistics are based solely on an examination of probate records.

[71]Ibid., 141, 148.

[72]N.Y. Wills, Liber 18:184–85, Oct. 13, 1752.

was more fortunate in several ways. Although he would not gain his freedom until after his mistress's death, she was already sixty-eight years old when her husband drafted his will in 1728. Clock also ordered his executors to set aside twenty-five pounds for his slave's "subsistence" as a freedman, and gave him "One good New Suit of Apparell from head to foot, three New Shirts, A New Hatt & Cap And All the Wearing Apparell he . . . then hath belonging to his body as Well of Linnen as Woolen."[73]

Twelve of the twenty-three testators who freed their slaves offered them a legacy for their subsequent maintenance or education. Samuel Bowne, a wealthy Quaker merchant, was unique among masters in offering his slave woman, Isabella, her choice of being freed or remaining in bondage after his death. If she elected freedom, she was to receive the annual interest from a £150 cash sum during the rest of her life. Acknowledging that Isabella might decline this opportunity because she was infirm and growing old, Bowne advised his wife to be a kind mistress to her in that case. The £150 was then to be divided among his heirs as part of the estate.[74] Some slaveholders adopted special measures to ensure that their executors or heirs would cooperate in the manumission of slaves. Mary Kennedy offered a bequest of one thousand pounds to her stepson on condition that he free her elderly slave woman and pay one hundred pounds for her support.[75] William Walton manumitted (at his wife's death) eleven slaves, including a mother and her six children, and ordered his executors to give security that the blacks would not become dependent on public welfare. He also offered small annuities to support the black children's education and set aside twenty-five pounds to each freedman or woman at age twenty-one. These bequests testify to Walton's kindness, but they hardly taxed his estate considering the £15,500 in cash legacies given to his nephews and nieces.[76]

Although several persons offered some degree of material support to their newly freed slaves, other testators hoped to reward their bondsmen in order to encourage their future loyalty. James McEvers gave five pounds to each of five slaves for their "faithful service"; he also conveyed ownership of these blacks to his wife and five children.[77] Bernard Rynlander voiced his concern for his slave's welfare but expressed a stronger commitment to his children's inheritance: "I give my Negrow York unto my three Sons in the following Manner that is as long as hee

---

[73]Ibid., 1st ser., no. 873, Dec. 6, 1728.
[74]Ibid., Liber 36:272–76, Nov. 5, 1771, codicil Jan. 4, 1784.
[75]Ibid., Liber 24:408–9, May 23, 1764.
[76]Ibid., Liber 26:318–22, June 8, 1768.
[77]Ibid., Liber 26:385–87, Aug. 12, 1768, codicil Sept. 4, 1768.

can bring any profit it shall be divided between them & so in like manner they shall join for his support, & that so as to make the remainder of his Days as comfortable as possible."[78] Few testators were inclined to free their slaves, and the likelihood of manumission became even more remote when owners were also parents.

A similar pattern also characterized the ninety-five persons (only 6 percent of all testators) who left behind charitable bequests. Forty-three of all sixty-nine male donors had no surviving children, and twenty-four had neither a wife nor any offspring. Of all twenty-six female philanthropists, four were single, and thirteen were widows without any children. Faced with the problem of how to dispose of their property, most fathers and mothers defined their goals in an uncompromising, single-minded manner.[79]

As further proof of their priorities, several testators ruled out any charitable bequests unless all their principal heirs should die. William Boyle, a cordwainer, left one hundred pounds to the city's poor in case his wife remarried and his two children died during their minority and without any offspring of their own.[80] William Ricketts, the absentee owner of a West Indian plantation, made certain that a small charitable legacy interfered as little as possible with his children's and grandchildren's inheritance. His will set aside three pounds for the poor "Communicants of Trinity Church . . . to be paid by my Executors the Same Day that I shall Depart this Life Every Year During the Minority of my Son William but no Longer unless he Consents to the Same." Should this only son die without "lawful issue," Ricketts ordered, an annuity of six pounds was to be given for the same purpose during the minority of his next heir, his daughter Mary's eldest child. Being as circumspect as possible, he also inserted a provision that ended any charitable outlay "if my Estate in Jamaica Should happen to fall under Some great misfortune."[81]

Philanthropists comprised an unrepresentative segment of the will-writing population in several important respects. Most of the men among them died without leaving behind either a wife or children; they also tended to belong to the city's upper class of well-to-do mariners, merchants, landholders, and attorneys. Members of these groups and their widows comprised a considerable majority of all persons who left charitable bequests; merchants alone accounted for more than half of

[78]Ibid., Liber 28:205–6, Dec. 13, 1771.
[79]Farmers in Bucks County, Pennsylvania, were even less inclined to make charitable bequests than New York City residents. See Shammas, Salmon, and Dahlin, *Inheritance in America*, 48.
[80]N.Y. Wills, Liber 14A:157–59, June 2, 1691.
[81]Ibid., 1st ser., no. 970, 1734.

the donors whose occupations can be determined.[82] Although a direct connection existed between increased wealth and the granting of charity, the possession of a sizable fortune did not itself determine the decision to give alms. The bequest of charity was also a highly personal act that depended greatly on the individual's sense of communal or civic responsibility.

During the period 1664–1725, writes Joyce Goodfriend, nearly all charitable bequests were given to churches that represented the testator's own ethnic group. While some donors contributed to the support of the ministry, a considerable number of philanthropists directed that their gifts be used to assist the poor of the congregation. Whatever a legacy's particular purposes, concludes Goodfriend, the general "pattern of philanthropic activity . . . affirms the importance of ethnic consciousness in the community." Not all donations, however, followed strictly along ethnic lines. Ties of kinship or political self-interest influenced several persons to bridge these divisions and to forge links to the congregations of other nationalities.[83]

During the years between 1710 and 1750, a series of broad cultural and religious developments led to an eventual change in patterns of almsgiving. This period witnessed the growth of religious toleration, the erosion of ethnic exclusiveness, and the beginnings of a common culture based on English standards, particularly among the colonial elite. As the cohesiveness of the French and Dutch communities gradually weakened, fewer persons channeled their charitable bequests through the churches of these groups. During the period 1697–1727, fifteen testators (about one-third of all French colonists who left wills) gave money to the Huguenot churches of New York City or New Rochelle. Between 1728 and 1775, however, only two persons made such bequests. The level of almsgiving was particularly high during the early 1700s because of the poverty of many newly arrived immigrants and the strong sense of group solidarity among French Huguenot colonists. By the mid-1720s, however, internecine strife had destroyed much of this unity and led many members of l'Eglise françoise à la Nouvelle York to shift their allegiance to Trinity Church.[84]

[82]The donors included 31 merchants, 11 artisans, 9 mariners, 3 laborers, 2 shopkeepers, 2 attorneys, 1 minister, 1 butcher, and 9 men who did not identify themselves by occupation. I have also been able to determine the occupations of 14 husbands of the 22 widows who left charitable bequests. These 14 men included 4 merchants, 2 high government officials, 2 attorneys, 2 ministers, 2 shopkeepers, 1 mariner, and 1 artisan.

[83]Joyce Diane Goodfriend, "'Too Great a Mixture of Nations'": The Development of New York City Society in the Seventeenth Century" (Ph.D. diss., UCLA, 1975), 234–39.

[84]See Michael Kammen, *Colonial New York: A History* (New York: Charles Scribner's Sons, 1975), 232–33. The assimilation of Huguenots in English colonial culture is analyzed in Jon Butler, *The Huguenots in America: A Refugee People in New World Society* (Cambridge: Harvard University Press, 1984).

The Dutch Reformed church suffered a similar decline as a beneficiary of charitable bequests. Between 1684 and 1722, ten testators contributed to the support of the ministry or congregation; only two did so between 1723 and 1775. One very obvious sign of cultural assimilation was the decline in the use of the Dutch language—a process that was already well advanced by the mid-1720s.[85]

As evidence of the growing dominance of English culture, Trinity Church had emerged by 1760 as the city's most important charitable organization. Although English colonists formed a considerable majority of all donors, several persons of Dutch and French stock also offered legacies through this tax-supported establishment.[86] The favorite recipient of many testators was the church's Charity School, dedicated to educating the city's poor children. Founded in 1710 by the Society for the Propagation of the Gospel, the school followed a policy of admitting pupils from dissenting as well as Anglican families. Beginning in 1764, however, a new directive provided that preference be given to children of members of Trinity Church whenever a vacancy arose in the student body. This policy, writes William Webb Kemp, evidently led to a considerable decline in the number of students of nonconformist background.[87]

Several testators during the late colonial era expressed a desire to transcend sectarian divisions and to encourage the process of assimilation. Ann (née Heathcote) De Lancey, the widow of the former lieutenant governor, directed her executors to give one hundred pounds to the city's poor "without any regard to religious denomination[s]."[88] The will of Elias Brevoort, Jr., placed the sum of three hundred pounds "out to interest" for the purpose of teaching the English language to the poor children of the "Protestant Dutch Church."[89] Other persons granted charity for purely secular purposes or left bequests that reflected their

---

[85]For the changing loyalties of the ethnic Dutch, see Joyce D. Goodfriend, "The Social Dimensions of Congregational Life in Colonial New York City," *William and Mary Quarterly*, 3d ser., 46 (1989): 252–78. See also Goodfriend, "'Too Great a Mixture,'" 232–33; Kammen, *Colonial New York*, 236–37. The Albany Dutch maintained their traditional culture and the use of the Dutch language while their Manhattan counterparts were assimilating English ways. See Alice P. Kenney, *The Gansevoorts of Albany: Dutch Patricians in the Upper Hudson Valley* (Syracuse: Syracuse University Press, 1969), 44–47, 61–63.

[86]See the wills of Frances Auboyneau and Samuel Van Horne, N.Y. Wills, Liber 21:544, Jan. 23, 1760; Liber 38:409–11, Oct. 16, 1771.

[87]William Webb Kemp, *The Support of Schools in Colonial New York by the Society for the Propagation of the Gospel in Foreign Parts* (New York: Teacher's College, Columbia University, 1913), 100, 105–6. Trinity Church's charity school received fifteen of all forty-three charitable bequests made between 1751 and 1775.

[88]N.Y. Wills, Liber 32:64–66, Aug. 12, 1760, codicil Sept. 7, 1767.

[89]Ibid., Liber 40:539–42, May 15, 1775. See also the will of Helena McPheadris, a widow of Dutch ancestry who had been formerly married to a Scotsman. She gave one hundred pounds to the Dutch Reformed church for the same purpose as Brevoort. Liber 36:528–31, Feb. 21, 1770, codicil May 23, 1772.

own special personal concerns. James Tucker, a physician, bequeathed "my Collection of Insects" to the College of New York, and Lawrence Reade, a merchant, left one hundred pounds to "a Society who call themselves the Governors of the Hospitall for Sick Persons, lately founded."[90] Several widows focused their attention on the needy members of their own sex. Anna Pritchard bequeathed fifty pounds to poor widows "of good character," to be selected at her executors' discretion.[91] Ann (née Van Cortlandt) Chambers, the widow of a wealthy attorney, gave the principal sum of five hundred pounds to Trinity Church and ordered that the interest be applied "towards the support of the Girls only, belonging . . . to the Charity School . . . and in rewarding such of the Girls, upon their leaving the said School, as . . . the presiding officers shall Judge deserving thereof in such Proportions as they shall think proper either in Cash or otherwise, which I intend for their Diligence and direct and orderly Behavior during their Continuance in the said School."[92]

Although secularization and cultural assimilation represented two important trends during the mid-eighteenth century, these developments did not affect all segments of the population to the same extent. Some individuals and groups remained firmly committed to the preservation of their distinctive ethno-religious traditions. Elias Desbrosses, for example, granted one thousand pounds to Trinity Church for the maintenance of a French clergyman and the performance of services in the French language according to the rites of the Church of England.[93] The city's German inhabitants, who probably included many recent immigrants, tended to give charity to their own Lutheran church alone.[94] Jewish residents also directed their philanthropy to the support of their own congregation, the Shearith Israel, or "Remnant of Israel." Joseph Bueno de Mesquita left twenty pounds to the "poor of the Jewish nation," and Joshua Isaacs, another merchant, bequeathed fifty pounds to the "Congregation of Jews . . . to be put out to use to support the Hebrew school and teach poor children the Hebrew tongue."[95]

---

[90]Ibid., Liber 26:509–10, Feb. 6, 1769; Liber 29:318–23, Nov. 6, 1773. As further proof of his liberality, Reade left one hundred pounds to the poor "of [the] several churches" of New York.

[91]Ibid., Liber 21:358–60, June 7, 1759.

[92]Ibid., Liber 29:77–82, June 11, 1767, codicil Apr. 9, 1774.

[93]Ibid., Liber 37:58–59, June 1773.

[94]Seven persons of German descent left charitable bequests between 1751 and 1775. Five legacies were given to the Lutheran church, one to the German Reformed church, and one to general charitable purposes. German donors were generally of a much more modest social rank than most philanthropists. They included two laborers, one gardener, tailor, currier, and glazier.

[95]Hershkowitz, *Wills of Jews*, 15–17, 69–71. Joseph Bueno drafted his will in October

A study of patterns of inheritance raises several important questions concerning the nature of civic responsibility in colonial New York City. Rather than leave a gift, however small, for some broadly charitable purpose, most heads of families focused virtually their entire energies on providing for their wives and children. Kenneth Lockridge, discerning a similar pattern in colonial New England, attributes the lack of charitable bequests to the influence of parochial social attitudes—the absence of a "modern" outlook that might lead persons to direct their concerns beyond their immediate surroundings.[96] An examination of New York wills confirms at least one part of this thesis. Persons without a wife or children showed a markedly greater tendency than the heads of families to leave something to charity. I am skeptical, however, whether this depth of commitment to one's own family indicates the absence of a "modern spirit." According to several historians, the emergence of the "modern" family has meant the strengthening of the emotional bonds between husband, wife, and children and the weakening of ties to more distant kin and the wider community.[97] By these criteria one can hardly accuse New York testators of failing the test of modernity.

In another sense, theories about modernization bear little relevance to the specific historical reality of family life in eighteenth-century New York. One of the most significant changes in social attitudes during this period involved the weakening of traditional ethnic loyalties, particularly among persons of French Huguenot and Dutch origin. These groups, which had formed ethno-religious communities in early New York, gradually lost some of their distinctive social characteristics. Being of Dutch stock ceased by itself to determine how a person would leave his property after death. By the 1750s, a testator of French descent proved as likely to grant charity through the Anglican establishment as through the Huguenot church of his parents. As the process of cultural

---

1708 and Joshua Isaacs composed his testament in July 1744. Jews were the most likely of all ethnic or religious groups to leave a charitable bequest.

[96]Kenneth A. Lockridge, *Literacy in Colonial New England: An Enquiry into the Social Context of Literacy in the Early Modern West* (New York: Norton, 1974), 33–36, 84–87, 94–97. For an important discussion of charitable bequests, see W. K. Jordan, *Philanthropy in England, 1480–1660: A Study of the Changing Pattern of English Social Aspirations* (1959; rpt. New York: Russell Sage, 1964). Charitable bequests were far less commonly made in colonial New York than in Tudor and Stuart England.

[97]For three distinct historical approaches to this general theme, see Philip Ariès, *Centuries of Childhood: A Social History of Family Life,* trans. Robert Baldick (New York: Vintage, 1962); Edward Shorter, *The Making of the Modern Family* (New York: Basic Books, 1975); Lawrence Stone, *The Family, Sex, and Marriage in England, 1500–1800* (New York: Harper & Row, 1977). Bequests to kin in one English town declined significantly after the Civil War. See Richard T. Vann, "Wills and the Family in an English Town: Banbury, 1550–1800," *Journal of Family History* 4 (1979): 346–67.

assimilation advanced, members of the upper classes began to model their behavior on commonly accepted English standards of conduct and decorum. More often than others, these individuals would bestow legacies on persons outside the nuclear family: kin who had special need of assistance or friends (usually persons of a similar social background) who might perform some useful service. The breadth of these concerns grew over time, sometimes extending by the mid-1700s, to a worthwhile project of social improvement: the education of the poor or the support of the city's college or hospital. In these important ways, changes in patterns of inheritance reflect the breakdown of ethnic divisions among the upper classes in eighteenth-century New York City.

But the history of inheritance cannot be reduced to a single strand. Although cultural assimilation had proceeded furthest among the upper classes, certain ethnic groups remained more closely wedded to their traditional ethnic and religious heritage. This pattern held true for recent immigrants from Germany, Scotland, and Northern Ireland and also characterized social relations among the small Jewish community. Then, too, persons of more modest social position, such as seamen and artisans, remained considerably more likely than merchants to select executors from persons of a similar ethnic background.

The bequest of property depended on a series of factors, including economic status, occupation, ethnic origin, length of settlement in New York, and perhaps most important, the extent of a person's familial responsibilities. A man with a wife alone, for example, was considerably more likely to appoint his kin as heirs than an individual who had left some surviving children. Because a father owed his primary loyalty to his offspring, the failure to leave property to other persons did not itself mean the absence of more extensive ties of kinship. Many of these same testators relied on their kin and friends to serve as their executors; other parents appointed their relatives as heirs should all their children die. These measures indicate that the well-being of the nuclear family often depended on the maintenance of meaningful ties to a wider social network.

# Conclusion

New York City was a vastly different urban society on the eve of the Revolution than it had been when the English conquered New Netherland in 1664. The city had not only grown in size, wealth, and sophistication; it had also changed in cultural orientation and outlook. Manhattan had once been part of "Holland on the Hudson," an immigrant society that was a crude and primitive offshoot of Dutch civilization. In 1775, New York City was a major commercial center about to break free of its colonial bonds. After the destruction of war and British occupation, it would soon begin an era of unprecedented growth. A town of some 22,000 residents at the close of the colonial era became a city of 300,000 in 1840 and a sprawling metropolis of more than 800,000 in 1860.[1]

The evolution of inheritance practices in colonial New York City was directly related to broader currents of social change, especially the Dutch accommodation to English rule. The introduction of English law during the late seventeenth century was a gradual, unsystematic process that allowed Dutch colonists a considerable degree of freedom to maintain their own traditions concerning inheritance. Rather than adopt alien social customs at once, the Dutch learned how they might use English legal procedures to serve their own purposes. While some burghers continued to write mutual wills with their wives, a growing number of men followed the English practice of preparing their own

---

[1]For population figures, see Edward K. Spann, *The New Metropolis: New York City, 1840–1857* (New York: Columbia University Press, 1981), 430.

testaments. By the mid-1690s, the mutual will had disappeared from use in New York City and had even become a rarity in predominantly Dutch Albany. Despite this change, the great majority of Dutch colonists adhered for some time to Netherlandish customs of bequeathing property: the transfer of the family estate to the surviving spouse, the postponement of the children's inheritance until the widowed party's death or remarriage, and the equal or nearly equal division of property among sons and daughters.

The hybrid legal system of the late seventeenth century itself mirrored the confused and unsettled nature of New York City society and politics. Dutch resentment at English power undoubtedly fueled Leisler's Rebellion in 1689, an event that determined allegiances in Manhattan throughout the next decade. Still, this uprising was by no means simply a result of clear-cut ethnic conflict. Many burghers joined Leisler's cause in order to forestall an alleged Catholic conspiracy rather than merely to express hatred of the English. It should also be emphasized that the New York City Dutch were divided in their response to English rule and culture. A minority of wealthy merchants such as Frederick Philipse and Stephanus Van Cortlandt had risen to power by cooperating with English governors, and they readily accepted new political offices after Leisler's downfall. Other Dutchmen initially supported the rebellion but soon turned against it. As John Murrin has written, the 1690s was a time when "loyalties were malleable" and when colonists "had choices, not only among competing ethnic groups but within them."[2] Ethnic pride seldom led to strict social exclusiveness because an individual's economic success was based on forging ties across national boundaries. Jacob Leisler, himself a German immigrant who married into a Dutch family, had three daughters who wed Englishmen. (English colonists themselves commonly married Dutch women, joined the Dutch Reformed church, and adopted Dutch social customs regarding inheritance.) Johannes De Peyster was another prominent Dutch colonist whose political loyalties did not always dictate social conduct. While he belonged to a predomi-

[2]John M. Murrin, "English Rights as Ethnic Aggression: The English Conquest, the Charter of Liberties of 1683, and Leisler's Rebellion in New York," in William Pencak and Conrad Edick Wright, eds., *Authority and Resistance in Early New York* (New York: New-York Historical Society, 1988), 66. Important books on this era include Joyce D. Goodfriend, *Before the Melting Pot: Society and Culture in Colonial New York City, 1664–1730* (Princeton: Princeton University Press, 1992); Thomas J. Archdeacon, *New York City, 1664–1710: Conquest and Change* (Ithaca: Cornell University Press, 1976); and Robert C. Ritchie, *The Duke's Province: A Study of New York Politics and Society, 1664–1691* (Chapel Hill: University of North Carolina Press, 1977). Another study is David William Voorhees, "'In Behalf of the true Protestant religion': The Glorious Revolution in New York" (Ph.D. diss., New York University, 1988). Voorhees differs from Archdeacon and Ritchie by emphasizing the religious dimension of the rebellion, not its roots in ethnic conflict.

nantly Dutch faction, he engaged in trade in New England and wrote rather proudly about his young son's progress in the English language.[3] Unlike Dutchmen in rural New Jersey, the burghers of Manhattan had to assimilate some degree of English culture if they were to prosper as individuals. Dutch discontent was no longer a driving force of city politics after 1710 since economic and constitutional issues displaced ethnic rivalry as dominant concerns.[4]

The pace of Anglicization varied among Dutch and other non-English settlers according to several factors, such as the strength of ethnic ties within a given national group, the health of its religious and social life, and the availability of opportunities for advancement within colonial society. The timing of immigration was also an important influence on cultural orientation. For example, Huguenot settlers in New Netherland commonly had refugee roots in the Low Countries, intermarried with Dutch colonists in the New World, and became members of the Dutch Reformed church. It is therefore not surprising that these French Protestants often bequeathed property just as the Dutch did. Huguenot immigrants to New York City in the late seventeenth century became more rapidly assimilated than previous arrivals into English colonial culture. The Anglicization of these colonists was quite pronounced by 1720 given their integration within the urban economy, election to political offices, the decline of the French church, and the high rate of intermarriage between the French and other groups.[5] There was little, if any, discernible French influence on inheritance practices in eighteenth-century New York City. Rural New Paltz, New York, was an exception to the rule of Huguenot assimilation in colonial America. Founded in the 1670s, this community maintained strong links to neighboring Dutch towns but also retained its own distinctive ethnic identity.[6]

[3]David E. Narrett, "Dutch Customs of Inheritance, Women, and the Law in Colonial New York City," in Pencak and Wright, *Authority and Resistance*, 40–41.

[4]The movement of some Leislerian families out of the city to New Jersey furthered this trend. See Murrin, "English Rights," p. 77. The difference in cultural orientation between Manhattan and rural areas is analyzed in Randall Balmer, *A Perfect Babel of Confusion: Dutch Religion and English Culture in the Middle Colonies* (New York: Oxford University Press, 1989). For the changing political atmosphere, see Adrian Howe, "The Bayard Treason Trial: Dramatizing Anglo-Dutch Politics in Early Eighteenth-Century New York City," *William and Mary Quarterly*, 3d ser., 47 (1990): 57–89. For more general accounts, see Patricia U. Bonomi, *A Factious People: Politics and Society in Colonial New York* (New York: Columbia University Press, 1971), 75–81; and Michael Kammen, *Colonial New York: A History* (New York: Charles Scribner's Sons, 1975), chap. 6.

[5]Jon Butler, *The Huguenots in America: A Refugee People in New World Society* (Cambridge: Harvard University Press, 1983), chap. 5.

[6]David E. Narrett, "Men's Wills and Women's Property Rights in Colonial New York," in Ronald Hoffman and Peter J. Albert, eds., *Women in the Age of the American Revolution* (Charlottesvile: University Press of Virginia, 1989), 98–100.

It is instructive to compare the Dutch response to English legal institutions in New York with the reaction of German immigrants in eighteenth-century Pennsylvania. Like the Dutch, the Germans were extremely fearful about the imposition of foreign inheritance law, particularly about laws favoring the eldest son. (While New York instituted strict primogeniture, Pennsylvania awarded a double portion of both real and personal property to the eldest son in case of intestacy.) One German immigrant, the author of a popular almanac, also complained that English law offered inadequate protection to widows. Viewing such practice as unchristian, he strongly advised his fellow immigrants to write wills in order to circumvent colonial intestacy law. New social conditions required the development of new social habits, especially since many Germans came from villages where customary law dictated inheritance and where will writing was virtually unknown. Ironically, German settlers learned how to use their freedom of testation under English law in order to preserve their own native traditions.[7]

The German experience in Pennsylvania differed, of course, from that of Dutch New Yorkers in one basic respect. While the Germans came to a province where the English were already well established, the Dutch had to cope with the problem of foreign conquest. The Dutch, too, came to appreciate the importance of will writing given their initial antagonism to English inheritance law. Though the proportion of Dutch settlers who left wills was not generally higher than among other New Yorkers, the practice of will writing did become much more widespread following the English conquest, especially after 1675. As English law was established, the Dutch could no longer safely assume that their own social customs would be respected if they died intestate. A few colonists even openly expressed their defiance of the legal system by declaring their wills according to the rule of the Dutch nation regardless of any contrary provincial statute.

The evidence of Anglicization in Manhattan wills was quite limited prior to 1720 because most testators were fairly elderly men and women who had grown up, and even come to maturity, in a predominantly Dutch

[7]A. G. Roeber, "The Origins and Transfer of German-American Concepts of Property and Inheritance," *Perspectives in American History*, new ser., 3 (1987): 115–71. See also Roeber, "'The Origin of Whatever Is Not English among Us': The Dutch-Speaking and German-Speaking Peoples of Colonial British America," in Bernard Bailyn and Philip D. Morgan, eds., *Strangers within the Realm: Cultural Margins of the First British Empire* (Chapel Hill: University of North Carolina Press, 1991), 230. Daniel Snydacker has found a low rate of testation among Germans in York County, Pennsylvania. He attributes this fact to the presence of a language barrier and the cost of translating German documents into an official English register. See Snydacker, "Kinship and Community in Rural Pennsylvania, 1749–1820," *Journal of Interdisciplinary History* 13 (1982): 41–61.

society. During the first half-century of English rule, Dutch colonists followed a nearly uniform manner of bequeathing property to their wives and children. Whether writing a mutual will or declaring their own testament, they generally conveyed the entire estate to the spouse during widowhood, thereby postponing their children's inheritance until the widow's death or remarriage. This practice reflected the strength of the marital bond within the Dutch colonial family and the persistence of Netherlandish customs of community property within marriage. It is especially significant that these New York City burghers followed virtually the same inheritance practices as other Dutch colonists—whether in rural Long Island, the mid–Hudson Valley, or the Albany region. *Boedelhouderschap*—the retention of the *boedel* or estate by the surviving spouse—supported a system of family relations in which parental authority during widowhood had priority over children's claims to property.

During the early colonial period, the ethnic Dutch adhered to quite different methods of bequeathing property than did English settlers in either New York or other regions. In communities from New England to South Carolina, the widow's share of the estate tended to vary significantly according to the age, gender, and even the number of the testator's surviving children. Her portion was usually restricted if her husband left behind some adult heirs, particularly sons, or if there were several surviving children as opposed to one or two.[8] New England farmers, for example, commonly distinguished between the widow's property rights during the children's minority and after the eldest son came of age. The widow might serve as caretaker of family property, but she was no longer the head of household once the male heir assumed control.[9] In the Dutch system, by contrast, sons did not generally acquire

---

[8]Carole Shammas, Marylynn Salmon, and Michel Dahlin, *Inheritance in America: From Colonial Times to the Present* (New Brunswick: Rutgers University Press, 1987), 51–55. See also Daniel Scott Smith, "Inheritance and the Social History of Early American Women," in Hoffman and Albert, *Women in the Age of the American Revolution*, 58. Smith analyzes essays in the same volume by Gloria L. Main, Carole Shammas, and Lois Green Carr, as well as by David Narrett. See Main, "Widows in Rural Massachusetts on the Eve of the Revolution," in ibid., 67–90; Shammas, "Early American Women and Control over Capital," in ibid., 134–54; Carr, "Inheritance in the Colonial Chesapeake," in ibid., 155–208. Two other important essays bearing on this issue are Linda E. Speth, "More Than Her 'Thirds': Wives and Widows in Colonial Virginia," *Women and History* no. 4 (1982): 5–41; and John E. Crowley, "Family Relations and Inheritance in Early South Carolina," *Histoire Sociale* 27 (1984): 35–57.

[9]Main, "Widows in Rural Massachusetts," 80–82. See also Alexander Keyssar, "Widowhood in Eighteenth-Century Massachusetts: A Problem in the History of the Family," *Perspectives in American History* 8 (1974): 83–122. Toby L. Ditz has also found that landowners in Connecticut towns tended to limit their widows' rights to real estate during the late colonial era. See Ditz, *Property and Kinship: Inheritance in Early Connecticut, 1750–1820* (Princeton: Princeton University Press, 1986), 130–31. For the early colonial period, see Kim Lacy Rogers, "Relicts of the New World: Conditions of Widowhood in Seventeenth

ownership of family land until their widowed mother's death or remarriage. The widow's legal control of the estate meant that she was truly her deceased husband's successor, not simply an elderly female dependent—literally a "relict"—entitled to little more than a decent maintenance.

The respect for female property rights in Dutch law undoubtedly strengthened some women's loyalty to their own ethnic community and church. Joyce Goodfriend has shown that Dutch women were strongly inclined to retain their membership in Manhattan's Reformed church, even when they wed Englishmen.[10] While women's identity was shaped by English law in the public sphere, it was defined by Dutch traditions in the church. By the 1690s, for example, widows who wrote wills adopted the English custom of identifying themselves by the deceased husband's surname. In the Dutch church, however, the baptismal registers continued throughout the colonial era to list the mother's and father's name at birth.[11]

The demise of the Dutch mutual will in the 1690s did not lead to a sudden decline in widows' rights, though it marked a turning point toward the assimilation of English property law by Dutch townsmen and farmers. Once men became accustomed to preparing wills without their wives, they began to develop an individualistic sense of ownership quite different from the Dutch system of community property within marriage. Though wives might still be awarded possession of the entire estate during widowhood, they were now dependents who had no guaranteed right of survivorship except for dower, a life-interest in one-third of the deceased husband's real estate. Men might choose in their wills to be either generous or rather stingy based on their own personal preferences. By the 1730s, they increasingly began to use their power to advance their children's inheritance and to restrict their widows' control of property. Whereas Dutch colonists had followed a nearly uniform manner of bequeathing property in the 1600s, they now began to vary their approach according to economic or social class. Wealthy city dwellers within diverse ethnic groups became the most likely to limit their wives' portion of the estate to the benefit of the younger generation. The link between wealth and patterns of bequests cannot be precisely calculated

---

Century New England," in Mary Kelley, ed., *Woman's Being, Woman's Place: Female Identity and Vocation in American History* (Boston: Hall, 1979), 26–52.

[10]Joyce D. Goodfriend, "The Social Dimensions of Congregational Life in Colonial New York City," *William and Mary Quarterly*, 3d ser., 46 (1989): 252–78.

[11]See "Baptisms from 1639 to 1800 in the Reformed Dutch Church, New York," in *Collections of the New York Genealogical and Biographical Society* (1901–3; rpt. Upper Saddle River, N.J., 1968).

given the limited documentation concerning property holdings. Unquestionably, however, merchants and other professionals—generally the most affluent colonists—advanced their children's inheritance more rapidly and fully than did other occupational groups. These men, of course, possessed sufficient wealth to provide amply for their spouses while conveying most of the estate directly to their heirs.[12]

While Dutch colonists in eighteenth-century New York bequeathed varying shares of wealth to their wives, they generally moved away from the idea of community property. For example, the great majority of testators in rural areas as well as New York City chose to limit their widows' rights upon remarriage to either a minimal portion (often no more than a single child's share) or nothing at all—rather than the one-half of the family estate guaranteed by Dutch customary law. Men also generally denied their spouses any discretionary power to sell real estate during widowhood. It should be emphasized that fathers usually included these provisions in their wills in order to protect their children's inheritance rather than to express any intrinsic disregard for their wives. Men tended to allow their widows unrestricted control of the estate, or at least a major portion of it, if they left behind no surviving children.

The decline in the widow's authority can be traced to distinct causes in various colonies. In the Chesapeake, for example, women's property rights diminished over time because of improvements in life expectancy and the changing age structure of the population. As men lived longer, they tended to leave behind more adult heirs who were capable of managing their own inheritance and could be entrusted with the responsibility of executorship. The goal of transmitting real estate to sons also became increasingly important with the development of the plantation regime.[13] In New York City, by contrast, the widow's sphere of responsibility contracted because of the decline of Dutch customs of community property and the concurrent growth of a more individualistic, commercially oriented society. As in other regions, a sharply declining percentage of men appointed their spouses as sole executors of their estates.[14] A

[12]Wealthy men in other colonial regions were also the most likely to restrict the widow's share of the estate. See Shammas, Salmon, and Dahlin, *Inheritance in America*, 53; Crowley, "Family Relations in Early South Carolina," 45.

[13]Carr, "Inheritance in the Colonial Chesapeake," 171–79; James W. Deen, Jr. [Jamil Zinaildin], "Patterns of Testation: Four Tidewater Counties in Colonial Virginia," *American Journal of Legal History* 16 (1972): 172–76; Speth, "More Than Her 'Thirds,'" 22–23.

[14]Shammas, Salmon, and Dahlin, *Inheritance in America*, 59–61. See also Shammas, "Early American Women," 134–54. Additional evidence on this point is found in Lisa Wilson Waciega, "A 'Man of Business': The Widow of Means in Southeastern Pennsylvania, 1750–1850," *William and Mary Quarterly*, 3d ser., 44 (1987): 40–64; Deborah Mathias Gough, "A Further Look at Widows in Early Southeastern Pennsylvania," in ibid., 829–39. Gough disputes Waciega's argument that widows had a major economic role, and also shows a decline in their appointment as executors.

considerable minority of testators, particularly among the well-to-do, declined to name their wives as executors at all. Since the settlement of a substantial estate was especially complex, merchants and other affluent professionals relied increasingly on their principal business associates, male kin, and adult sons to administer their property. The widow's role in commerce was still important in numerous urban households, but it was more limited within most leading merchant families than it had been in New Netherland or early New York.

The evolution of inheritance practices in eighteenth-century New York coincided with the emergence of a new style of family life among the gentry and professional classes throughout America. Historians such as Daniel Blake Smith and Philip Greven have characterized the emotional quality of domestic relations during this period as increasingly "child-centered," or oriented toward satisfying the individual needs of children.[15] Parents openly expressed their love for their young offspring in affectionate and sentimental language influenced by English cultural standards. Fathers aimed to cultivate both a sense of duty and self-discipline in their children, and to encourage their sons toward individual advancement. This goal could be served only indirectly if men offered the entire estate to the widow on condition that it pass eventually to the children after her remarriage or death.

Religious values, rather than simply secular concerns, shaped the ways that some colonists satisfied their parental obligations. Quaker men in Pennsylvania, for example, were intensely concerned with cultivating their children's spiritual growth as well as with protecting and promoting their inheritance. They tended, therefore, to restrict the widow's share of the estate and her control of property, while appointing men as guardians over their minor heirs. Quaker testators encouraged their wives to be moral instructors of the young but curtailed their economic authority within the family. Their social practices anticipated what would be the prevailing view of women's domestic role in nineteenth-century America.[16]

Few married women in colonial New York City or elsewhere in the province escaped the common law restrictions on their control of property, including the authority to make a valid will. Though some widows

[15]Daniel Blake Smith, *Inside the Great House: Planter Family Life in Eighteenth-Century Chesapeake Society* (Ithaca: Cornell University Press, 1980), 40–46. Philip J. Greven, Jr., *The Protestant Temperament: Patterns of Child-Rearing, Religious Experience, and the Self in Early America* (New York: Knopf, 1977), 269–74. Similar cultural trends are analyzed in Lawrence Stone, *The Family, Sex, and Marriage in England, 1500–1800* (New York: Harper & Row, 1977), chaps. 6, 9.

[16]Barry Levy, *Quakers and the American Family: British Settlement in the Delaware Valley* (New York: Oxford University Press, 1988), 196–98.

entered into marriage contracts to preserve their independence within a new union, this was not the general practice even in cases of remarriage. The expanding rights of married women under English equity law therefore had little impact on New York women. Marriage settlements or trusts were not nearly as common as in late colonial South Carolina, where they safeguarded women's interest in slaves.[17] Though such legal agreements were more frequently utilized in the early nineteenth century, the loosening of the bonds of coverture was quite limited until the passage of the New York married women's property act of 1848. This statute established equity as the general rule by giving all married women separate ownership of both property brought to marriage and property received by gift or inheritance during marriage. This significant advance in women's rights was itself made necessary by widows' economic vulnerability as dependents in a commercial society.[18]

Given the disabilities of married women at common law, widows comprised the great majority of female testators during the colonial era. In New York and other colonies, women's wills differed from men's principally in the importance they attached to personal property. Since widows had ownership primarily of household goods, clothing, and other personal effects, they devoted considerable attention to the bequest of such items to daughters, female relatives, or friends. They frequently offered these gifts, moreover, as a means of expressing affection as well as conveying valuable property.[19] Though widowed mothers sometimes favored daughters with a special bequest, they usually distributed wealth among all their surviving children. Women's sense of equity was somewhat different from their husbands', but no less compelling.

One of the most striking features of colonial inheritance practices is the discrepancy between intestacy law and actual patterns of devising land by last will and testament. In New York and the South, the English custom of primogeniture was the law of intestacy by the early 1700s. Most northern colonies, influenced by Puritan or other dissenting values, allowed the eldest son a double share of both real and personal property. Whatever the prevailing intestacy law, most testators utilized their right to declare a will in order to apportion their wealth in a more

[17]Marylynn Salmon, "Women and Property in South Carolina: The Evidence from Marriage Settlements, 1730 to 1830," *William and Mary Quarterly*, 3d ser., 39 (1982): 675–77. See also her important book *Women and the Law of Property in Early America* (Chapel Hill: University of North Carolina Press, 1986).

[18]Norma Basch, *In the Eyes of the Law: Marriage and Property in Nineteenth-Century New York* (Ithaca: Cornell University Press, 1982). See also Marylynn Salmon, "Republican Sentiment, Economic Change, and the Property Rights of Women in American Law," in Hoffman and Albert, *Women in the Age of the American Revolution*, 447–78.

[19]For evidence of this trend in New England, see Main, "Widows in Rural Massachusetts," 88–89.

egalitarian manner among their children, especially among sons.[20] The particular method of distribution varied significantly according to the individual testator's ethnic and religious traditions as well as economic circumstances.

Dutch customs of inheritance in early New York were distinctively more advantageous to daughters than were English practices, especially in rural areas. While the typical Dutch colonist might give a token gift to the eldest son in recognition of his birthright, he generally divided the great portion of his wealth equally among sons and daughters. This practice prevailed, moreover, among yeomen in Long Island and the Hudson River Valley as well as among New York City burghers. It was not until the early 1700s that Dutch farmers in rural Ulster County, New York, began to move away from a strictly equal division of real estate among their children. While men increasingly desired to limit the fragmentation of family land, they remained committed to their own ethnic traditions of equity regarding inheritance. Privileged male heirs, usually two or more sons, were nearly always required to make substantial compensatory payments to their sisters for the land. Daughters received, moreover, an equal share of personal property with sons in addition to the special payment for family real estate. This degree of support for female heirs was greater than that gained by daughters in most colonial English households whether in New York or other regions.[21] For example, English settlers in eastern Long Island followed the same customs in bequeathing property as most rural New Englanders. While Yankee farmers attempted to convey land to as many sons as possible, they generally gave only personal property to their daughters. Though daughters might receive a substantial amount in cash, livestock, or household goods toward a dowry, their overall share of wealth was considerably less than their brothers' inheritance.[22]

[20]Shammas, Salmon, and Dahlin, *Inheritance in America*, 30–35, 42–50. For the avoidance of primogeniture by Virginia testators, see C. Ray Keim, "Primogeniture and Entail in Colonial Virginia," *William and Mary Quarterly*, 3d ser., 25 (1968): 545–86; Deen, "Patterns of Testation," 170–76.

[21]Narrett, "Men's Wills and Women's Property Rights," 119–30.

[22]Philip J. Greven, Jr., and John J. Waters are among numerous scholars who have emphasized the patrilineal basis of inheritance practices in rural New England. See Greven, *Four Generations: Population, Land, and Family in Colonial Andover, Massachusetts* (Ithaca: Cornell University Press, 1970); Waters, "Family, Inheritance, and Migration in Colonial New England: The Evidence from Guilford, Connecticut," *William and Mary Quarterly*, 3d ser., 39 (1982): 64–86; Waters, "Patrimony, Succession, and Social Stability: Guilford, Connecticut in the Eighteenth Century," *Perspectives in American History* 10 (1976): 131–60. Waters maintains that daughters usually obtained real estate only when there were no surviving sons—the same trend that prevailed in eastern Long Island. Toby Ditz, analyzing wills in another Connecticut region, has found that daughters were somewhat more likely to receive real estate but that their portions were of considerably less value than sons'. See Ditz, *Property and Kinship*, 66–70.

Most city dwellers found it easier than rural heads of households to reconcile their sons' and daughters' interests as heirs. Since land was not the primary means of sustenance in an urban environment, it could be readily partitioned into fractional shares and sold for the benefit of all family members. Irrespective of ethnic origin, the great majority of New York City testators divided their wealth in an equal or nearly equal manner among all their children. Relatively few fathers or mothers expressed an interest in reserving particular houses for certain sons or daughters. Inheritance therefore encouraged the fragmentation of family wealth and the establishment of separate households by adult siblings.[23] While equality of division remained the general rule, a growing number of fathers during the 1700s came to favor the eldest son as an heir to real estate. This tendency was especially pronounced among well-to-do colonists who wished to preserve a residence or business for a single heir. Even in these cases, however, fathers generally required the recipient to offer compensatory payments to his siblings for the inheritance. Dutch colonists were especially insistent that the male heir's privileges not come at the expense of other family members.

Dutch hostility to primogeniture was so great that it is doubtful that this law was actually applied in many cases of intestacy. There is some limited, though suggestive, evidence that families in New York City and rural areas deliberately avoided primogeniture after the head of household died without a will. Since the vast majority of intestacy cases were not supervised by courts, it cannot be assumed that New Yorkers generally followed an aristocratic English custom that violated their own sense of equity. A significant number of Dutch men and women from the 1670s through 1710s threatened the eldest son with disinheritance if he attempted to claim his full legal privileges. Given the uncertain nature of provincial law during this period, these settlers were justifiably fearful that they lacked the power to defeat primogeniture by a last will and testament. They therefore took no chances with the law, relying on family discipline rather than the court system to enforce their own values. Primogeniture itself would remain the official rule of descent in New York until the revolutionary era.[24]

Given the limitations of the colonial legal system, New Yorkers often decided issues pertaining to inheritance within the private rather than public sphere. Consider, for example, the question of guardianship and

[23]This pattern was also evident in colonial Germantown, Pennsylvania. See Stephanie Grauman Wolf, *Urban Village: Population, Community, and Family Structure in Germantown, Pennsylvania, 1683–1800* (Princeton: Princeton University Press, 1976), 310–25.

[24]For changes in inheritance law during the revolutionary period, see Shammas, Salmon, and Dahlin, *Inheritance in America*, 63–67. See also Stanley N. Katz, "Republicanism and the Law of Inheritance in the American Revolutionary Era," *Michigan Law Review* 76 (1977–78): 1–29.

the protection of children's property rights. Although an Orphan Masters Court was established in New Amsterdam during the early 1650s, it was dissolved soon after the English conquest. The new legal system sanctioned a far more limited degree of communal involvement in family affairs. In the Dutch system, courts had closely monitored the conduct of widowed parents through the appointment of male guardians who were the minors' relatives or friends. Since children inherited property from both parents, their interests as heirs were protected in the event that either father or mother died. Under a New York statute of 1692, however, courts assumed direct responsibility only for the care of orphans who had lost both parents and who had no surviving kin. The appointment of guardians in other cases depended on petitions from the interested parties themselves rather than mandatory court action. Though the provincial Chancery Court assumed a growing role in protecting minors' inheritances during the late colonial period, its jurisdiction was by no means as comprehensive as that of the Orphan Masters Court in New Amsterdam.

Few parents in eighteenth-century New York City chose to appoint guardians by last will and testament. The decline of this practice is especially striking among the Dutch, who had commonly selected overseers in seventeenth-century wills. It may then be asked why so few parents, whether married or widowed, appointed individuals who might assume special legal obligations toward their children. Though there is no obvious answer to this question, two possible explanations should be considered: first, that the great majority of testators trusted their spouses, kin, or other executors to care for their offspring in a responsible manner; second, that testators were reluctant to choose guardians because they recognized that few men were willing to serve in that position. Disdaining public supervision, colonists seemingly preferred to entrust family members or friends with considerable discretionary power in overseeing their minor children's welfare. The institution of guardianship was generally weak in eighteenth-century America except among groups such as the Quakers that maintained a strong sense of communal responsibility over the young.[25] The trend toward private supervision strengthened the widowed mother's parental authority since

[25]The weakness of guardianship as a legal institution is discussed in Shammas, Salmon, and Dahlin, *Inheritance in America*, 58–59. For Quaker practices, see Levy, *Quakers and the American Family*, 197–204. Early Maryland had an active Orphan's Court, though justices seldom appointed guardians if the widowed mother had children under her care. See Lois Green Carr, "The Development of the Maryland Orphan's Court, 1654–1715," in Aubrey C. Land, Lois Green Carr, and Edward C. Papenfuse, eds., *Law, Society, and Politics in Early Maryland* (Baltimore: Johns Hopkins University Press, 1977), 41–62. Linda Speth has found that only the wealthiest testators in eighteenth-century Virginia tended to appoint guardians other than their wives. See Speth, "More Than Her 'Thirds,'" 21–22.

it allowed her to raise her children without accounting to other individuals, especially her deceased husband's male kin.

The transmission of property across the generations fostered a sense of autonomy and individual responsibility among children. Apart from some early Dutch colonists who opposed primogeniture, parents very rarely threatened their children with disinheritance. Like most testators in northern colonies, New Yorkers tended to convey unrestricted ownership of property to their offspring. Only a few of the very wealthiest landed families such as the Philipses attempted to entail estates within the male line over the course of several generations. A more significant minority of city residents bequeathed property to their married daughters on condition that it descend automatically to their grandchildren on the mother's death. This device, the life estate, protected the interests of the lineage against sons-in-law who might abuse their legal power over their wives' inheritance. New Yorkers did not, however, utilize the life estate nearly to the same degree as southern colonists, who were especially concerned about the transmission of land and slaves to their lineal descendants.[26]

Most New York City residents resembled colonists in other regions by defining their family responsibilities in a narrow manner. For example, only 13 percent of fathers bequeathed any property to individuals besides their wives, children, or grandchildren. It was extremely uncommon for men to offer kin or friends a major share of the estate when they had immediate domestic obligations.[27] Women were somewhat more likely than men to offer legacies outside the nuclear family, largely because of their close personal relationship to female relatives or acquaintances. While wealthy testators tended to distribute their possessions more broadly than other colonists, most merchants and affluent professionals still bequeathed property to their spouses and lineal descendants alone. Among the city's ethnic or religious groups, only the

[26]For the importance of conditional bequests in the South, see Shammas, Salmon, and Dahlin, *Inheritance in America*, 56–57. The granting of land and slaves in fee tail to sons and daughters was common among the great planter class in Tidewater Virginia, but this practice was not typical among small holders in that colony. See C. Ray Keim, "Primogeniture and Entail in Colonial Virginia," *William and Mary Quarterly*, 3d ser., 25 (1968): 557–61.

[27]Less than one-fifth of testators in colonial Bucks County, Pennsylvania, gave any significant legacies to kin other than children or grandchildren or wives. See Shammas, Salmon, and Dahlin, *Inheritance in America*, 48. For New England practices, see Ditz, *Property and Kinship*, 54–56. The tendency to keep property within the bloodline became more pronounced in eighteenth-century Virginia. See Deen, "Patterns of Testation," 157–62. John Crowley assesses references to kin in South Carolina wills, though he does not offer any precise statistics about the frequency of bequests to relatives. See Crowley, "The Importance of Kinship: Testamentary Evidence from South Carolina," *Journal of Interdisciplinary History* 16 (1986): 559–77.

small Jewish community recognized the claims of kin on a customary basis. The Jewish testator's sense of social obligation commonly extended to the poor of his community as well as relatives, though he naturally left most of his wealth to his wife and children.

Men's commitment to their own family was so paramount that they usually named the spouse as principal heir if they had no children. A substantial group of these testators named their blood relations as beneficiaries but postponed their inheritance until the widow's death.[28] Among single men, only common sailors tended to bequeath property to friends or acquaintances rather than kin. Since these men had little attachment to urban society, they frequently left their meager possessions, including future wages and prize money, to a fellow mate, a female friend on shore, or an innkeeper to whom they owed money. The mariner's declaration of a will expressed his own special sense of mortality since it was often made just before putting off to sea, especially when embarking on privateering voyages against His Majesty's enemies.[29]

The bequest of property to kin and neighbors was undoubtedly limited in colonial America because of the high degree of economic self-sufficiency within the free population. Most households could support themselves without direct communal assistance, and therefore people may have felt little need to help others beyond the immediate family. This trend is also apparent in certain areas of Britain during the seventeenth and eighteenth centuries, particularly among the middle classes. Testators increasingly directed all their energies toward providing for their wives' and children's needs rather than acknowledging communal claims to their wealth.[30]

The bequest of property to kin in colonial New York, as elsewhere in early America, was strongly biased toward consanguineal kin or blood relations, rather than kin through marriage. Indeed, the position of the latter became weaker over time because of the displacement of Dutch by English law. Since husbands and wives held equal shares of the family

[28]Crowley, "Family Relations and Inheritance in Early South Carolina," 45. Main, "Widows in Rural Massachusetts," 80.

[29]The seaman's cultural values are eloquently discussed in Marcus Rediker, *Between the Devil and the Deep Blue Sea: Merchant Seamen, Pirates, and the Anglo-American Maritime World, 1700–1750* (Cambridge: Cambridge University Press, 1987), chap. 4.

[30]Richard T. Vann, "Wills and the Family in an English Town: Banbury, 1500–1800," *Journal of Family History* 4 (1979): 346–67. Keith Wrightson and David Levine, *Poverty and Piety in an English Village: Terling, 1525–1700* (New York: Academic Press, 1979), 92–93. Barry Levy maintains that the Quaker movement in late seventeenth-century Britain was especially attractive to middle-class households that aimed to be economically independent of kin and neighbors. Pennsylvania Quakers dedicated their wills to the nuclear family's interest, while expressing their broader social concerns through the Monthly Meeting. See Levy, *Quakers and the American Family*, 37–39, 50–51, 91–92, 148–51.

estate according to Dutch law, the blood relations of each party had a claim to one-half of all wealth if the couple died with no children of their own. Male colonists in New Netherland and seventeenth-century New York commonly recognized their wives' kin as heirs in such cases. This practice became extremely rare by the 1720s since men ceased to regard their property as part of a jointly owned estate. Dutch colonists henceforth were just as unlikely as English settlers to offer bequests to the wife's kin, thereby excluding their own stepchildren.

While relatives did not ordinarily receive legacies, they often served as executors of the estate. Both men and women frequently appointed their kin through marriage (especially sons-in-law and brothers-in-law) as well as blood relations (most often brothers) to this important position. The health of the nuclear family therefore depended on the cooperation of a rather narrow range of kin. Even more commonly, testators selected male friends and acquaintances as executors. This same pattern is also evident in other colonial areas, ranging from Pennsylvania to South Carolina.[31] The reliance on nonrelatives as well as kin indicates that adults often formed their closest social ties on the basis of interest and affection, rather than on marriage or blood ties alone. Familial assistance within an urban environment was usually voluntary since heirs had few, if any, legal obligations toward their siblings. The appointment of executors in New York City also reveals the transition from a society based on national ties to one encouraging associations across such boundaries. Ethnic loyalties were the foremost influence on the choice of executors in the 1600s, while economic and occupational ties became more important by the mid-1700s, especially among merchants.

Though charitable bequests were not unknown in colonial New York, they were far less common than in English and western European communities during the sixteenth and seventeenth centuries. In the Old World, both wealthy and poor testators often felt obliged to offer some charitable donation as a communal or religious responsibility.[32] This tradition was greatly diminished in the colonies. In New York, for example, charitable bequests were made in only 6 percent of Manhattan wills and in less than 3 percent of testaments drafted in rural areas. It should be emphasized that colonists usually donated charity by will only if they had limited family obligations. A considerable majority of New York City

[31] Wolf, *Urban Village*, 295–96; Crowley, "Importance of Kinship," 568–71.

[32] W. K. Jordan, *Philanthropy in England, 1480–1660: A Study of the Changing Pattern of English Social Aspirations* (New York: Russell Sage, 1959). Levy, *Quakers and the American Family*, 37–38. Sherrin Marshall, *The Dutch Gentry, 1500–1650: Family, Faith, and Fortune* (New York: Greenwood Press, 1987), 83–84, 88–91. Shammas, Salmon, and Dahlin, *Inheritance in America*, 48.

donors were men without wives or children, or widows without any surviving offspring. The small number of testators who freed their slaves also tended to be without lineal heirs.

Charitable bequests seem to have been more common in New York City than in rural areas for two main reasons. First, the city's population was more ethnically diverse than that of most rural towns and therefore more inclined toward mutual aid based on national or religious ties. Second, the city was also the scene of the most abject poverty and the most splendid displays of wealth in the province. The donation of charity enabled some prominent merchants, professional men, and their widows to demonstrate their civic leadership through philanthropy. The nature of charitable bequests in Manhattan itself reflected a shift in communal ties and social values among several ethnic groups, especially the Dutch and French. During the late 1600s and early 1700s, testators usually offered gifts to aid the poor of their own national churches— Dutch Reformed, French, or Anglican. By the mid-1700s, the Anglican Trinity Church had emerged as the city's leading charitable institution, and it commonly received gifts from persons of non-English origin. This trend again underscores the progress of ethnic assimilation and the emulation of English culture among the wealthy.

There is little evidence of systematic estate planning in colonial America because most persons drafted their wills shortly before death. About two-thirds of testators in New York City described themselves as sick or weak as they prepared their wills. Forty percent of all wills were probated within one year of being drafted. While one might expect merchants and other well-to-do men to plan their wills well in advance of a final illness, this was not generally the case. As in other colonies, New York wills had a religious as well as secular purpose since the great majority of men and women bequeathed their souls to God before disposing of their material possessions. The religious preamble to the will became somewhat less important and more formulaic over time, but it was still included in most wills on the eve of the Revolution.

This study of inheritance in early New York is based on the concept that certain social and cultural trends can be measured through the provisions of wills. Indeed, colonial wills are a rich historical source because they reveal how individuals were influenced by social conditions and values as they made fundamental decisions concerning their family's welfare. The bequest of property by last will and testament changed significantly from the conquest of New Netherland to the onset of the American Revolution. Ethnic divisions became less salient over time, especially among long-established families, as Dutch, French, English, and other city dwellers devoted their energies to the pursuit of wealth.

While New York remained a pluralistic society, its people came to share a common culture that fostered male control of property within marriage, individual advancement by the young, and the economic self-sufficiency of family households. By the time of the Revolution, a type of family life had developed that would serve as a model for future generations of immigrants and their descendants.

# Appendix

# New Yorkers Who Left Wills: A Social Profile

The execution of a will was a commonplace, though by no means the only, method by which New Yorkers transmitted property to their descendants. During much of the colonial period, from one-fifth to one-fourth of all men—and a much smaller portion of women—dictated or drafted any such legally binding instructions. Since much more is known about the types of persons who left wills than those who died intestate, it is not always possible to determine how representative testators were of the general population. Despite some gaps in the historical record, however, there is little doubt that will writing was fairly widespread among diverse economic and occupational groups rather than simply confined to a small elite.

The number of persons who left wills increased fairly steadily as New York developed into a major commercial center during the course of the colonial period. Between 1664 and 1775, the city grew from a town of about fifteen hundred inhabitants to a thriving port of some twenty-two thousand, the second largest urban concentration in Britain's mainland colonies.[1] During the 1670s, one or two residents might draft or dictate a will during a single year. One hundred years later, more than thirty persons a year would do so. Almost 70 percent of all colonial wills were drafted between 1726 and 1775; 47 percent of them were executed within the final quarter-century of the colonial period (see Table A.1).

---

[1]Bureau of the Census, *A Century of Population Growth* (Washington, D.C., 1909), 170–83. For an analysis of the size and growth of the colony's population, see Robert V. Wells, *The Population of the British Colonies in America before 1776* (Princeton: Princeton University Press, 1975), 111–14.

**Table A.1** Wills executed in colonial
New York City

| Period | No. wills* | Percent |
|--------|-----------|---------|
| 1664–95 | 137 | 8.7 |
| 1696–1725 | 336 | 21.4 |
| 1726–50 | 358 | 22.8 |
| 1751–75 | 741 | 47.1 |
| Entire period | 1,572 | 100 |

*Data taken from all 1,572 wills left by residents of
Manhattan's urban wards.

Rather than matching every yearly or decennial increase in population, the level of will writing sometimes rose suddenly during periods of extraordinary danger and high mortality due to an epidemic or war. The outbreak of yellow fever during the summer and early autumn of 1702 undoubtedly prompted an unusually high number of persons to settle their temporal affairs before death might strike. In little more than three months, the epidemic claimed 570 lives, about 10 percent of the city's population.[2] Thirty-one men and women executed wills from July through October—a 300 percent increase over the number of testaments usually drafted throughout an entire year during the early 1700s. The next sudden spurt in will writing occurred more than half a century later during the French and Indian War. As a preparation for battle and possible death, many seamen made certain to execute a testament before embarking on privateering voyages against the king's enemies. The years 1756–58 produced a greater number of testaments than any similar span throughout the colonial period.[3]

Because there are few extant records of deaths or burials, it is nearly impossible to determine the exact percentage of all men who executed wills rather than dying intestate in colonial New York City. Still, one can estimate the frequency of will writing by analyzing data from several city-wide assessment lists—by determining the number of taxpayers on any single list who had already executed wills or would do so in the future. This method is admittedly inexact because it fails to account for the movement of taxpayers in or out of the city after an assessment was taken. One must also face the very real problem of identifying certain ratepayers as the same individuals who might leave wills many years later. The major advantage of using tax lists, however, is that they are

[2]John Duffy, *A History of Public Health in New York City, 1625–1866* (New York: Russell Sage, 1968), 35–36.
[3]From 1756 through 1758, 144 wills were prepared, 35 more than the next highest three-year total.

among the few historical sources that record the names of the great majority of adult male residents at any given time. Although there is only one known listing of individuals by census, there are several extant tax lists from the 1670s and an annual series during the periods 1695– 1709 and 1721–34.[4] By analyzing several lists over a considerable span of years, one can determine whether there were any major changes in the frequency of will writing as New York developed from a trading outpost into a major colonial port.

The assessment list of 1677 records the amount of taxation paid by some 298 men who owned houses and vacant lands within the city.[5] Eighty of these ratepayers, 26.8 percent of the entire group, would execute wills. Two subsequent tax lists, compiled in 1701 and 1730, assess the property of all inhabitants, tenants as well as owners of real estate. Since these assessments are more inclusive than the valuation of 1677, one cannot precisely compare findings from all the lists. There is little doubt, however, that the frequency of will writing did not increase and may have even decreased over time. Only 24.7 percent of all male taxpayers in 1701 would execute testaments; this ratio fell to 20.9 per- cent in 1730.[6] Because of the methodological problems discussed above, I do not offer these figures as precise statistics but as estimates of the percentage of all adult white males who left wills.

These findings are comparable to several assessments of the incidence of will writing in colonial New England, Pennsylvania, and Maryland. After examining probate records in nine diverse areas of Massachusetts, Connecticut, and New Hampshire, Kenneth Lockridge concludes that no more than one-fifth of all adult males left wills over the period 1650– 1762. Daniel Scott Smith estimates that testators accounted for about 36 percent of all men who died in the town of Hingham, Massachusetts, between 1726 and 1786. In Bucks County, Pennsylvania, about one-fifth of all men who died in 1751 left wills. Lois Green Carr estimates that testators comprised from 20 to 40 percent of the adult male population in three colonial Maryland counties, though the typical rate of testation was closer to the former figure than the latter.[7] It should also be noted

[4]The assessment lists of 1695–1734 are recorded on microfilm reel AR-1, Paul Klapper Library, Queens College, New York City. The 1703 census is printed in E. B. O'Callaghan, ed., *The Documentary History of the State of New York,* 4 vols. (Albany: Weed, Parsons, 1849– 51), 1:611–24.

[5]See Herbert L. Osgood, ed., *Minutes of the Common Council of the City of New York, 1665– 1776,* 8 vols. (New York: Dodd, Mead, 1905), 1:50–62. A tax list of 1674 is printed in *Collections of the New-York Historical Society,* 2d ser. (New York, 1891), 1:387–88.

[6]Among 781 male taxpayers on the 1701 list, 193 left wills; 246 testators are found among 1,175 male taxpayers in 1730.

[7]See Kenneth A. Lockridge, "A Communication," *William and Mary Quarterly,* 3d ser., 25 (1968): 516–17; Daniel Scott Smith, "Underregistration and Bias in Probate Records: An

that the frequency of will writing among adults in the twentieth-century United States is not generally higher than the frequency among colonial men. The preparation of a last will and testament is still primarily a concern of an affluent minority. Indeed, the rate of testation among the wealthy is especially high in contemporary society because of the need to avoid inheritance taxes—a problem that colonists did not confront.[8]

If a minority of men in New York and elsewhere left wills, why should studies of inheritance emphasize those documents? One way of answering this question is to contrast the number of wills that were probated with the number of cases of intestacy that came under the supervision of public officials. When a person died without leaving a will, his next of kin were entitled to petition for letters of administration from a duly authorized court. After an administrator posted bond as security for the execution of his duties, he possessed the legal authority to sue on behalf of the estate, settle outstanding credits and debts, and distribute the deceased's personal property according to the laws of intestate succession. While one-fourth to one-fifth of men executed wills, a far smaller portion left behind properties that were administered through official intestacy procedures. From 1664 through 1775, local and provincial courts issued 640 letters of administration concerning the estates of New York City men. During the same period, 1,339 male residents prepared wills. The ratio between will writing and intestacy was more than 2:1 for most of the colonial era.[9] It is therefore evident that many families settled questions of inheritance without direct recourse to legal institutions. This tendency was more pronounced in New York than in other colonies—undoubtedly because of the disparity between provincial law and popular customs regarding inheritance, especially among the ethnic Dutch.[10]

Analysis of Data from Eighteenth-Century Hingham, Massachusetts," *William and Mary Quarterly*, 3d ser., 32 (1975): 100–110; see also in the same issue, Gloria L. Main, "Probate Records as a Source for Early American History," 88–89. For data on will writing in colonial Bucks County and in recent America, see Carole Shammas, Marylynn Salmon, and Michel Dahlin, *Inheritance in America: From Colonial Times to the Present* (New Brunswick: Rutgers University Press, 1987), 15–17, 221. Lois Green Carr's statistics pertain to the period 1670–1776; see Carr, "Inheritance in the Colonial Chesapeake," in Ronald Hoffman and Peter J. Albert, eds., *Women in the Age of the American Revolution* (Charlottesville: University Press of Virginia, 1989), 199–201.

[8]Only 10.6 percent of all adult decedents in New York County, N.Y., left wills during the period 1914–29. Testators comprised 14.9 percent of adult decedents in Los Angeles County in 1980. The rate of testation among the same group in affluent Bucks County was 36 percent in 1979. See Shammas, Salmon, and Dahlin, *Inheritance in America*, 15–17.

[9]See David Evan Narrett, "Patterns of Inheritance in Colonial New York City, 1664–1775: A Study in the History of the Family (Ph.D. diss., Cornell University, 1981), 56–57.

[10]Carole Shammas estimates that testators numbered from one-fourth to one-half of all those whose estates went through probate in most colonial jurisdictions. Unlike the situation in New York City, probate records therefore generally included more cases of intestacy than testacy. See Shammas, Salmon, and Dahlin, *Inheritance in America*, 41.

Colonial records indicate that cases of intestacy were especially likely to come under court supervision under certain circumstances. I have determined the occupations of three-fourths of all men whose estates passed through official intestacy procedures. More than two-thirds of this group were mariners—surely a much greater ratio than the percentage of seamen among all white males. Why should mariners have constituted such a disproportionately high number of men whose estates were administered through the legal system? Since sailors were far more likely to die as bachelors than members of most other occupations, their friends or creditors would probably have to lodge a formal petition with a court in order to gain access to their estates. When a man was survived by a wife or children, however, the members of his family could more readily distribute his property among themselves without requesting the permission of public officials.

Among certain groups, cases of intestacy very seldom passed through legal channels. The records of the Dutch Reformed congregation list some 718 men who were buried by the church between 1731 and 1775.[11] Although 567 of these persons (or 79 percent of the entire group) died without having made a will, only 25 intestate men left properties that would be managed by a court-appointed administrator. The remaining 151 men (or 21 percent) executed testaments. These findings indicate that the laws of succession may have actually been applied in relatively few cases of intestacy. By avoiding court supervision and legal fees, colonial families could determine the course of inheritance according to their particular needs rather than necessarily complying with a uniform rule of law. This goal was especially important to Dutch New Yorkers who wished to maintain their distinctive social customs without official interference.

Since the succession to property was often decided upon in a strictly private setting, wills provide most of our knowledge about popular attitudes and practices concerning inheritance. As we examine how testators disposed of their property, it is also essential to analyze their social and economic backgrounds—to determine the extent to which wealth may have shaped the decision to execute a will.

One means of measuring the economic status of testators is to analyze inventories of estates—itemized and appraised listings of an individual's property at death. Although this method has several advantages, I have not selected it because of lack of sufficient evidence. There are simply not enough inventories to permit reasonably precise comparisons be-

---

[11] "Records of Burials in the Dutch Church, New York," *Year Book of the Holland Society of New York* (New York, 1899), 139–211. The list of burials begins in 1727, but I begin my analysis in 1731 in order to correlate mortality records with extant probate records.

tween the property holdings of testators and persons who died intestate.[12] Instead, I have chosen tax lists as my principal source for measuring the economic status of testators. By identifying all ratepayers on a given list who had executed wills or would subsequently do so, one can determine whether will writing was largely confined within certain social classes.

While testators occupied nearly all ranks on the economic scale, they constituted a disproportionately high share of the wealthiest men. Nearly half of the city's upper tenth of taxpayers in 1677 eventually executed wills; more than 60 percent of this portion of property holders in 1701 and 1730 also drafted testaments. The incidence of will writing among the most affluent residents far exceeded the rate among all taxpayers.[13] It should be emphasized, however, that will writing was practiced among a broad spectrum of property holders rather than being limited to a small elite. The markedly unequal distribution of wealth among testators in eighteenth-century New York City roughly paralleled the degree of economic stratification within the community.[14]

In a study of eighteenth-century Hingham, Massachusetts, Daniel Scott Smith also concludes that wealth was the single most important factor in determining whether an individual would leave a will: "A man in the wealthiest 40 percent on a tax list was eight times more likely to leave a will . . . as a man without property or in the poorest 20 percent of those owning real property."[15] This difference between the social habits of rich and poor was of a similar magnitude in eighteenth-century New York City. Almost one-half of the wealthiest 30 percent of all male taxpayers in 1701 and 1730 executed wills. Only about one-twentieth of the poorest 30 percent did so.[16]

Those men who did leave wills varied greatly in economic status and also practiced a wide range of occupations (see Table A.2). Despite the representation of many different trades, however, a disproportionately high number of testators belonged to the city's most prestigious professions. Merchants alone accounted for about one among every three men

[12]Kenneth Scott has compiled a complete listing of all colonial inventories on file in the New-York Historical Society and the Paul Klapper Library, Queens College. See "Early New York Inventories of Estates," *National Genealogical Society Quarterly* 53 (1965): 133–43; "New York Inventories," in ibid., 54 (1966): 246–59.

[13]For a more detailed analysis of testators' economic status, see Narrett, "Patterns of Inheritance," 58–65.

[14]See Bruce Wilkenfeld, "The Social and Economic Structure of the City of New York, 1695–1796" (Ph.D. diss., Columbia University, 1973), 22, 80.

[15]Smith, "Underregistration in Probate Records," 516–17. Testators also owned a disproportionately high percentage of wealth in colonial Pennsylvania and Maryland. See Shammas, Salmon, and Dahlin, *Inheritance in America*, 18–19. Carr, "Inheritance in the Colonial Chesapeake," 202–8.

[16]Narrett, "Patterns of Inheritance," 64–65.

**Table A.2** Occupational status of male testators*

| Occupation | 1664–95 N | % | 1696–1725 N | % | 1726–50 N | % | 1751–75 N | % | Entire period N | % |
|---|---|---|---|---|---|---|---|---|---|---|
| Artisans | 20 | 23.2 | 69 | 27.2 | 78 | 28.0 | 155 | 27.3 | 322 | 27.1 |
| Merchants | 29 | 33.7 | 84 | 33.1 | 76 | 27.2 | 105 | 18.5 | 294 | 24.8 |
| Mariners | 13 | 15.1 | 46 | 18.1 | 42 | 15.0 | 162 | 28.6 | 263 | 22.2 |
| Professionals** | 10 | 11.6 | 26 | 10.2 | 29 | 10.4 | 42 | 7.4 | 107 | 9.0 |
| Shopkeepers*** | 5 | 5.8 | 11 | 4.3 | 19 | 6.8 | 36 | 6.3 | 71 | 6.0 |
| Processors of food and drink | 5 | 5.8 | 8 | 3.1 | 19 | 6.8 | 29 | 5.1 | 61 | 5.1 |
| Laborers | 2 | 2.3 | 4 | 1.6 | 13 | 4.7 | 30 | 5.3 | 49 | 4.1 |
| Others | 2 | 2.3 | 6 | 2.4 | 3 | 1.1 | 8 | 1.4 | 19 | 1.6 |
| Totals | 86 | 99.8 | 254 | 100 | 279 | 100 | 567 | 99.9 | 1186 | 99.9 |

*Data have been gathered for 88.6 percent of all men who left wills during the colonial period.
**Includes attorneys, government officials, ministers, physicians, and men who identified themselves by the titles of "gentleman" or "esquire."
***Includes shopkeepers, innkeepers, tavern keepers, and traders.

who left wills between 1664 and 1725—clearly a much higher ratio than the proportion of merchants among all adult white males.[17] Although merchants continued to be among the largest groups of testators, they accounted for a smaller share of the will-leaving population during the next fifty years: 27 percent between 1726 and 1750, 18 percent between 1751 and 1775.

Since we might expect that the wealthiest men would be most likely to leave wills, it is especially noteworthy that the middling strata of skilled craftsmen and shopkeepers also executed a major share of all testaments. Artisans, a highly diverse group of craftsmen, accounted for about one-fourth of all testators throughout the colonial period.[18] Other

[17]In 1701, merchants accounted for 15.9 percent of all taxpayers whose occupations are known; they numbered 15.1 percent in 1730. See Wilkenfeld, "Social and Economic Structure," 28, 87.
[18]I have defined the term "artisan" to include the following types of skilled craftsmen: workers in wood or stone (joiner, carpenter, cooper, turner, wheelwright, mason, blockmaker); smiths and metal workers (blacksmith, brazier, ironmonger, silversmith, goldsmith, gunsmith, cutler); workers in leather (saddler, glover, tanner, currier, cordwainer [i.e., shoemaker]); shipyard workers (ropemaker, shipwright, ship carpenter, sailmaker); workers in cloth and finery (tailor, weaver, staymaker, hatmaker, feltmaker, wigmaker); miscellaneous trades (chandler, limeburner, painter or glazier [lymner], pipemaker, potter, printer). These occupations comprise a great diversity of individuals of varying wealth and status. Silversmiths and goldsmiths, for example, generally occupied the highest ranks within these categories; the lowest were commonly held by blacksmiths and tailors. Since even members of the same craft often held different levels of wealth, "artisan" should be understood primarily as an occupational rather than an economic catetory. This group does not include persons who were primarily concerned with the processing of food and drink: brewers, bakers, butchers, millers (bolters). These tradesmen generally occupied a higher economic position than most skilled craftsmen. Joyce Goodfriend has analyzed the relative economic status of various professions in seventeenth-century New York City. See

groups of tradesmen were also well represented. Shopkeepers, innkeepers, tavern owners, and small traders together numbered about 6 percent of all men who left wills. The processors of food and drink (brewers, bakers, butchers, millers) accounted for 5 percent of testators.

Unskilled workmen, however, seldom made wills. Only six common laborers left wills between 1664 and 1725, amounting to less than 2 percent of testators during this period. More workmen prepared wills during the next fifty years because they formed an increasingly large element within the city's population.[19] They still accounted, however, for only 5 percent of testators between 1726 and 1775.

Although occupational status is often a useful indicator of social position, one cannot simply equate certain trades with a definite level of wealth. As one of the most highly diverse professional groups, "mariners" ranged from ship captains and sponsors of trading ventures to common sailors. Men who described themselves as mariners accounted for more than one-fifth of all colonial New York City testators whose occupation is known. This group prepared an especially high proportion of wills during the period 1751–75—a trend connected to the expansion of trade and privateering, particularly during the French and Indian War. There is some evidence that common sailors constituted a much larger share of the will-leaving population during the mid-1700s than they had previously formed. Between 1664 and 1725, more than four-fifths of all mariners who left wills were heads of households—men who bequeathed property to wives or children. Between 1751 and 1775, however, few seamen showed any signs of establishing permanent roots in the city. Fifty-seven percent of all mariners who left wills during this period failed to mention either a wife or any children.

LITERACY

Probate records offer an obvious and useful measure of literacy—the capacity of individuals to sign their wills. Nearly four-fifths of New York City men who left wills from 1664 through 1695 were literate. This proportion rose to 86 percent between 1696 and 1725 and remained fairly constant during the remainder of the colonial era (see Table A.3).

---

"'Too Great a Mixture of Nations': The Development of New York City Society in the Seventeenth Century" (Ph.D. diss., UCLA, 1975), 35–39. Bruce Wilkenfeld has done much the same task for eighteenth-century New York. See Wilkenfeld, "Social and Economic Structure," 28, 87.

[19]After the mid-1740s, an increasing proportion of city residents registered for freemanship under the designation of "laborer." See "The Burghers of New Amsterdam and New York, 1675–1866," *Collections of the New-York Historical Society for the Year 1885*, vol. 18 (New York, 1886).

**Table A.3** Literacy rate among men who left wills

| Period | N* | Sign | | Mark | |
|---|---|---|---|---|---|
| | | N | % | N | % |
| 1664–95 | 89 | 71 | 79.8 | 18 | 20.2 |
| 1696–1725 | 232 | 200 | 86.2 | 32 | 13.8 |
| 1726–50 | 282 | 242 | 85.8 | 40 | 14.2 |
| 1751–75 | 603 | 502 | 83.2 | 101 | 16.7 |
| Entire period | 1,206 | 1,015 | 84.2 | 191 | 15.8 |

*Slightly more than 90 percent of all wills contain data concerning literacy. This information is missing wherever the original will has been lost and a copy exists only in abstract form.

Mariners were the only major occupational group whose literacy rate declined over time. Although 92.5 percent of seamen signed wills from 1664 through 1725, only 76.7 percent could do so during the period 1751–75. This trend is undoubtedly linked to the increasing number of common sailors who left wills during the late colonial era.

The overall rate of literacy among New York City testators was quite similar to the general level in colonial Boston. Basing his findings exclusively on an examination of wills, Kenneth Lockridge concludes that male literacy was about 75 percent in Boston during the 1660s and rose slowly to just over 80 percent during the latter part of the eighteenth century. In the New England countryside, the literacy of farmers increased from 45 percent in 1660, to 60 percent in 1710, and to 80 percent in 1760.[20] Examining deeds as well as probate records, Ross W. Beales, Jr., has found an even higher rate of literacy in Grafton, Massachusetts, during the mid-eighteenth century: 97.9 percent of all men whose names appear on an assessment list of 1747 were literate.[21] Although Grafton may have had an unusually high level of literacy, there is some evidence that the ability to read and write was somewhat more widespread in New England and New York City than in rural Pennsylvania during the mid-eighteenth century. Alan Tully has determined that 72 percent of Chester County men were able to sign their wills between 1729 and 1774; the rate of literacy in Lancaster County was about 63 percent during that same period.[22]

[20]Kenneth A. Lockridge, *Literacy in Colonial New England: An Enquiry into the Social Context of Literacy in the Early Modern West* (New York: Norton, 1974), 21.

[21]Ross W. Beales, Jr., "Studying Literacy at the Community Level: A Research Note," *Journal of Interdisciplinary History* 9 (1972): 98–99.

[22]Alan Tully, "Literacy Levels and Educational Development in Rural Pennsylvania, 1729–1775," *Pennsylvania History* 39 (1973): 304. The rate of male literacy in two rural New York counties, Suffolk and Ulster, was above 80 percent during the period 1729–75. The literacy rate had been 67 percent in Suffolk and 72 percent in Ulster during the years 1664–95. See Narrett, "Patterns of Inheritance," 312.

**Table A.4** Literacy rate among
occupational groups

| Occupation | N* | Wills signed | |
| --- | --- | --- | --- |
| | | N | % |
| Professionals | 94 | 92 | 97.9 |
| Merchants | 276 | 265 | 96.0 |
| Processors of food and drink | 53 | 47 | 88.7 |
| Shopkeepers | 65 | 55 | 84.6 |
| Mariners | 232 | 189 | 81.5 |
| Artisans | 301 | 237 | 78.7 |
| Laborers | 46 | 23 | 50.0 |

*Data have been compiled for 90 percent of all
testators who practiced these professions.

The ability to write varied considerably among diverse occupational
and economic groups in colonial New York City. As in contemporary
Boston, literacy was nearly universal at the top of the social pyramid:
more than 95 percent of all merchants and professional men signed
their wills (see Table A.4). Tradesmen and skilled craftsmen showed a
somewhat lesser level of literacy. About 89 percent of all processors and
85 percent of all shopkeepers were able to sign their testaments. The
ability to write was fairly general among skilled craftsmen but dropped
off significantly among testators at the lower end of the occupational
scale. Although nearly four-fifths of artisans signed their wills, only one-
half of laborers did so.

Artisans were the only occupational group that showed a significant
increase in its level of literacy. Between 1664 and 1695, only ten among
nineteen artisans were able to sign their wills. The level of literacy within
the group climbed to nearly 80 percent between 1696 and 1725 and rose
even higher toward the end of the colonial period.[23] Because of the
small number of wills executed during the seventeenth century, one
hesitates to generalize about the increase in literacy among artisans.
These findings do, however, closely parallel patterns of literacy among
skilled craftsmen in rural New England. Although little more than one-
half of New England artisans could sign their wills during the 1660s,
about three-fourths were literate by the 1720s, and more than 85 percent by the 1760s. In Boston, the rate of literacy among artisans remained fairly close to 75–80 percent from the mid-seventeenth to mid-
eighteenth centuries.[24]

[23]Forty-six among fifty-nine artisans (or 78 percent of the entire group) signed wills
drafted between 1669 and 1725. Fifty-five of seventy-two (or 76 percent) signed between
1726 and 1750, while 126 of 151 (or 83 percent) signed from 1751 through 1775.
[24]Lockridge, *Literacy*, 21–22, 25, 54.

**Table A.5** Literacy rate among women who left wills

|  |  | Sign | | Mark | |
| --- | --- | --- | --- | --- | --- |
| Period | $N*$ | N | % | N | % |
| 1664–95 | 28 | 14 | 50.0 | 14 | 50.0 |
| 1696–1725 | 46 | 32 | 69.6 | 14 | 30.4 |
| 1726–50 | 54 | 43 | 79.6 | 11 | 20.4 |
| 1751–75 | 104 | 71 | 68.3 | 33 | 31.7 |
| Entire period | 232 | 160 | 69.0 | 72 | 31.0 |

*Probate records yield information concerning the literacy of 91.3 percent of all female testators.

While male literacy in New York City increased from the 1660s to the 1720s, the rate among women rose much more sharply (see Table A.5). Between 1664 and 1695, only 50 percent of women were able to sign their wills. This percentage increased to 69.9 percent between 1696 and 1725 and fluctuated around a similar level during the remainder of the colonial period. Although female literacy also rose significantly in eighteenth-century Boston, this trend developed later than in New York City. Basing his findings on a sample of wills, Lockridge concludes that 40 percent of Boston women were literate between 1650 and 1715. The signature rate among females climbed to 65 percent during the period 1758–92.[25]

By the mid-eighteenth century, a significant discrepancy had developed in female literacy between urban and rural areas. While the signature rate among city women rose to between 65 and 70 percent by the end of the colonial period, the literacy of females in rural New England showed little change at all, increasing from less than 40 percent during the early 1700s to perhaps 45 percent by the 1770s.[26] Ross Beales estimates that only 46 percent of all women in Grafton, Massachusetts, could write in 1747.[27] Female literacy was even lower in two Pennsylvania counties than in rural New England during the mid-eighteenth century. While 42 percent of women in Lancaster and Chester counties signed their wills between 1765 and 1774, the overall average was only 31 percent during the period 1729–74.[28] Although few women in rural New York left wills, my data suggest that female literacy was much higher among Dutch colonial farm women than among Yankees. Seventeen of twenty-four female testators (or 71 percent) in predominantly Dutch Ulster County signed wills, while only eight among twenty-eight women (29 percent) did so in Suffolk County, an area settled by New En-

[25]Ibid., 38–43.
[26]Ibid.
[27]Beales, "Studying Literacy at the Community Level," 98–100.
[28]Tully, "Literacy Levels," 304.

glanders. Perhaps the privileged position of women in Dutch colonial society was based on literacy as well as the tradition of community property.[29]

Some of the distinctive cultural characteristics of eighteenth-century urban life—the proliferation of newspapers and other printed materials, the increased opportunities for learning through social intercourse as much as through formal educational institutions—may help to explain why such a high percentage of women were able to sign their wills in New York City as compared to Grafton, Massachusetts, or Lancaster County, Pennsylvania. Although his study is based on a limited sample, Lawrence Cremin has found a signature rate of 79 percent among female testators in Philadelphia between 1773 and 1775.[30] The cultural advantages of city life may have had an especially great impact on female literacy because women generally had fewer opportunities for social intercourse than men did. Unlike the rural housewives who seldom left the farm, city women were almost daily participants in the market economy.

As one might expect, female literacy in New York City varied considerably according to social class. Forty-two women in my sample were the wives or widows of merchants; thirty-eight of these women signed their wills. By contrast, only twenty-four of the forty-two wives and widows of tradesmen (artisans, shopkeepers, and processors) were literate. None of the three women who had been married to laborers could sign their testaments.

Although wills clearly provide a great deal of useful information about literacy in colonial society, do they actually yield reliable data concerning the ability to read and write among the general population? Despite the fact that wealthy men were considerably more likely to execute wills than the poor, Kenneth Lockridge argues that the literacy rate of testators was similar to that of the entire adult white male population of New England. While the generally high economic status of testators undoubtedly tended to raise their level of literacy, this upward bias was offset by an equally strong bias in the opposite direction. Many testators were aged, ill men who lacked enough strength to sign their wills or who had forgotten how to write. Other elderly men may not even have had the opportunity to become literate because of the inferior quality of education during their youth. After balancing the negative effects of sickness and

---

[29]Narrett, "Patterns of Inheritance," 315.

[30]Although Cremin makes some valid generalizations about literacy in an urban environment, his sample considerably overestimates the level of literacy in New York City during the 1690s and the first decade of the eighteenth century. See Lawrence A. Cremin, *American Education: The Colonial Experience, 1607–1783* (New York: Harper & Row, 1970), 540–41.

old age against the considerable wealth of testators, Lockridge concludes that wills provide an accurate measure of the rate of literacy among all adult white males.[31]

Although Lockridge offers some important points about analyzing wills, I am skeptical whether his argument sufficiently considers the disproportionately high number of wealthy men who left wills. In colonial New York City, about seven times as many merchants as laborers executed testaments. Since probate records undoubtedly underrepresent poor persons who were likely to be illiterate, it is highly probable that testators had a higher rate of literacy than other men. As Lockridge himself suggests, will writing may have been a "selective process" that partially depended on literacy. Persons who could read and write were more likely than illiterates to grasp the significance and potential uses of legal documents such as wills.[32]

## Ethnic Origins

Though will writing was most common among the middle and upper social classes, testators formed a fairly representative cross-section of the city's ethnic groups from the late 1670s to 1730s. By analyzing surnames, I have determined the ethnic origins of about 90 percent of all male taxpayers on the assessment lists of 1677, 1701, and 1730 (see Table A.6). The ethnic balance among testators roughly paralleled the shifting percentage of Dutch, British, and French Huguenot colonists within the entire population (compare Tables A.6 and A.7). As patterns of colonization changed, the British gradually supplanted the Dutch as the most numerous group in New York City. French Huguenot colonists, the victims of religious persecution in Europe, formed about 10 percent of the population during the early eighteenth century. New York's small Jewish community was overrepresented among testators because many of its members were affluent merchants.

Because of a lack of tax lists or censuses, one cannot precisely determine the ethnic composition of New York's population during the mid-eighteenth century. An analysis of wills, however, can provide at least some measure of major changes in the relative numbers of certain groups (see Table A.7). Since few Dutch or French Huguenot colonists settled in New York City during this period, these groups formed a

[31]Lockridge, *Literacy*, 7–12.
[32]Ibid., 11. For a similar critique of Lockridge's analysis, see Harvey J. Graff, "Literacy in History," *History of Education Quarterly* 15 (1975): 472. See also Beales, "Studying Literacy at the Community Level," 95.

**Table A.6** Ethnic composition of New York City's adult
white male population

| Ethnic group* | 1677 | | 1701 | | 1730 | |
|---|---|---|---|---|---|---|
| | N | % | N | % | N | % |
| Dutch | 189 | 69.7 | 355 | 51.8 | 399 | 38.6 |
| English-British | 68 | 25.1 | 253 | 36.9 | 506 | 49.0 |
| French | 13 | 4.8 | 68 | 9.9 | 100 | 9.7 |
| German** | — | — | — | — | 10 | 1.0 |
| Jewish | 1 | 0.4 | 9 | 1.3 | 18 | 1.7 |
| Totals | 271 | 100 | 685 | 99.9 | 1,033 | 100 |

*By analyzing surnames, I have determined the national origins of about 90 percent of all male taxpayers on the assessment lists of 1677, 1701, and 1730.

**Early German and Scandinavian immigrants to New Amsterdam were rapidly assimilated into the city's Dutch majority. Because many of these colonists belonged to the Dutch Reformed church and adopted Dutch-style names, it is especially difficult to distinguish between them and settlers from the Netherlands. German residents emerged as a more distinct group during the first half of the eighteenth century, a period of increased immigration from continental Europe to New York. There is little doubt that this table underrates the number of city residents of German origin. For a discussion of early German and Scandinavian colonists, see John O. Evjen, *Scandinavian Emigrants in New York, 1630–1674* (Minneapolis, 1916).

steadily declining share of all testators.[33] A nearly opposite trend characterized British immigration. Colonists of British stock numbered about 45 percent of male testators between 1726 and 1750 but more than 60 percent during the next quarter-century. Because of the inherent difficulties, I have not attempted to differentiate among Englishmen, Welshmen, Scotsmen, and Scots-Irish. The latter two groups, not well represented before 1720, formed a major element in the city's population by the 1760s.[34]

As early as the late 1600s, certain ethnic groups began to dominate distinct sectors of Manhattan's economic life. Through the apprenticeship system and ties of kinship, Dutch residents established a mastery of the leather, wood, metal, and stone crafts. English settlers accounted for a disproportionately high number of seamen and workers involved in shipbuilding.[35] Although a detailed analysis of the ethnic composition

[33] For an overview of Dutch immigration to America, see Gerald F. De Jong, *The Dutch in America, 1609–1974* (Boston: Twayne, 1975). For an important study of French immigration, see Jon Butler, *The Huguenots in America: A Refugee People in New World Society* (Cambridge: Harvard University Press, 1984).

[34] Two scholarly treatments of Scots and Scots-Irish colonization are found in R. J. Dickson, *Ulster Emigration to Colonial America, 1718–1775* (London: Routledge and Kegan Paul, 1966); and Ian Charles Cargill Graham, *Colonists from Scotland: Emigration to North America, 1707–1783* (Ithaca: Cornell University Press, 1956). Forrest McDonald and Ellen Shapiro McDonald estimate that Welshmen, Scots, and Irishmen accounted for slightly more than one-fourth of New York State's population in 1790. See "The Ethnic Origins of the American People, 1790," *William and Mary Quarterly*, 3d ser., 37 (1980); 179–99.

[35] Goodfriend, "'Too Great a Mixture,'" 146–53.

**Table A.7** Ethnic composition of male testators

| Ethnic group* | 1664–95 | | 1696–1725 | | 1726–50 | | 1751–75 | | Entire period | |
|---|---|---|---|---|---|---|---|---|---|---|
| | N | % | N | % | N | % | N | % | N | % |
| Dutch | 62 | 53.9 | 116 | 41.3 | 121 | 42.0 | 164 | 27.5 | 463 | 36.1 |
| English-British | 48 | 41.7 | 122 | 43.4 | 128 | 44.4 | 366 | 61.3 | 664 | 51.8 |
| French | 5 | 4.3 | 37 | 13.2 | 24 | 8.3 | 22 | 3.7 | 88 | 6.9 |
| German | — | — | — | — | 6 | 2.1 | 39 | 6.5 | 45 | 3.5 |
| Jewish | — | — | 6 | 2.1 | 9 | 3.1 | 6 | 1.0 | 21 | 1.6 |
| Totals | 115 | 99.9 | 281 | 100 | 288 | 99.9 | 597 | 100 | 1,281 | 99.9 |

*By analyzing surnames, I have determined the ethnic origins of 95.7 percent of all men who executed wills. The ethnic balance among testators corresponded fairly closely to the distribution of national groups within the entire white male population (see Table A.6).

of specific occupations is not one of my primary concerns, it is important to indicate that several national groups tended to gravitate toward certain vocations throughout the colonial period. While about 85 percent of all mariners were of British origin, more than 80 percent of all shoemakers were of Dutch ancestry. These enduring patterns remind us that inheritance often involves the transmission of status and privilege within a particular social group as well as within an individual family.[36]

## AGE AND MARITAL STATUS

Through a study of church records and genealogies, I have determined the ages of about one-fourth of all men who left wills during the colonial period (see Table A.8). Although we might expect testators to be an especially elderly group, fewer than one-third had reached age sixty and less than 13 percent were age seventy or older. More than two-fifths of testators were between forty and fifty-nine years old. The average man in our sample was just 51.2 years old when he executed his will and the typical life span no greater than fifty-five years. Seventy-four percent of all wills were probated within five years after being drafted, and more than three-fifths were validated within two years. This pattern remained quite stable throughout the colonial period and varied little among diverse ethnic or occupational groups.

Because the vital registers of the Dutch Reformed church are far more comprehensive than the records of other congregations, Dutch settlers account for about 70 percent of all testators whose ages have been deter-

[36]For a general discussion of this aspect of inheritance, see E. P. Thompson, "The Grid of Inheritance: A Comment," in Jack Goody, Joan Thirsk, and E. P. Thompson, eds., *Family and Inheritance: Rural Society in Western Europe, 1200–1800* (Cambridge: Cambridge University Press, 1978), 358–60.

**Table A.8** Age of male testators*

| Age (in years) | No. testators | Percent |
|---|---|---|
| Under 30 | 23 | 7.1 |
| 30–39 | 59 | 18.2 |
| 40–49 | 72 | 22.2 |
| 50–59 | 67 | 20.7 |
| 60–69 | 62 | 19.1 |
| 70 and above | 41 | 12.6 |
| Totals | 324 | 99.9 |

*I have compiled data concerning 324 testators, 24.2 percent of all men who left wills during the colonial period (1664–1775).

mined. I have also been more successful in finding this kind of information about men who left wills in the eighteenth than in the seventeenth century. Despite these limitations, I have collected sufficient data to contrast the average age of testators during three periods: 1696–1725, 1726–50, and 1751–75. The average age of these men increased from 47.1 years during the first period to 52.3 years during the next, and then leveled off to 52.9 years during the late colonial era. Only one among every five testators was 60 or older between 1696 and 1725. This proportion increased to 35 percent during the next half-century.[37]

Although the longevity of New York City testators rose during the first half of the eighteenth century, the average man still died at a considerably younger age than his counterpart in several New England villages.[38] The typical life span of Manhattan men was closer to the norm in late eighteenth-century Germantown, Pennsylvania (where the average age of men at death ranged from 54.0 to 57.8 years between 1760 and 1800).[39] It is even more striking that testators in two rural New York counties were significantly older than their city counterparts.[40] During the entire English colonial era, 32 percent of city testators (in my sample) were at least sixty years old when they prepared their wills. Sixty-six percent of Suffolk County men and 45 percent of Ulster County men had reached this age (see Table A.9). These statistics suggest that the

[37]For a more detailed analysis of testators' ages, see Narrett, "Patterns of Inheritance," 83–88. Mariners were the only group that fell far below the norm in age.

[38]Philip J. Greven, Jr., *Four Generations: Population, Land, and Family in Colonial Andover, Massachusetts* (Ithaca: Cornell University Press, 1970), 26–27, 108–9, 192–94. See also John J. Waters, "Patrimony, Succession, and Stability: Guilford, Connecticut, in the Eighteenth Century," *Perspectives in American History* 10 (1976): 146.

[39]Stephanie Grauman Wolf, *Urban Village: Population, Community, and Family Structure in Germantown, Pennsylvania, 1683–1800* (Princeton: Princeton University Press, 1976), 283–84.

[40]Narrett, "Patterns of Inheritance," 318–20.

**Table A.9** Age of male testators by region*

| | Under 30 | | 31–39 | | 40–49 | | 50–59 | | 60–69 | | 70 and above | | Totals | |
|---|---|---|---|---|---|---|---|---|---|---|---|---|---|---|---|
| | N | % | N | % | N | % | N | % | N | % | N | % | N | % |
| New York City | 23 | 7.1 | 59 | 18.2 | 72 | 22.2 | 67 | 20.7 | 62 | 19.1 | 41 | 12.6 | 324 | 99.9 |
| Suffolk County | 6 | 2.0 | 13 | 4.4 | 33 | 11.2 | 49 | 16.6 | 91 | 30.8 | 103 | 34.9 | 295 | 99.9 |
| Ulster County | 6 | 5.0 | 16 | 13.4 | 17 | 14.3 | 27 | 22.7 | 24 | 20.2 | 29 | 24.4 | 119 | 100 |

*Data have been determined for 24 percent of all male testators in New York City, 56 percent in Suffolk County, and 55 percent in Ulster County in the period 1664–1775.

rural areas were considerably more healthful than the environment of New York City.

More than 70 percent of all New York City men were married and almost 12 percent were widowed when they executed their wills (see Table A.10). Mariners were both the youngest group of testators and the only major occupational group having many members who never married. While 46 percent of all mariners were bachelors, only 10 percent of all other testators were single.

Despite the predominance of married men, the proportion of bachelors among the male population was significantly higher in New York City than in rural New York counties. Only 6 percent of testators were single in five Ulster County towns and only 1 percent in three Suffolk county towns throughout the colonial era. Men who prepared wills in rural areas were nearly all heads of families.[41] While members of certain occupational groups within New York City (processors, shopkeepers, and laborers) almost always married, others (artisans, professional men, and merchants) tended to include a somewhat higher percentage of single men (see Table A.10).

More than 90 percent of all Dutch and German testators in Manhattan were either married or widowed. Single men, by contrast, accounted for more than one-fourth of all Britons who left wills. If one excludes the large number of seamen from our survey, however, the proportion of bachelors falls to 13 percent of all Britons. Though Dutch and German testators were the most likely to have married, few men (excluding mariners) remained single throughout life.

To determine how many testators married more than once, we need to examine vital records and genealogies rather than relying on probate records alone. The marriage registers of the Dutch Reformed church between 1640 and 1730 are our single most valuable source of information concerning this question.[42] Ministers regularly inscribed the dates of marriage of the members of their congregation, and frequently they noted whether the bride and groom were single or previously wed. The clerical register provides the most thorough information about couples who wed after the publication of banns rather than simply after obtaining a marriage license from the government. Since this last practice became increasingly common after 1700, it is often difficult to determine

[41] See ibid., 321–22. The percentage of men who never wed was very small in other rural and semi-urban areas. See Waters, "Patrimony," 148; Wolf, *Urban Village*, 254.

[42] See *Marriages from 1639 to 1801 in the Reformed Dutch Church, New Amsterdam, New York City*, Collections of the New York Genealogical and Biographical Society, 9 (New York, 1940). See also *Names of Persons for whom Marriage Licenses were Issued by the Secretary of the Province of New York, Previous to 1784* (Albany: Weed, Parsons, 1860).

**Table A.10** Marital status of male testators

| Occupation* | Single | | Married | | Widowed | | Totals | |
|---|---|---|---|---|---|---|---|---|
| | N | % | N | % | N | % | N | % |
| Laborers | 2 | 4.1 | 41 | 83.7 | 6 | 12.2 | 49 | 100 |
| Shopkeepers | 3 | 4.2 | 60 | 84.5 | 8 | 11.3 | 71 | 100 |
| Processors of food and drink | 3 | 4.9 | 46 | 75.4 | 12 | 19.7 | 61 | 100 |
| Artisans | 29 | 9.0 | 256 | 79.5 | 37 | 11.5 | 322 | 100 |
| Professionals | 12 | 11.2 | 73 | 68.2 | 22 | 20.6 | 107 | 100 |
| Merchants | 38 | 13.3 | 209 | 73.1 | 39 | 13.6 | 286 | 100 |
| Mariners | 120 | 46.1 | 128 | 49.2 | 12 | 4.6 | 260 | 99.9 |
| All occupations** | 207 | 17.9 | 813 | 70.3 | 136 | 11.8 | 1,156 | 100 |
| All testators | 234 | 17.7 | 937 | 70.8 | 153 | 11.5 | 1,324 | 100 |

*Each group has been ranked (in ascending order) according to the proportion of single men within each occupation. Data have been compiled for nearly 99 percent of all testators (1,324 among all 1,339 men who left wills).

**This category reflects totals for 1,156 testators whose occupations are known.

the marital status of brides and grooms in eighteenth-century New York City. The evidence, however, is sufficient for us to contrast the frequency of remarriage among testators who wed during three successive thirty-year periods: 1640–69, 1670–99, and 1700–1729. Since 77 percent of the men in my sample were of Dutch origin, the findings apply principally to that group.

Remarriage was a very common occurrence among testators who first wed between 1640 and 1669. Thirty percent of these men married twice and an additional 15 percent married three times (see Table A.11). The frequency of remarriage declined dramatically among testators who first married during the next thirty years. Less than 14 percent of this group wed twice and none are known to have had three wives. This newly established pattern remained dominant among testators who first wed between 1700 and 1729. Only about one among every six of these men married more than once. Although these statistics may overstate the

**Table A.11** Frequency of remarriage among male testators, by data of first marriage

| No. times married | 1640–69 | | 1670–99 | | 1700–1729 | |
|---|---|---|---|---|---|---|
| | N | % | N | % | N | % |
| Once | 18 | 54.5 | 90 | 86.5 | 115 | 83.9 |
| Twice | 10 | 30.3 | 14 | 13.5 | 20 | 14.6 |
| More than twice | 5 | 15.1 | 0 | 0 | 2 | 1.5 |
| Totals | 33 | 99.9 | 104 | 100 | 137 | 100 |

degree of change among the general population, they do indicate a major and far-reaching shift in the social experience of the city's Dutch settlers. Testators who first wed during the late 1600s were far less likely to remarry than members of the preceding generation.

A brief survey of the records of the Dutch Reformed church indicates that the frequency of remarriage declined among the congregation as a whole rather than simply among testators. I have compared the marital status of all persons listed in the clerical register during three five-year spans: 1661–65, 1691–95, and 1721–25. During the first period, more than one-half of marriages involved at least one widowed person (see Table A.12). This proportion declined to 31 percent of all weddings between 1691 and 1695 and dropped even further between 1721 and 1725. During this last span, fewer than one-fourth of couples included a previously wed party. Though my data are limited, it is striking that marriages between widows and single men were more common than unions between widowers and single women. These findings suggest that some widows were attractive marriage partners because of the property acquired from their deceased spouses.

The overall decline in the frequency of remarriage in eighteenth-century New York City may be traced to several factors: improved life expectancy, changes in the sex ratio, and the use of testamentary provisions that deprived widows of property rights upon remarriage. If the experience of testators is typical of the general population, the increase in men's life span meant that more women were widowed at a fairly advanced age—fifty years old or above. Since women outnumbered men in eighteenth century New York City, these older widows were quite unlikely to attract a new spouse. The ratio of women to men had become a mirror image of the situation in New Netherland, an immigrant society composed largely of young males.[43] Whereas Dutch custom in the early colonial period had guaranteed widows one-half of the family estate upon remarriage, this was no longer the case under English law. By the 1730s, many testators of Dutch ancestry declined to offer their widows any legacy if they should remarry.[44] Though more research needs to be

[43]For an analysis of New Netheland's population, see Oliver A. Rink, *Holland on the Hudson: An Economic and Social History of Early New York* (Ithaca: Cornell University Press, 1986), chap. 6. The 1698 census was the first city-wide enumeration to count women as well as men. The ratio of white men to women was .98 in 1698, .81 in 1703, .85 in 1723, .86 in 1731, .91 in 1737, .78 in 1746, .90 in 1749, and .68 in 1756. Despite some rather sudden fluctuations in the sex ratio, there were often fewer than nine men for every ten women in eighteenth-century New York City. See Bureau of the Census, *A Century of Population Growth*, 170–83. For corrections in the census figures of 1731, see Robert V. Wells, "The New York Census of 1731," *New-York Historical Society Quarterly* 59 (1973): 255–59.

[44]See above, Chap. 3.

**Table A.12** Marital status of couples wed in the Dutch Reformed church*

| Marital status | 1661–65 | | 1691–95 | | 1721–25 | |
|---|---|---|---|---|---|---|
| | N | % | N | % | N | % |
| Both single | 37 | 48.7 | 101 | 68.7 | 61 | 76.2 |
| Widower–single woman | 10 | 13.2 | 7 | 4.8 | 6 | 7.5 |
| Single man–widow | 16 | 21.0 | 23 | 15.6 | 9 | 11.2 |
| Both widowed | 13 | 17.1 | 16 | 10.9 | 4 | 5.0 |
| Totals | 76 | 100 | 147 | 100 | 80 | 99.9 |

*The total number of marriages (in this sample) declined during the eighteenth century because ministers recorded the marital status of only those couples who wed after the publication of banns rather than after obtaining a marriage license.

done on this problem, the decline in remarriage in New York City conforms to trends in other areas of America and western Europe from the 1600s through the 1800s. According to Daniel Scott Smith, remarriage was generally more common in most regions for widowers than widows, except for women under thirty. As colonial societies matured, the widow's chance for remarriage became quite limited—far narrower than historians had previously thought.[45]

## CHILDREN

Since children often failed to survive their parents, wills seldom reflect the full number of children born to married couples. Probate records do, however, provide an accurate measure of the extent of the average testator's parental responsibilities. Few testators failed to mention all their surviving children, even when the latter had previously received most of their inheritance. Parents felt legally bound to provide at least a token bequest for each child lest an heir claim to be neglected and challenge the will's validity.[46]

Most fathers tended to have relatively few children by the time that they executed their wills. The average testator (among men who married) bequeathed property to either two or three children. This pattern changed little throughout the colonial era.[47] Nearly 75 percent of all

[45]Daniel Scott Smith, "Inheritance and the Social History of Early American Women," in Hoffman and Albert, *Women in the Age of the American Revolution*, 55–57. See also Susan Grigg, "Toward a Theory of Remarriage: A Case Study of Newburyport at the Beginning of the Nineteenth Century," *Journal of Interdisciplinary History* 8 (1977): 183–220.
[46]Stephanie Grauman Wolf reaches a similar assessment about the use of wills as a source of information about family size. See *Urban Village*, 266.
[47]I have determined the number of children named by 995 testators (or 91 percent of all 1,090 married and widowed men who drafted wills from 1664 through 1775). On average,

married and widowed men in New York City named at least one child in their wills (see Table A.13). About half designated between one and four children as heirs. Only 19.9 percent mentioned between five and seven children and just 3.4 percent bequeathed property to more than seven offspring.

New York City testators tended to distribute their estates among a similar, if somewhat smaller number of children than did their counterparts in eighteenth-century Germantown, where 42 percent of all married men named two or fewer children in their wills.[48] Fifty-two percent of New York testators fell into that same category. It is even more striking that family size in New York City was significantly smaller than among rural households in either eastern Long Island or the mid–Hudson Valley (see Table A.13). One-fourth of all city men who had married failed to mention any children in their wills, yet just 10 percent of Ulster County men and 7 percent of Suffolk men were childless. Though only 23 percent of the city's testators had five or more children, nearly 60 percent of all Ulster and Suffolk County men had families of that size. Although it is not clear why there was such a substantial disparity in family size between these rural and urban areas, it is possible that New York City testators generally had fewer children because of a higher rate of mortality on Manhattan Island than in either Suffolk or Ulster counties. Unlike the more homogeneous small towns and villages, the city's population included several groups that differed greatly in family size. While certain types of skilled tradesmen named an average of 3.6 children in their wills, mariners mentioned only 1.3. More than half of all mariners (among those who had married) failed to name any children in their wills; less than one-fourth had more than two offspring. Many of these men prepared wills soon after marriage and probably had little time for family responsibilities given the nature of their work.[49]

Since more than 80 percent of all mariners were of British origin, it is no surprise that Britons had a substantially smaller number of children than persons of other nationalities. Even if one were to exclude seamen from our survey, however, the family size of British testators would still be considerably smaller than that of their Dutch counterparts (see Table A.14). Although there is no obvious explanation for this substantial discrepancy, it is possible that married couples of Dutch ancestry had more

2.7 children were named in these wills. See Narrett, "Patterns of Inheritance," 96. In addition to wills, a basic source of demographic data is found in *Baptisms from 1639 to 1800 in the Reformed Dutch Church, New York,* Collections of the New York Genealogical and Biographical Society, 2 vols. (New York, 1901–3; rpt. Upper Saddle River, N.J., 1968). For other vital records analyzed in this study, see Narrett, "Patterns of Inheritance," 351–55.
[48]Wolf, *Urban Village,* 266.
[49]Narrett, "Patterns of Inheritance," 98–99.

**Table A.13** Number and proportion of men naming children in their wills (1664–1775)*

| Region | 0 | | 1–2 | | Number of children named 3–4 | | 5–7 | | 8–14 | | Totals | |
|---|---|---|---|---|---|---|---|---|---|---|---|---|
| | N | % | N | % | N | % | N | % | N | % | N | % |
| New York City | 252 | 25.3 | 268 | 26.9 | 243 | 24.4 | 198 | 19.9 | 34 | 3.4 | 995 | 99.9 |
| Suffolk County | 32 | 6.7 | 60 | 12.5 | 106 | 22.1 | 188 | 39.2 | 94 | 19.6 | 480 | 100.1 |
| Ulster County | 19 | 9.9 | 21 | 11.0 | 38 | 19.9 | 76 | 39.8 | 37 | 19.4 | 191 | 100 |

*All men considered here were either married or widowed.

**Table A.14** Average number of children named by testators within five ethnic groups*

|                              | No. testators | Ave. no. children |
|------------------------------|:-------------:|:-----------------:|
| Jews                         |      17       |        3.6        |
| Dutch                        |      386      |        3.4        |
| Germans                      |      43       |        2.7        |
| French                       |      62       |        2.4        |
| British                      |      428      |        2.1        |
| British (excluding mariners) |      343      |        2.4        |

*All testators considered were either married or widowed.

children because of greater longevity. Since the great majority of the ethnic Dutch had been settled in New York for several generations by the mid-eighteenth century, these colonists and their offspring may not have been as susceptible to certain diseases as more recent immigrants.


WOMEN WHO LEFT WILLS

Women prepared by themselves 15 percent of all New York City wills during the colonial period (see Table A.15). Although this percentage may at first appear to be small, it was significantly greater than the share drafted by females in rural areas of the province.[50] One reason for this discrepancy may be that women were more likely to be heads of households in the city than in the countryside. Robert Wells has determined that 16.7 percent of all city households were headed by women in 1703. This percentage was markedly higher than the comparable figure in other regions during the period 1697–1714: 9.2 percent in Albany County, 7.7 percent on Long Island and in Westchester, and 4.5 percent in Orange and Dutchess counties.[51] New York City was also the only area of the colony that had a markedly greater number of adult white females than males during much of the colonial period, partly because of the tendency among widows in outlying rural areas to move to the city in search of increased economic opportunity. Because urban women were especially likely to participate in the market economy and to be literate, they may have also been more apt to declare wills than their rural counterparts.

[50]Women alone executed 5.6 percent of 557 wills left in three Suffolk County towns between 1664 and 1775. They executed 6.6 percent of 228 wills in five Ulster County towns. See Narrett, "Patterns of Inheritance," 316.

[51]Wells, *Population of the British Colonies*, 122–23, 128. For population figures, see also Bureau of the Census, *A Century of Population Growth*, 170–83.

**Table A.15** Number of wills executed by men and women

| Period | Men | | Women | | Married couples* | | Totals | |
|---|---|---|---|---|---|---|---|---|
| | N | % | N | % | N | % | N | % |
| 1664–95 | 99 | 72.3 | 17 | 12.4 | 21 | 15.3 | 137 | 100 |
| 1696–1725 | 285 | 84.8 | 51 | 15.2 | 0 | 0 | 336 | 100 |
| 1726–50 | 300 | 83.8 | 58 | 16.2 | 0 | 0 | 358 | 100 |
| 1751–75 | 634 | 85.6 | 107 | 14.4 | 0 | 0 | 741 | 100 |
| Entire period | 1318 | 83.8 | 233 | 14.8 | 21 | 1.3 | 1572 | 99.9 |

*Husbands and wives who jointly executed their testaments.

While widows were by far the most likely of New York City women to execute wills, unmarried women (or "spinsters") formed an increasingly large percentage of female testators during the mid-eighteenth century. Between 1664 and 1725, only two single women left wills. During the period 1751–75, they numbered about one among every five female testators (see Table A.16). Although no obvious factor underlies this trend, at least one possible explanation can be offered. Many single women who executed wills during the 1750s and 1760s had come to maturity during the first half of the century, a period when adult white females generally outnumbered men among the city's inhabitants. As the chances for marriage diminished, more single women asserted their own preferences by bequeathing property to their kin and friends.

Widows, the great majority of all female testators, formed a distinct segment of the will-leaving population in several respects. For one, these women tended to be considerably older than most men who drafted or dictated a testament. Almost 70 percent of the widows in my sample were at least sixty years old, and 45 percent had passed their seventieth

**Table A.16** Marital status of women who left wills*

| Period | Married | | Widowed | | Single | | Status unknown | | Total | |
|---|---|---|---|---|---|---|---|---|---|---|
| | N | % | N | % | N | % | N | % | N | % |
| 1664–95 | 22 | 57.9 | 15 | 39.5 | 0 | 0 | 1 | 2.6 | 38 | 100 |
| 1696–1725 | 1 | 2.0 | 48 | 94.1 | 2 | 3.9 | 0 | 0 | 51 | 100 |
| 1726–50 | 1 | 1.7 | 50 | 86.2 | 6 | 10.3 | 1 | 1.7 | 58 | 99.9 |
| 1751–75 | 4 | 3.7 | 83 | 77.6 | 20 | 18.7 | 0 | 0 | 107 | 100 |
| Entire period | 28 | 11.0 | 196 | 77.2 | 28 | 11.0 | 2 | 0.8 | 254 | 100 |

*The number of single women, although never a large portion of the whole, increased markedly over time.

**Table A.17** Ages of men and widows who left wills*

| Testators | Under 30 | | 31–39 | | 40–49 | | 50–59 | | 60–69 | | 70 and above | | Total | |
|---|---|---|---|---|---|---|---|---|---|---|---|---|---|---|
| | N | % | N | % | N | % | N | % | N | % | N | % | N | % |
| Men | 23 | 7.1 | 59 | 18.2 | 72 | 22.2 | 67 | 20.7 | 62 | 19.1 | 41 | 12.6 | 324 | 99.9 |
| Widows | 2 | 3.8 | 4 | 7.5 | 3 | 5.7 | 7 | 13.2 | 13 | 24.5 | 24 | 45.3 | 53 | 100 |

*I have been able to determine the ages of nearly one-quarter of all men and somewhat more than one-fourth of all widows (324 of 1,339 men or 24.2 percent and 53 of 196 widows or 27.0 percent).

birthday. By contrast, only 32 percent among men had reached age sixty and fewer than 13 percent were seventy years old or above (see Table A.17).

Attaining an advanced age was not an unmixed blessing for those women who lived through the death of several children. Although it is not usually possible to determine how many times mothers had to endure this misfortune, the small size of many widows' families indicates that it must have been a fairly common experience. Throughout the colonial period, 36.2 percent of all widows failed to mention any children in their wills; only 17.9 percent had more than four children (see Table A.18). As in other areas of Britain's mainland and island colonies, families headed by women were generally smaller than those in which a man was in charge.[52]

In addition to their relatively advanced age, many female testators occupied a fairly high social position. I have been able to determine the occupational status of nearly three-fifths of the former husbands of all widows who left wills (see Table A.19). Almost one-half of the women in my sample had been wed to members of the upper echelon of colonial society: merchants and professionals, including government officials. Thirty-two percent of the sample had been married to artisans, shopkeepers, or processors, men who generally occupied the broad middle strata of the city's class structure. Although a considerable number of women had been wed to mariners, most of the latter were ship captains or sponsors of commercial ventures rather than common sailors. Among all widows who executed wills, I have found only three who were married to common laborers. Because it is easier to find information concerning the social backgrounds of prominent women, these statistics probably understate the number of female testators of modest means.

Female testators were a highly diverse group that appears to have included many women at the top of the social pyramid, a substantial number in the middle, but relatively few at the bottom. It is also significant that one-half of all widows who left wills had been married to at least one man who had executed a testament. More than three-fourths of these husbands asked their wives to serve as an executor; 45 percent requested that the wife act as sole executor. Since the position of executor carried important administrative duties, these women may have been especially likely to assume the responsibility of making their own

[52]Wells, *Population of the British Colonies,* 58–59, 108, 129–30, 186, 190–92, 204–6, 223, 225, 232, 248–49, 317–19. Wells points out, however, that "while women had smaller households than men, they were generally similar enough so that families headed by women were more like those headed by men in the same colony than they were like households headed by women elsewhere" (319).

**Table A.18** Number and proportion
of widows naming children in their wills*

| No. children named | No. testators | Percent |
|---|---|---|
| None | 71 | 36.2 |
| 1–2 | 48 | 24.5 |
| 3–4 | 42 | 21.4 |
| 5–7 | 29 | 14.8 |
| 8–12 | 6 | 3.1 |
| Totals | 196 | 100 |

*I have compiled data on all 196 widows who ex-
ecuted testaments between 1664 and 1775.

wills. After receiving generous bequests from their husbands, widows
would also need to dispose of their property in a legally proper and
orderly manner.

New York City assessment lists confirm that female testators were a
select group of women. Indeed, the gap in wealth between these testators and other women exceeded the disparity in property between male
and female taxpayers. An assessment list of 1701 indicates that women
comprised 11.7 percent of all assessed persons and held 9.0 percent of
taxable wealth. By 1730, women comprised 17.8 percent of the assessed
but owned just 12.6 percent of taxable wealth.[53] As the number of poor
female residents swelled, the frequency of will writing declined among
all women. I have identified 15 testators among 104 assessed women in
1701, but only 23 testators among 254 assessed women in 1730. The
frequency of will writing among these Manhattan women was about half
the rate among men during the mid-eighteenth century. While female
testators were considerably wealthier than the average male taxpayer,
they were more than twice as affluent as those women who died intestate.[54] Thirty-seven women in 1730 (or 15 percent of all assessed

[53] The assessment of Feb. 25, 1701, lists 104 women among 885 residents in the city's
urban wards (including all wards except the Bowery and Harlem). These women's property was assessed at £3,755 out of a total of £41,822. The assessment of Feb. 28, 1730, lists
254 women among 1,429 residents in the urban wards. The women's holdings were valued
at £4,675 out of a total of £37,001. The decline in total assessed value from 1701 to 1730
undoubtedly reflects changes in methods of assessment rather than actual decline in the
value of taxable property. Both tax lists record assessments of real and personal property
for the maintenance of the Anglican ministry and the city's poor. See microfilm reel AR-1,
Paul Klapper Library, Queens College, New York City. New York City women owned a
somewhat higher percentage of taxable wealth than women in other colonies owned of
inventoried wealth after probate. See Carole Shammas, "Early American Women and
Control over Capital," in Hoffman and Albert, *Women in the Age of the American Revolution*,
138.

[54] The average assessment of twenty-three female testators in 1730 was £43, while the
average for 231 women who did not prepare wills was £16. The average assessment among

**Table A.19** Occupational status of the former husbands of female testators*

| Occupation | No. husbands | Percent |
|---|---|---|
| Merchants | 40 | 34.8 |
| Artisans | 24 | 20.9 |
| Mariners | 19 | 16.5 |
| Professionals | 16 | 13.9 |
| Shopkeepers | 9 | 7.8 |
| Processors of food and drink | 4 | 3.5 |
| Laborers | 3 | 2.6 |
| Total | 115 | 100 |

*When a woman had more than one husband, I have listed only the profession of her last spouse. Information has been obtained for 58.7 percent of all widows who left wills.

females) were so poor that their property was deemed nontaxable. Only one of these women prepared a will. It is also striking that women who prepared wills tended overwhelmingly to be heads of households. Fourteen among fifteen female testators assessed in 1701 were taxed on the possession of real estate as well as personal property. Twenty-one among twenty-three women who declared wills were assessed in the same manner in 1730. This type of ownership was far less common among all female taxpayers. At least one-fifth of all assessed women in 1701 were boarders who held no real estate, while one-third belonged to this group in 1730. Female poverty was becoming more deeply entrenched in eighteenth-century New York City—a trend that was also apparent in Philadelphia and eastern Massachusetts.[55]

Quantitative analysis is useful in determining the frequency of will writing, but it alone cannot explain why certain individuals executed wills while others of a similar social background did not. Is the failure to leave a will evidence of a lack of concern about one's descendants or does

246 male testators was £63, while that of all 1,175 men was £27. Men who did not prepare wills held property assessed at an average of £18.

[55]Twenty-one among 104 assessed women in 1701 were not taxed on real estate. Eighty-five among 254 women in 1730 fall into this category. For evidence of female poverty, see Carole Shammas, "The Female Social Structure of Philadelphia in 1775," *Pennsylvania Magazine of History and Biography* 107 (1983): 69–84; Alexander Keyssar, "Widowhood in Eighteenth-Century Massachusetts: A Problem in the History of the Family," *Perspectives in American History* 8 (1974): 83–119; Smith, "Inheritance and Social History," in Hoffman and Albert, *Women in the Age of the American Revolution,* 59–63.

it simply indicate that heads of households generally preferred less formal, less legalistic means of distributing their property among their families? My own research suggests that men seldom neglected to make a will because they had already given away the greater portion of the estate to their children. Rather than yield most of their property prematurely, most heads of households retained a sizable amount of goods for their own well-being and the security of their wives in old age. The question of the succession to property after death was probably less important to many men than the acquisition of wealth for their more immediate concerns. Although New Yorkers were an extremely acquisitive people from all accounts, many heads of families engaged in little deliberate economic planning for the more distant future. Unlike our own world in which persons often write wills while they still enjoy good health and are relatively young, the typical man or woman of the colonial era did not declare a testament until he or she felt a premonition of death. In this sense, many New Yorkers were perhaps closer to the mind-set of fifteenth- or sixteenth-century western Europeans than to the ways of thinking of bourgeois Americans in the late twentieth century.

# Index

*Library of Congress Cataloging-in-Publication Data*

Narrett, David E., 1951–
   Inheritance and family life in colonial New York City / David E.
Narrett.
     p.  cm.
   Includes bibliographical references and index.
   ISBN 0-8014-2517-4 (alk. paper)
    1. Inheritance and succession—New York (City)—History.
2. Wills—New York (City)—History.  3. New York (City)—Social life
and customs.  I. Title.
KFN5200.N37   1992
346.747′1052—dc20
[347.4710652]                              92-7680